"This book takes readers beyond the hyperbole. It is an impressive early analysis of some of the ways in which these new organizations are, and are not, changing American politics. Specialists will be returning to the book's themes for years. They will want to read Dowling and Miller before doing so."

—Michael J. Malbin,   *The Campaign Finance Institute and University at Albany, SUNY*

"The rise of Super PACs is a monumental development with wide-ranging implications for the future of American democracy. Yet, until the publication of *Super PAC!*, very little was known about how Super PACs operate, and the influence that Super PACs have had on public opinion and voting behavior. Conor M. Dowling and Michael G. Miller fill this void by writing what can only be described as a pioneering and must-read book for all who care about campaign finance, organized interests, and U.S. elections."

—Peter L. Francia,   *East Carolina University*

Super PAC!

Recent federal court activity has dramatically changed the regulatory environment of campaign finance in the United States. Since 2010, the judiciary has decided that corporations and labor unions may freely spend in American elections, and that so-called "super PACs" can accept unlimited contributions from private citizens for the purpose of buying election advertising.

Despite the potential for such unregulated contributions to dramatically alter the conduct of campaigns, little is known about where super PACs get their money, where they spend it, or how their message compares with other political groups. Moreover, we know almost nothing about whether individual citizens even notice super PACs, or whether they distinguish between super PAC activity and political activity by other political groups.

This book addresses those questions. Using campaign finance data, election returns, advertising archives, a public opinion survey, and survey experiments, *Super PAC!* provides unprecedented insight into the behavior of these organizations, and how they affect public opinion and voting behavior. The first in-depth exploration of the topic, this book will make significant contributions in both political science and applied policy.

Conor M. Dowling is Assistant Professor of Political Science at the University of Mississippi.

Michael G. Miller is Assistant Professor of Political Science at the University of Illinois, Springfield.

Routledge Research in American Politics and Governance

1 **Lobbying the New President**
Interests in Transition
Heath Brown

2 **Religion, Race, and Barack Obama's New Democratic Pluralism**
Gastón Espinosa

3 **Direct Democracy in the United States**
Petitioners as a Reflection of Society
Edited by Shauna Reilly and Ryan M. Yonk

4 **American Exceptionalism in the Age of Obama**
Stephen Brooks

5 **"An Empire of Ideals"**
The Chimeric Imagination of Ronald Reagan
Justin D. Garrison

6 **Resisting Injustice and the Feminist Ethics of Care in the Age of Obama**
"Suddenly, . . . All the Truth Was Coming Out"
David A. J. Richards

7 **Interfaith Advocacy**
The Role of Religious Coalitions in the Political Process
Katherine E. Knutson

8 **Social Contract Theory in American Jurisprudence**
Too Much Liberty and Too Much Authority
Thomas R. Pope

9 **Voting and Migration Patterns in the U.S.**
George Hawley

10 **Democracy, Intelligent Design, and Evolution**
Science for Citizenship
Susan P. Liebell

11 **Inventive Politicians and Ethnic Ascent in American Politics**
The Uphill Elections of Italians and Mexicans to the U.S. Congress
Miriam Jiménez

12 **Competitive Elections and Democracy in America**
The Good, the Bad, and the Ugly
Heather K. Evans

13 **Gender, Race, and Office Holding in the United States**
Representation at the Intersections
Becki Scola

14 **The Latino Gender Gap in U.S. Politics**
Christina E. Bejarano

15 **Perspectives on Presidential Leadership**
An International View of the White House
Edited by Michael Patrick Cullinane and Clare Frances Elliott

16 **Super PAC!**
Money, Elections, and Voters after *Citizens United*
Conor M. Dowling and Michael G. Miller

Super PAC!

Money, Elections, and Voters after *Citizens United*

By Conor M. Dowling and Michael G. Miller

 Routledge
Taylor & Francis Group

NEW YORK AND LONDON

First published 2014
by Routledge
711 Third Avenue, New York, NY 10017

and by Routledge
2 Park Square, Milton Park, Abingdon, Oxon OX14 4RN

*Routledge is an imprint of the Taylor & Francis Group,
an informa business*

Library of Congress Cataloging-in-Publication Data

Dowling, Conor M.
  Super Pac! : money, elections, and voters after citizens united / Conor M.
Dowling, Michael G. Miller.
    pages cm. — (Routledge research in American politics and governance ; 16)
  1. Campaign funds—United States.   2. Campaign funds—Law and
legislation—United States.   3. Political action committees—United
States.   4. Political action committees—United States—Public
opinion.   5. United States—Politics and government.   I. Miller, Michael
Gerald.   II. Title.
  JK1991.D685 2014
  324'.40973—dc23
  2013044560

ISBN: 978-0-415-83302-8 (hbk)
ISBN: 978-0-203-50907-4 (ebk)

Typeset in Sabon LT
by Apex CoVantage, LLC

To Our Families

Contents

List of Figures		*xiii*
List of Tables		*xv*
Acknowledgments		*xvii*
	Introduction	1
1	*Citizens United*	7
2	Rise of the Super PAC	35
3	Money in Elections	54
4	Does It Matter Where Money Comes From?	77
5	Super PAC Ads in the 2012 Presidential Election	105
6	Public Opinion of Campaign Finance after *Citizens United*	132
7	Prospects for Campaign Finance Reform	155
	References	*167*
	Appendixes	*175*
	Index	*187*

Figures

2.1   Number of Registered PACs, by Type   39

3.1   Total Cost of Federal Elections, 1998–2012   58

3.2   Total Committee Financial Activity (in Millions of Dollars), 2012 Federal Elections   60

3.3   Mean Receipts (2012 Dollars), by Source and Candidate Status, U.S. House General Election Candidates   62

3.4   Percentage of Independent Expenditures Made to "Oppose" General Election Candidates for U.S. House, 2004–2012   67

3.5   Mean Independent Expenditures 2008–2012 (in 2012 Dollars), by Candidate Status, in U.S. House Races Where Expenditures Were Made   69

3.6   Daily Advertising Expenditures by Campaigns and Outside Groups, 2012 U.S. House Elections   73

4.1   Independent Expenditures and Campaign Spending for Incumbents and Challenger's Ultimate Share of the Two-Party Vote, 2008–2012   83

5.1   Evaluations of Eight Presidential Ads Used in Study 1   115

5.2   Difference in Evaluations of Ads Attacking Romney (Obama – Super PAC), by Respondent Party Identification   118

5.3   Difference in Evaluations of Ads Attacking Obama (Romney – Super PAC), by Respondent Party Identification   119

5.4   Difference in Evaluations of Ads Attacking Romney (Obama – Super PAC), by Respondent Party Identification: "Election Day" Ads   122

5.5   Difference in Evaluations of Ads Attacking Obama (Romney – Super PAC), by Respondent Party Identification: "Election Day" Ads   123

5.6   Evaluations of Presidential Ads from Study 2, Randomly Assigned Sponsor   128

6.1   Support for the *Citizens United* Decision (in November 2011 Survey)   138

xiv *Figures*

6.2   Support for the *Citizens United* Decision (in November 2011
      Survey), by Respondent Party Identification   140
6.3   Beliefs about the First Amendment Rights of Corporations
      Compared to Individuals   142
6.4   Beliefs about the First Amendment Rights of Corporations
      Compared to Individuals, by Respondent Party Identification   144
5.1A Evaluations of Eight Presidential Ads Used in Study 2,
      Randomly Assigned Sponsor   181

Tables

2.1	Key Contribution and Expenditure Rules in 2012	50
3.1	Purpose of Expenditures Made by U.S. House Candidates in 2012	65
3.2	Purpose of Independent Expenditures Made to Support/ Oppose Federal Candidates in 2012	71
4.1	Challenger's Vote Share as a Function of Challenger and Incumbent Spending, 2008–2012 U.S. House Elections	80
4.2	Effect of Funding Source Treatments on Candidate Evaluations	90
4.3	Effect of Funding Source Treatments on Candidate Evaluations, for Full Sample and by Extra Information Conditions	94
4.4	Effect of Super PAC v. Interest Group Funding Source Treatment on Candidate Evaluations	97
5.1	Number of Unique Ads and Total Number of Ads Aired in the 2012 Presidential Election, by Sponsor	107
5.2	Presidential Ads Used in Study 1	110
5.3	Presidential Ads Used in Study 2	127
6.1	Knowledge of Campaign Finance Rules Pertaining to Corporations and Citizens	147
6.2	Knowledge of Campaign Finance Rules Pertaining to Corporations and Citizens, by Respondent's Level of Political Interest	149
4.1A	Experimental Designs and Question Wording for Studies Reported in Chapter 4	177
5.1A	Average Evaluations of the Eights Presidential Ads Used in Study 1	180
6.1A	Predicting Beliefs about the Rights of Corporations Compared to Individuals	182
6.2A	Selected Demographic and Political Characteristics of the 2012 CCES and CCAP Sample	183
6.3A	Additional Question about Legality of Super PACs	184

Acknowledgments

In a way, this book was born at Miller's Pub (unfortunately, no relation to Miller the author) in Chicago, coincidentally around the same time the *Citizens United* case began its odyssey through the federal courts. Political scientists tend to congregate at Miller's every April during the annual meeting of the Midwest Political Science Association, and that is where we met for the first time, in 2008. Our professional and personal interests were oddly similar, and we resolved that day to always be working on something together. We have kept that promise and have met at Miller's every April since. So long as the MPSA meets in Chicago, we will be found there each spring, planning our next year. We thank the friendly staff of Miller's for accommodating us through the years as many of the ideas in this book took root at their bar, and for introducing us to the joy of smelt as a food.

We jointly incurred many debts in writing this book, and several individuals and organizations deserve special recognition for their support of our work. Peter Francia read several of our chapters and provided many helpful comments. His help was crucial as we navigated the sometimes byzantine landscape of campaign finance regulations, and he graciously provided feedback on tight deadlines. We want to thank him especially, as he truly went above and beyond.

Parts of the book appeared as a paper at the 2010 annual meeting of the Midwest Political Science Association. We thank Scott Desposato for improving that paper (which subsequently became part of Chapter 4) in his capacity as discussant at that meeting. We also benefitted—either separately or collectively—from productive conversations with Adam Brown, Alan Gerber, Mike Henderson, Seth Hill, Greg Huber, Jonathan Krasno, Ray La Raja, Adam Seth Levine, Michael Malbin, Walter Mebane, Christopher Mooney, David Racine, John Transue, and Jon Winburn. David Doherty has long been a good friend and colleague to us both, and deserves special recognition for his insight and willingness to tell us when we are wrong. Chanse Travis and Logan Woods proved to be capable research assistants; we appreciate their attention to detail and their patience with us. Our colleagues at the University of Illinois, Springfield and the University of Mississippi have provided substantial support at the early stage of our careers, and we are most thankful for it. Two anonymous reviewers were also integral to the direction of the project, and we thank them for their feedback. Finally, at Routledge, we thank Darcy Bullock and Natalja Mortensen for their early belief in the project, and their patience with us during the process.

Collection of our original data was funded via the generosity of the institutions with which one of us has been affiliated during the previous three years. Specifically, the University of Mississippi provided funding for a number of our surveys, and its College of Liberal Arts provided a summer research grant that greatly aided the writing process. Yale University's Center for the Study of American Politics also kindly granted us survey time on a number of national surveys, and the Institute for Legal, Legislative, and Policy Studies at the University of Illinois, Springfield graciously funded collection of some our survey data via a public affairs research grant.

Several people and organizations also provided us with data, without which this project would not have been possible. In this area, we want to acknowledge Gary C. Jacobson for sharing his personal data on congressional elections. Adam Bonica also deserves recognition for compiling and making available the Database on Ideology, Money in Politics, and Elections, as well as for clarifying some points for us as we worked with it. Both the Center for Responsive Politics and the Campaign Finance Institute have long provided scholars with reliable data and/or summary reports on federal campaign finance. We thank them for their work.

Finally, we recognize that producing this book has made us somewhat less available to our families, particularly at the end. We thank our spouses, Carey Dowling and Laura Miller, for their patience and support over many long hours as this manuscript came together, and we look forward to much more time in the immediate future to spend with our children, Anorah and Larkin Dowling, and Ava, Carli, and Landon Miller. These seven people have supported us each separately for much longer than our own five-year friendship, and have continuously reminded us what all the work is for.

Though this book would not have been possible without the contributions of those listed above, any errors, omissions, or oversights herein, like our tab at Miller's Pub, are our responsibility alone unless someone else is willing to claim them.

Introduction

February 6, 2012, was a big day for President Barack Obama. As his 2012 reelection campaign loomed in the fall, the Republican nomination process to choose his opponent was well underway. The candidates vying for the GOP nomination had been campaigning for the better part of a year, and with no primary contest on the Democratic side, all eyes were on the Republican primaries. Some of the candidates had proven to be serious contenders, at least when it came to the capacity to raise money. Presumed front-runner Mitt Romney had raised $57 million in 2011, before the Iowa Caucuses marked the opening of voting on January 3, 2012. And former House Speaker Newt Gingrich's campaign had taken in almost $10 million in the last three months of 2011 alone (Confessore and Luo 2012).

The numbers were formidable in their own right, but the Republican primary candidates had also demonstrated an impressive capacity to generate money from "super PACs." Those groups were not formally affiliated with the presidential campaigns—they were legally barred from coordinating their message with the campaigns at all—but were nonetheless proving to be a serious vehicle for campaign cash in the presidential election. Like the campaigns, there was no limit on the amount of money that super PACs could spend on advertising naming a candidate, either to attack or support him/her. But unlike the campaigns, political action committees, and parties, all of which were restricted in the size of contributions they were able to receive from individuals, the super PACs could accept contributions of any size, from nearly anyone, including from the treasuries of corporations and labor unions.

There was vast potential for the presidential candidates to leverage the capacity of super PACs to help their campaigns. Even in the absence of communication between the two entities, a campaign could ensure that a friendly super PAC was headed by someone who knew what the candidate's organization thought the core message *should* be. For instance, Romney's super PAC, Restore Our Future, was founded and run by several of the top aides from his previous campaign—a failed bid for the 2008 Republican presidential nomination (Eggen and Cillizza 2011). With the ability to leverage unlimited contributions into ads that could expressly say "Vote for Romney" or "Don't Vote for Gingrich," super PACs were therefore a powerful weapon for the Republican candidates as they fought it out on the airwaves in the early primary states. Although the Romney campaign itself was restricted to receiving contributions from individuals of no more than $2,500—and could receive no corporate money—Restore Our Future raised $18 million from about 200 donors (including corporations) in the last six months of 2011, just prior to the Iowa caucuses (ibid.). For comparison, the Romney campaign would have needed to collect the maximum donation of $2,500 from 7,200 individuals to raise that amount.

Restore Our Future's success should have forced any of Romney's rivals to take notice. His nomination was hardly certain on February 6, but he had at that point won three of the five nominating contests and looked to be in the race for the long haul. Moreover, with unlimited contributions still flowing to his super PAC, there was no obvious reason to expect the stream of pro-Romney advertising to ebb any time soon. Further, regardless of whether Romney's nomination campaign was successful, his rivals all had super PACs of their own. The writing was on the wall for the general election: Whoever emerged to take on the president in the fall would likely be well-funded and would almost certainly have a very wealthy advocate in the form of a friendly super PAC.

Until that time, the president had been resistant to jumping on the super PAC bandwagon. He had long favored raising money from small donors, and had set precedents in his first campaign by refusing not only contributions from lobbyists and interest groups, but also presidential public funding. These stances had hardly hampered his fundraising success though, as Obama's campaign raised more than $650 million from individuals in 2008.[1] With a demonstrated ability to eschew traditional funding sources that might create the perception of entanglement with "special interests," Obama's hesitancy to embrace super PACs seemed reasonable. In an interview with Matt Lauer of NBC's *Today Show* that aired on the morning of February 6, the president underscored his distaste for super PACs, saying,

> One of the worries we have obviously in the next campaign is that there are so many of these so-called super PACs, these independent expenditures that are going to be out there. There is going to be just a lot of money floating around, and I guarantee a bunch of it is going to be (funding) negative (ads). (Epstein 2012)

No doubt many viewers heard the president's remarks while they ate their breakfast on the morning of February 6, and as they went about their day, little had apparently changed inside the president's campaign: Obama's team had stood on principle to that point, and had resisted endorsing a super PAC to raise unlimited money for pro-Obama ads. But by the time those people were getting ready for bed that evening, things appeared to have changed dramatically. In a stunning reversal, the Obama campaign had decided that the strategic realities of competing with a super PAC–enhanced opponent must trump principled resistance to unlimited, possibly corporate donations.

Around 10:00 p.m. on that February 6, the Obama campaign informed its top contributors that the president would endorse super PAC Priorities USA Action, with the aim of benefitting from its fundraising capacity. In an email later that evening, Obama's campaign manager Jim Messina wrote to supporters that given the financial dynamics apparent in the Republican primaries, something had to give:

> In 2011, the super PAC supporting Mitt Romney raised $30 million from fewer than 200 contributors. Ninety six percent of what they've spent so far, more than $18 million, has been on attack ads. The main engine of Romney's campaign has an average contribution of roughly $150,000. The stakes are too important to play by two different sets of rules. If we fail to act, we concede this election to a small group of powerful people intent on removing the president at any cost. (Thrush 2012)

The age of the super PAC in presidential politics had begun.

* * *

The emergence of super PACs represented a new era of American campaign finance. Prior to some groundbreaking federal court decisions in early 2010, almost all money that was funneled into the political system was subject to "hard money" limitations. That is, since the passage of the Bipartisan Campaign Reform Act in 2002, anyone wishing to donate to a political committee (such as a campaign, PAC, or "527" organization) was constrained by campaign finance law.[2] Candidates, for instance, could only accept limited contributions from individuals, parties, and political action committees (PACs), and the latter two groups were in turn bound by the same rules. In short, any money that found its way into the bank account of a campaign would have been subject to strict limits designed to prevent any one donor from "buying" either the election or the candidate. And, although so-called 527 groups were able to accept unlimited contributions, they could only engage in "issue advocacy" and voter mobilization efforts. Such groups were not allowed to give any of their money to candidates, nor could they spend it on advertising naming a candidate close to an election. Furthermore, like campaigns, they had to publicly disclose their donors' identities. Finally, corporations had limited opportunities to influence elections: Like 527s, they were banned from "express advocacy" that mentioned a candidate near an election, and could not directly contribute to campaigns at all.

A series of events in 2010, however, significantly changed the dynamics regarding American campaign finance, expanding the opportunities for corporations and wealthy individuals alike to spend money during election campaigns. The Supreme Court decided in *Citizens United v. FEC* (558 U.S. 310 (2010)) that although corporations and labor unions were still barred from contributing money directly to federal candidates, they *could* spend funds from their treasury to purchase advertising to support or attack candidates by name. At the heart of the Court's logic was the holding that corporate spending—so long as the money did not go to campaigns as contributions—was tantamount to political speech, which was subject to First Amendment protections and could therefore not be lawfully limited. Following the lead of the Supreme Court on this question, subsequent lower court decisions held that *any* group wishing to spend money to communicate a message (but not to contribute to candidates) could therefore raise unlimited contributions from both private citizens and corporations. This was an unprecedented expansion of not only outside groups' ability to spend money in federal elections, but also of the capacity of donors to channel their money to groups with the aim of communicating a political message.

Thus, although 2010 was rightfully seen by many as unexplored territory, few doubted the potential for super PACs to transform large donations into advertising on a massive scale. Anxiety about accountability is typical of critics, who worry that unlimited contributions will lead to nefarious outcomes ranging from disproportionate influence of wealthy donors to outright bribery. Yet, much of this prognostication remains speculative, as there has been to date no large-scale analysis of the role of super PACs (and similar groups) in contemporary American politics. We know very little about how, when, or where outside groups have spent their money, whether their spending alters the outcome of elections, or whether the public at large notices or cares. In short, it is not terribly difficult to collect financial data on the activities of outside groups. It is a considerably more complicated task to determine how the federal court activity in 2010–2011 ultimately changed the conduct of elections and the manner in which voters orient to them.

That is the main goal of this book. In the following pages, we examine the role and effects of unregulated money from outside groups after *Citizens United*. We took on this task because we believe that a close look at both the behavior of outside groups and voters' reactions to them will yield answers about the extent to which the emergence of super PACs and related groups have altered American public life. We not only analyze donation and spending patterns, but also move beyond those evaluations, focusing on the manner in which outside groups change the tone of political campaigns, affect election outcomes, and provoke a reaction from voters. In short, we explore the monetary, communications, and behavioral effects of outside group spending, because a deeper understanding in these areas can help to determine what reforms (if any) are likely to be effective in the future, or whether such reforms are even necessary.

Our findings no doubt confirm some of the fears of those who oppose the core holding in *Citizens United*. Namely, we observe nearly $1 billion in spending during the 2012 elections by outside groups that did not legally exist in the 2008 campaign. The vast majority of this money was spent on advertising, and as Election Day neared, outside groups combined to spend more on advertising than campaigns (at least in House elections) on a day-to-day basis. Moreover, consistent with President Obama's belief that super PACs would fuel negative campaigning, the advertising that groups funded was overwhelmingly intended to attack candidates with whom the group disagreed. We also find some evidence that those ads make a difference, at least in certain situations: Challengers for U.S. House seats who are heavily backed by outside spending (again, the vast majority of which was spent on advertising), for instance, appear to perform better on Election Day.

But it is in our view premature to conclude either that super PACs are "buying" elections or that their advertising is perceived by voters as more misleading or negative. For one, in a study of presidential ads aired in 2012, we find little consistent evidence that super PAC ads are more negative or misleading than candidate ads. That is, the content of super PAC ads is not necessarily all that different from those of candidate ads, and some candidate ads are perceived to be more misleading and negative than super PAC ads. So, although super PACs do predominantly choose to run ads attacking candidates, these ads are not necessarily any "worse" than the ads the candidates choose to run themselves. In fact, some super PAC attack ads were perceived to have more information content than candidate attack ads.

In addition, we find evidence that voters downgrade their assessment of candidates when they are informed about various aspects of the candidate's financial backers. Namely, either taking contributions from special interests or having outside groups spend on a candidate's behalf appears to provoke a negative reaction from the electorate, as voters' perception of whether the candidate would be beholden to special interests increases, and their estimation of whether they would vote for him decreases. Simply, when informed that a candidate is backed by outside money, his reputation takes a hit, and people are less likely to vote for him. This suggests that so long as information about funding sources reaches voters, they take it into consideration when evaluating candidates, with heavily interest-backed candidates suffering in comparison to those who receive more funding from individual citizens.

The downgraded assessments of interest-backed candidates are consistent with public opinion about *Citizens United* and corporate speech rights. Specifically, we find that only about one-third of the public agreed with the *Citizens United* decision, and more than 60 percent feel that corporations should not have speech rights akin to those of a private citizen when it comes to elections. Still, although many people are dissatisfied with the notion of corporate election spending on First Amendment grounds, we also find that they seem to lack knowledge of current campaign finance law. For example, in the weeks before the 2012 federal elections, only about 40 percent of the public knew that corporations and citizens could contribute unlimited sums of money to groups who buy political advertising in presidential elections. In other words, less than half of the public knew what a super PAC was in legal terms. And so, although there is clear public disagreement with the Court's decision in *Citizens United*, it is not clear that there is strong public support for implementing new reforms of the campaign finance system given the relatively low level of knowledge of how the current system operates.

It is not our intention to comment on campaign finance law in a normative sense; whether one thinks increased corporate and other group activity *should* be permissible in politics is in some ways beside the point given that the Supreme Court has, at least for now, settled that argument. Moreover, our findings are neither universally positive nor negative with regard to the effects of the activities of corporations, super PACs, and other outside groups on the whole. However, understanding the altered politics in the new campaign finance world is crucial to evaluating the capacity of unregulated money to change electoral competition, campaign tone, public policy, and mass orientation to political events. Simply, if we are to consider reform, we ought to know what we are reforming and whether the public would be supportive of such reform efforts.

NOTES

1. Center for Responsive Politics. www.opensecrets.org/news/2008/06/obama-puts-lobbyists-pacs-on-d.html.
2. We describe these political committees at length in Chapters 1 and 2.

1 *Citizens United*

On January 27, 2010, President Barack Obama went before a joint session of Congress to deliver his first State of the Union address. The event played in a fashion familiar to observers of American politics: The president, flanked by the vice president and Speaker of the House, was frequently interrupted by applause as he commented both on his legislative ideas and his foreign policy objectives. As is typical in such speeches, the president laid out a broad policy agenda, touching on economic recovery, health care reform, and energy policy (among other topics), using the theme "Rescue, Rebuild, Restore" as a rhetorical guide (Zeleny 2010). After the speech, the president gradually made his way out of the chamber, greeting well-wishers and signing programs, as the networks moved to coverage of Virginia Governor Bob McDonnell's Republican response. It was, in short, business as usual for an American president's State of the Union address.

But there was one moment in the president's address that was decidedly atypical, even if it likely went unnoticed by many who watched from their homes. Midway through the speech, President Obama pivoted from a discussion of the nation's fiscal woes to discuss what he saw as a "deficit of trust" in government among the general public, characterized by "deep and corrosive doubts about how Washington works that have been growing for years." Obama proposed that in order to increase public confidence in government, Congress and the executive branch focus on working together "to end the outsized influence of lobbyists; to do our work openly; to give our people the government they deserve." Specifically, the president suggested greater disclosure rules for lobbyists, and noted that his administration had excluded them from the policymaking process. He then went much further:

> With all due deference to separation of powers, last week the Supreme Court reversed a century of law that I believe will open the floodgates for special interests—including foreign corporations—to spend without limit in our elections. I don't think American elections should be bankrolled by America's most powerful interests, or worse, by foreign entities. They should be decided by the American people. And I'd urge

Democrats and Republicans to pass a bill that helps to correct some of these problems. (ibid.)

This instant in the president's speech, while brief, was a notable one because presidents rarely use the State of the Union address as a vehicle to affect public opinion regarding the actions of the U.S. Supreme Court. Indeed, President Obama's remarks made him just the second president since 1960 to discuss federal court decisions during such an occasion (Parsneau 2013), and aside from Franklin Roosevelt's admonishment of the New Deal–averse Court in his 1937 address, Obama's direct characterization of a Supreme Court decision as a mistake was unprecedented in a State of the Union message (Barnes 2010). The rarity of such a moment is understandable; presidents frequently use their State of the Union address to suggest congressional action on future policy, but criticizing a Supreme Court decision is tantamount to arguing with an umpire after a call has been made. As the highest judicial authority in the land (and an unelected one at that), presidents have little to gain from twisting the arms of Supreme Court justices by influencing mass opinion with the so-called bully pulpit.

Moreover, the decision to which Obama was referring, *Citizens United v. Federal Election Commission* (558 U.S. 310 (2010)), may have seemed unlikely to have been the topic of conversation around many American dinner tables during the week between its release and the president's remarks, since its effect was to make changes to rules about who could spend money to promote campaigns or viewpoints during elections. Compared to regulatory policies that force people to change their behavior, or redistributive ones that raise taxes or change government benefits, the politics of campaign finance reform generally do not draw much attention from many people (see: Lowi 2009). Rather, changes to campaign finance policies are debated in the halls of government by elites, with commentary from cable news pundits that fails to rise to incendiary levels. Moreover, very few Americans typically contribute money to political organizations: Fewer than 5 percent gave money to politicians in 2008.[1] Simply, because changes to campaign finance laws affect few Americans in a direct way, it is difficult to provoke a strong mass reaction about them.

That he took on the Court anyway illustrated President Obama's deep frustration with its decision in *Citizens United*. The opinion in that case allowed both for-profit and nonprofit corporations, as well as labor unions, to spend money on communications during elections, even when their message expressly advocates the election or defeat of a candidate. The practical implication of the decision was that corporations and unions were allowed to either purchase advertising or other communications materials directly, or to donate funds to other groups so long as their money ultimately went only toward independent communications (and not to candidates or parties).

Given his remarks that evening, Obama appeared to have two concerns about the case's likely impact: First, he thought it possible that groups with access to vast resources might choose to spend a great deal of money during a given election, which could conceivably drown out the voices of candidates or interested, less-wealthy citizens. Second, the president expressed some worry that foreign-owned corporations could inject money into American politics via their subsidiaries within the United States. In either case, Obama likely reasoned that the viewpoint of the average voter was less likely to be expressed in the post–*Citizens United* world. Thus, Obama's position was that in allowing corporate spending during elections, the Supreme Court had favored the interests of small, relatively wealthy groups over those of individual American voters.

But the evening also demonstrated that there was a fair amount of disagreement among political elites about what *Citizens United* actually meant for the future of American elections. Such discord was on display even as the president made his remarks, as Associate Justice Samuel Alito—who had voted with the majority in the case—mouthed the words "not true" from his seat in the front row (Barnes 2010). It was less clear though *which* part of the president's statement Alito found to be untrue. Certainly, President Obama's contention that the decision "reversed a century of law" was dubious.[2] Bans on direct corporate donations to political candidates had been in effect for more than a century, but *Citizens United* did not enable corporations to contribute money to candidates for office. Alternatively, perhaps Alito took issue with Obama's assertion that *Citizens United* would render an environment in which "special interests . . . bankroll American elections." If corporations are merely groups of people with a common interest, Alito (and the rest of the justices in the majority) could argue that the Court's decision had merely made it possible for a wider range of voices to be heard.

The exchange between the president and Justice Alito underscored their very different personal orientations to campaign finance regulations. On one hand, Alito and his majority colleagues had crafted an opinion in accordance with the views of many civil libertarians. In this framework, political money is viewed as effectively the same thing as political speech, because the former presumably facilitates the dissemination of a specific message. Assuming that political speech is sacred in a free society, adherents to this viewpoint tend to view campaign finance regulations with skepticism, arguing that they complicate the act of speaking in a political setting. On the other hand, the president—like many other Americans who favor reforms geared toward making elections more competitive, transparent, and reflective of the "will of the people"—expressed a willingness to tolerate some restrictions on campaign spending in the interest of achieving those ends. Thus, the president might have argued that although money does largely equate to speech in American politics, it is still important to consider the implications of allowing money to freely enter the political system, regardless of its source and sum.

Most everyone agrees that free speech is a cornerstone of American democracy, but political equality is also valued, and it seems reasonable to argue that few Americans want their political system to be slanted in favor of the rich and powerful. Debates over campaign finance regulations therefore often pit free speech against fairness, and the public confrontation between the president and the Supreme Court in early 2010 certainly reflected that. Regardless of which side in the debate is correct, it is safe to say that 2009–2010 was a significant year in American campaign finance. Together with another federal court case (*SpeechNow.org v. Federal Election Commission*, discussed at length in Chapter 2), the *Citizens United* opinion substantially altered the regulatory landscape, allowing for a much wider range of groups to directly infuse money into the system. The president and the Supreme Court may have been at philosophical odds in early 2010, but neither could say for sure what the practical effects of those decisions would be. Before considering those effects, we examine the roots of the new campaign finance environment in the United States.

CITIZENS UNITED MAKES A MOVIE

The chain of events leading to President Obama's comments was preceded by several important cases dealing with campaign finance law, each of which ultimately had implications for *Citizens United v. Federal Election Commission*. Campaign finance rules are often reviewed by the courts to make certain they do not infringe upon an individual's or group's First Amendment speech rights. As such, campaign finance laws are typically subject to strict scrutiny, which necessitates that the government prove a law furthers a compelling government interest (for example, reducing the appearance of corruption) and is narrowly tailored to achieve that interest (*United States v. Carolene Products*, 304 U.S. 144 (1938), Footnote Four). With the federal courts applying strict scrutiny standards over the years, some campaign finance laws have been upheld, while others have been judged unconstitutional (for extended discussions, see: Gora 2011; Lowenstein et al. 2008). The principles of these cases are important for understanding why the Court made the decision it did in *Citizens United*, and we discuss them below. However, it is also important to understand the origins of the *Citizens United* case, which was set in motion two years before President Obama's comments when a nonprofit group made a movie.

The group, a conservative advocacy organization calling itself Citizens United, had since 1988 been dedicated to the advancement of American conservative principles such as "limited government, freedom of enterprise, strong families, and national sovereignty and security."[3] The organization pursued its objectives mainly through the utilization of so-called grassroots tactics, employing a mix of policy advocacy, organization, and mass education about public policy in an effort to influence public opinion. It also maintained a separate political action committee, Citizens United Political Victory Fund (CUPVF), which accepted contributions from like-minded individuals (subject to $5,000 limitations per election) and passed that money along to candidates it supported. During the 2008 election, for instance, CUPVF raised more than $3.5 million from private donors, and contributed about $250,000 to candidates running for federal offices. All of the recipients of CUPVF funds were Republicans.[4] In short, Citizens United was—and is—not unlike a myriad of other groups in Washington D.C., seeking to influence public policy by changing both the minds of voters and the composition of Congress.

One of its primary methods of speaking directly to the voting public was the production of books—and later, of documentary films—that promoted the group's viewpoint. Since 2000, for instance, Citizens United has released films detailing a conservative case for American energy and immigration policy changes, among others. The organization has also proven itself quite capable of assailing those on the other side of the political divide, from groups it views as adversarial like the American Civil Liberties Union to the United Nations, which it perceives as threatening American sovereignty. Left-leaning politicians are also fair game. Indeed, every Democratic presidential nominee from 2000 onward has been the subject of a highly critical Citizens United production, from the 2000 book *Prince Albert: The Life and Lies of Al Gore* to a film titled *Hype: The Obama Effect*.[5]

It was, however, a 2008 film about then–New York Senator Hillary Clinton that garnered Citizens United national attention and set the stage for significant changes to American campaign finance regulations. Clinton was running in the 2008 Democratic presidential primary, and in *Hillary: The Movie*, Citizens United advanced a sustained case against her nomination. Over its 90 minutes, *Hillary: The Movie* employed archival video intermingled with both critical narration and interviews conducted with Clinton detractors. The film unrelentingly assaulted Clinton's character, accusing her of untruths and obfuscation throughout her career not only as an Arkansas attorney, but also in public life as both first lady (of both Arkansas and the United States) and as a United States Senator.

The film's clear goal was to raise doubts about Clinton's honesty and capacity for leadership. It reminded viewers of her highly visible role in the failed attempt at large-scale health care reform during her husband's presidency, and questioned whether she truly possessed the policy credentials that she had allegedly claimed early in the primary. It also depicted her as, in the words of one interviewee, "steeped in sleaze," while speculating about her involvement in a number of scandals during her time in both Arkansas and Washington. The film was by any measure an effort to convince viewers that a Hillary Clinton presidency would result in policies antithetical to the beliefs of American conservatives. Dick Morris, former aide of President Bill Clinton turned critic, pointedly expressed such anxiety during an interview shown in the film, saying "Hillary is really the closest thing we have in America to a European socialist."[6]

Hillary: The Movie was certainly red meat for conservative anti-Clinton voters, but given the questions it introduced about Clinton's character in general, it held the potential to raise doubts about her even among less ideologically motivated viewers. Citizens United therefore wanted the film to reach as many eyes as possible, and so just before Democratic voters got the chance to start casting their presidential primary ballots in early 2008, the group began the process of marketing and distribution. This was a two-step process. First, Citizens United intended to sell DVDs of the movie directly to consumers through its website for $23.95, and also to screen the film in seven theaters nationally (*Citizens United v. Federal Election Commission*, 530 F. Supp. 2d 274 (D.D.C. 2008) [2008 BL 7985]). The second phase introduced some elements of broadcast media. Citizens United planned to place the film among the "on-demand" offerings of cable and satellite television providers, which would allow their customers to order the movie from their home TV and watch it at their convenience. To raise awareness about the movie—and to persuade people to purchase an on-demand viewing—Citizens United also created media advertising for it, which was intended to air in one 30-second and two 10-second advertisements during programs that promised to have healthy proportions of conservative viewers. These advertisements were intended to air both before and after the film's theatrical release date in January of 2008, which coincided with early Democratic nominating events.

These decisions were not without risk, since the Federal Election Commission (FEC)—the agency tasked with enforcing federal campaign finance laws—could very well have deemed them illegal and punishable with large fines and up to five years of jail time. Citizens United's immediate problem in 2008 was that it was itself a nonprofit corporation, while part of its funding—and, therefore, funding for the film—had also come from corporate sources. Thus, either advertising or broadcasting the film was likely to be judged as a violation of the Federal Election Campaign Act (FECA), which had banned direct corporate independent expenditures in the early 1970s, and the Bipartisan Campaign Reform Act (BCRA) of 2002, a set of reforms which became commonly known as "McCain-Feingold" after Senators John McCain (R-AZ) and Russell Feingold (D-WI) had sponsored similar legislation in the Senate.

The BCRA had made sweeping changes to campaign finance regulations in federal elections, including higher individual contribution limits and the banning of so-called soft money raised by parties in unlimited sums. Soft money was ostensibly for "party-building" activities such as phone banking or party (not candidate) advertising, but in practice, the line between "party" functions and "campaign" activities—that expressly advocated the election or defeat of an individual candidate—was often blurry (Magleby 2010). By the end of the 1990s, donors could write massive checks to aid the campaigns of their favored candidates (Gill and Lipsmeyer 2005). The Democratic and Republican Parties combined raised a little more than $85 million in soft money in 1992; in 2002 the combined figure was nearly $500 million (Gill and Lipsmeyer 2005, Table 1). By banning such funding, the BCRA was widely seen as an impediment to the ability of moneyed interests to "buy votes" (see: Corrado 2003; Malbin 2003).

But Citizens United had not contributed "soft money." Rather, it was concerned that advertising *Hillary: the Movie* would run afoul of Section 203 of the BCRA, which banned "corporate and labor disbursements for electioneering communications"—that is, an advertisement that mentions a specific candidate for federal office by name—within 30 days of a primary election and 60 days of a general election (2 U.S.C. § 441b). The BCRA also mandated that all electioneering communications disclose in the ad itself the individuals or groups that paid for the advertising. Like the ban on soft money, these provisions of the BCRA were intended to limit the ability of moneyed interests to leverage their war chests into votes. By prohibiting corporate- and labor-funded "issue advocacy ads," which could in theory allow a narrow interest to swing public opinion with a sensationalistic ad late in an election, the BCRA aimed to ensure that corporations and unions did not enjoy disproportionate influence over the political process due simply to the size of their treasuries.

Citizens United was no stranger to the rules governing electioneering communications. Indeed, it had previously alleged that left-leaning film-makers had violated them. During the 2004 election, the group had asked the FEC to prevent the broadcast and/or advertising of director Michael Moore's film *Fahrenheit 9/11*. Moore's documentary was highly critical of then-president George W. Bush's handling of events surrounding the terrorist attacks of September 11, 2001, the subsequent "War on Terror," and the Iraq War. The film was released in theaters late in June 2004, and was distributed on DVD in October of that same year—shortly before the presidential election. Given its anti-Bush slant, a number of conservative organizations sought to limit its release, while liberal groups rallied to the cause. For instance, the left-leaning organization MoveOn.org urged people to see the film, while Move America Forward, a right-leaning group, launched a letter-writing campaign designed to dissuade theater owners from screening it (Kasindorf and Keen 2004).

In a complaint submitted to the FEC the day before Moore's film was released, Citizens United made a legal challenge rooted in the newly enacted BCRA. The group argued that Moore had made the film "for the express purpose of influencing the outcome of the 2004 presidential election." There was certainly some veracity to this claim, as Moore had freely admitted that he hoped the film would contribute to President Bush's defeat in the 2004 election (Kasindorf and Keen 2004). Because it featured images of the president and other candidates for federal office, Citizens United claimed that *Fahrenheit 9/11* amounted to electioneering communications as defined by the BCRA if it—or related advertising featuring images of Bush—would be broadcast within 60 days of the November election or within 30 days of the Republican National Convention, which began on August 30. As such, Citizens United asserted that Moore, as well as his corporate producers and distributors, were "about to violate [the law] because the ads will be funded by corporate and foreign money, expenditures for the ads will not be reported to the Federal Election Commission, and the ads will not include the required disclosure statements."[7]

The FEC dismissed the complaint. It may have been reasonable to assert that as media companies whose primary mode of profit was the dissemination of films and related materials, the companies involved in marketing *Fahrenheit 9/11* qualified for a statutory "media exception" that would have allowed them to produce marketing materials containing Bush's image. However, the FEC exercised restraint in this area in ruling that such an exemption need not be granted for conduct that had not actually occurred. As Citizens United's complaint "present[ed] nothing more than idle, unsupported speculation," the FEC closed the matter, since guessing about what a corporation *might* do would "invite misuse of the enforcement process to harass political opponents engaged in legal conduct." No further actions were issued by the FEC relative to the film's marketing. *Fahrenheit 9/11* went on to gross nearly $120 million, making it the highest-earning documentary film of all time, more than $40 million ahead of the next-highest earning documentary, *March of the Penguins*, as of late 2013.[8]

Considering the long-shot nature of its petition against *Fahrenheit 9/11*, it is worthwhile to consider whether Citizens United was mainly interested in hectoring the marketing strategy for that film, or whether it had ulterior motives in mind. One possibility is that Citizens United had recognized an opportunity to test whether the FEC would grant a "media exception" from the electioneering rules to companies producing documentary films. The BCRA allowed such exemptions for material that appeared "in a news story, commentary, or editorial distributed through the facilities of a broadcast, cable, or satellite television or radio station." Though it was banned from traditional "electioneering" due to its corporate structure, Citizens United might have believed in 2004 that the FEC would distinguish between documentary films and campaign advertising, allowing corporate producers of the former to air ads with candidate images. Such a decision would have allowed it to create and market similar movies advocating conservative ideas.

If that was indeed Citizens United's true motivation for filing a complaint against *Fahrenheit 9/11*, then it did not take long for the group to get an answer. Its method this time was simple: Citizens United would simply ask the FEC if it would be allowed to market documentary films. In October 2004, Citizens United sought an advisory opinion from the FEC about whether it could pay providers to broadcast a documentary about Democratic presidential nominee John Kerry and his running mate, John Edwards, and also whether it could air advertisements for the movie.[9] The film would likely have been similar in tone to *Fahrenheit 9/11*; that is, it would probably not have painted Edwards and Kerry in the most flattering light. The ads that

Citizens United proposed were well within the definitions of "electioneering" in the BCRA; they mentioned both candidates by name, and would have aired close to the election. However, Citizens United asked the FEC to determine whether it could qualify for a media exemption to the electioneering rules. Like *Fahrenheit 9/11*, the film would be a "documentary," and the ads were directing people to buy it for home viewing.

The FEC failed to grant the media exception, however. According to the Commission, in order to be excepted from the electioneering rules, Citizens United would have to demonstrate that it regularly made and distributed films, which it did not do in 2004. The FEC went on to note that by paying to have the film broadcast (as opposed to the opposite arrangement), Citizens United was itself insinuating that it was not a media outlet, since it clearly had to rely on the services of other entities with broadcast abilities to disseminate the film. As a corporation that failed to meet the media exceptions, the FEC therefore ruled that Citizens United could neither pay to have the movie aired, nor could it finance broadcast advertising. Citizens United was allowed only to "disseminate the documentary through direct mail, print advertising, videocassette and DVD sales, the Internet and in theaters, without being affected by the electioneering communication provisions" (ibid.). It was back to the drawing board for the would-be conservative documentary filmmakers.

* * *

Given the FEC's previous refusal to grant Citizens United a media exception to disseminate its John Kerry movie, there was a high probability that *Hillary: The Movie* would meet a similar fate in 2008. Citizens United probably knew that the FEC was likely to claim that considering its exclusively negative tone and laser-like focus on Senator Clinton, *Hillary: The Movie* amounted to a 90-minute campaign commercial well within the BCRA definitions of "electioneering," and as such could neither be aired on broadcast outlets nor advertised over the airways within the applicable time limits. This presented an obvious marketing challenge. Were it limited to only movie theater screenings and online DVD sales, the film's audience would be considerably narrower than intended. Citizens United surely realized that the only way to proceed with its plans to market political documentaries was to change the rules of the game.

In December 2007, Citizens United brought suit against the FEC in the United States District Court for the District of Columbia. The purpose of the suit was to secure an injunction prohibiting the FEC from enforcing the electioneering provisions of the BCRA with regard to *Hillary: The Movie*. To that end, Citizens United made a First Amendment challenge, claiming that the BRCA's bans on electioneering communications amounted to an unconstitutional infringement on its members' freedom of speech. Moreover, the group alleged that because in its view its electioneering activities could not be banned, the disclosure requirements of the BCRA were also unconstitutional.

First Amendment speech protections have long clashed with the restrictions imposed by campaign finance regulations. The general conflict in American campaign finance case law is that restrictions on contribution and/or spending are viewed by some as unreasonable restrictions on political speech, which has traditionally garnered significant protection (for an excellent summary, see: La Raja 2008, Ch. 3). As such, the history of First Amendment litigation on campaign finance regulations is as old as campaign finance law itself. There was therefore no shortage of existing opinions to guide the interpretation of Citizens United's speech claims. Indeed, there are a number of cases that were so important to the federal court deliberations in *Citizens United v. FEC* that they merit some description here.

The seminal case in American campaign finance is *Buckley v. Valeo* (424 U.S. 1 (1976)), in which the contribution and spending limitations enacted in the early 1970s with the Federal Election Campaign Act (FECA) were challenged on First Amendment grounds. The FECA was a significant, wide-ranging reform that had for the first time created a meaningful regulatory environment in federal campaign finance. The law implemented statutory campaign contribution limits, and also originally mandated spending limitations for congressional campaigns. Moreover, the FECA barred all expenditures made by either private citizens or groups "advocating the election or defeat of (a) candidate" in excess of $1,000 per annum.

In *Buckley*, the Supreme Court held that while contribution limits were constitutional, there could be no prohibition on either individuals or candidates looking to spend their own money to directly communicate a political message. The distinction between contributions and direct spending in *Buckley* is based on two premises. First, the government has an interest in preventing instances of corruption, or even in limiting public *perceptions* of corruption. Second, money spent on election communications effectively equates to speech in the modern political realm, so more money spent in this manner is equivalent to more speech. In contrast, the act of contribution by an individual to a candidate, party, or PAC is itself an expressive act. This distinction allowed the court to strike down spending limits on individuals while upholding contribution limits: In the Court's framework setting limitations on the amount of money that a private citizen could spend would be tantamount to muzzling political speech, but the size of contributions can be limited in the interest of reducing corruption.

The Court in *Buckley* applied the same logic to independent expenditures. Although, as noted above, the FECA had originally sought to limit independent expenditures "relative to a clearly identified candidate," the Court held that no such limitation could pass constitutional scrutiny. However, the Court did determine that in the interest of reducing the appearance of untoward relationships, groups engaging in *express* advocacy—but not *issue* advocacy—could be subjected to disclosure and contribution requirements. The difference between express and issue advocacy is that in the former case, an ad would expressly advocate the election or defeat of a federal candidate (using words such as, "vote for," "elect," "support," "cast your ballot for," "vote against," "defeat," "reject," etc.), while in the latter, political issues or policy proposals might be discussed and the candidate need not appear at all.[10]

The Court's treatment of the FECA ban on independent expenditures from corporate treasuries has also displayed some nuance. In 1986, the Court heard arguments in *FEC v. Massachusetts Citizens for Life, Inc.* (479 U.S. 238 (1986)), in which the issue was whether Massachusetts Citizens for Life, Inc. (MCFL), a nonprofit corporation with no members, was subject to the ban on corporate election spending in the FECA. MCFL had printed a voter guide during the 1978 election that detailed the positions of candidates on abortion policies. The guide contained images of candidates that MCFL supported, and in some instances, used phrases such as "vote pro-life." The question before the Court was therefore whether MCFL had engaged in unlawful express advocacy, or only issue advocacy.

In a narrow decision, the Supreme Court determined that MCFL had violated the FECA by engaging in express advocacy with its treasury funds, but more importantly, that the FECA ban on independent expenditures amounted to an unconstitutional impediment to corporate speech. However, the Court held that only *a narrow set of corporate organizations* were exempt from the ban on direct corporate expenditures. Specifically, the Court formulated the "MCFL Test" that deemed only expenditures from nonprofit, politically oriented corporations allowable for express advocacy. For a corporate organization to fit this definition, the Supreme Court held that three criteria must be met: First, the main purpose of the organization must be "promoting political ideas," and not "business activities." Second, the group may have no shareholders that can take a part of its assets or income. Third, the group must not be affiliated with a business corporation or labor union, and may not accept contributions from those entities (see: Askin 2002).

The Supreme Court applied the MCFL Test in its 1990 opinion in *Austin v. Michigan Chamber of Commerce* (494 U.S. 652 (1990)). In that case, the Michigan Chamber of Commerce challenged a state law prohibiting independent expenditures made by corporations from their general funds. The basis for the Chamber's challenge was that as a nonprofit corporation focused on advancing member interests, it was more analogous to a traditional political advocacy organization than a business enterprise, and should therefore pass the MCFL Test.

The Court disagreed. Justice Marshall's opinion held that the typical wealth of a corporation—compared to that of most private citizens—created conditions in which the former could exert disproportionate influence over elections, relative to the latter. The Chamber of Commerce failed the MCFL Test because even though it had tax-exempt status, for-profit corporations provided a significant component of the Chamber's funding. The mere fact that they possess on average much deeper pockets than the typical citizen was sufficient for the Court in *Austin* to hold that "corporate wealth can unfairly influence elections" in a manner inconsistent with the public interest. Indeed, Marshall pulled no punches in describing "the corrosive and distorting effects of immense aggregations of wealth that are accumulated with the help of the corporate form and that have little or no correlation to the public's support for the corporation's political ideas." Suffice to say that the Supreme Court's opinion in *Austin* did not bode well for an expansion of corporate independent expenditures beyond the MCFL Test—at least with the composition of the Court in the early 1990s.

Equally salient to the *Citizens United* case was *McConnell v. Federal Election Commission* (540 U.S. 93), which had posed several direct challenges to the constitutionality of the BCRA in 2003, shortly after its passage. The most pertinent BCRA challenge in *McConnell* for Citizens United's subsequent argument was that of the electioneering rules. The Supreme Court upheld the BCRA's electioneering provisions (described above) in *McConnell*. Consistent with its findings in both *Buckley* and *Austin*, the Court held that the BCRA electioneering restrictions combat the "appearance of corruption" that might result from large expenditures made by corporations on behalf of candidates for federal office. The ban on electioneering by most corporations—and certainly for-profit business corporations—was therefore upheld.

By the time Citizens United's case reached the federal court system, however, there were signs that the Supreme Court might be willing to soften its position on direct corporate expenditures. In its 2007 opinion in *Federal Election Commission v. Wisconsin Right to Life, Inc.* (551 U.S. 449), the Court carved out some significant exemptions that allowed corporate funding for express advocacy. In that case, Wisconsin Right to Life, Inc. (WRTL) had run afoul of the FEC for airing ads that were critical of Democratic Wisconsin Senator Russell Feingold's voting record on abortion, even though the group did not explicitly tell voters to withhold support from him. The group's defense was that because its ads were ostensibly informative on a policy dimension, they should not be considered "electioneering" and should be protected speech. The Court agreed, holding that in order to be banned under the BCRA electioneering rules, an ad's *only* purpose must be to expressly advocate the election or defeat of a named candidate. In formulating their opinion in the case, Chief Justice John Roberts and his colleagues in the majority positioned themselves as defenders of speech rights, writing that "the First Amendment requires us to err on the side of protecting political speech rather than suppressing it."

* * *

Given the Supreme Court's apparent willingness to consider as-applied challenges to the electioneering rules in the BCRA, Citizens United's attempt to prohibit the FEC from penalizing it was not wholly unreasonable. In weighing whether to issue a preliminary injunction, the District Court's task was to judge whether, given the manner in which the Supreme Court had interpreted the BCRA rules, Citizens United was likely to win its challenge on First Amendment grounds. Unfortunately for Citizens United, the District Court justices held that the film could not be reasonably interpreted as anything other than a focused attempt to thwart Clinton's effort to become president. The District Court wrote that,

> After viewing *The Movie* and examining the 73-page script at length, the court finds (that) . . . *The Movie* is susceptible of no other interpretation than to inform the electorate that Senator Clinton is unfit for office, that the United States would be a dangerous place in a President Hillary Clinton world, and that viewers should vote against her. *The Movie* is thus the functional equivalent of express advocacy.

Simply, because the Supreme Court had previously ruled clearly and consistently that the electioneering rules set forth in the BCRA were allowable restrictions on speech rights, the District Court could find little rationale that were the Supreme Court to take the case, it would see *Hillary: The Movie* as an allowable communication. As such, it refused to stop the FEC from enforcing the BCRA.

Citizens United was undeterred. The group took its challenge to the United States Supreme Court, making essentially the same claims as it had in the District Court. In persuading the Court to hear the case, Citizens United argued that the electioneering provisions of the BCRA impeded it from adding its voice to the public debate, amounting to an unconstitutional infringement on its First Amendment rights. Despite having ruled previously on the legality of the electioneering rules, the Supreme Court agreed to hear the case, and scheduled the argument for March 24, 2009. Initially, the case—a narrow claim against a rather esoteric component of federal campaign finance law—attracted relatively little attention outside of academic circles. However, its humble beginning belied its significance: Before all was said and done, the proceedings in *Citizens United v. FEC* would consume two oral arguments, and would attract briefs from more than three dozen outside parties. The Supreme Court's opinion in the case would ultimately spark a visible public debate involving even the president of the United States, and would lay the groundwork for a fundamental shift in the conduct of American elections.

* * *

Citizens United got its day in court on March 24, 2009. Its counsel, Theodore Olson, got straight to the point in arguing that byzantine federal campaign finance rules were infringing on the First Amendment rights of citizens and groups alike. Freedom of speech, he said, was "being smothered by one of the most complicated, expensive, and incomprehensible regulatory regimes ever invented by the administrative state." Olson argued that it was unfair to exempt media corporations (whose primary focus was disseminating information) from penalty while punishing a group like Citizens United, which had done nothing more than create a film that was "the very definition of robust, uninhibited debate about a subject of intense political interest that the First Amendment is there to guarantee."

The justices immediately seized on Citizens United's corporate status. The first question, from Justice Souter, was whether Citizens United would hold the same position if *Hillary: The Movie* had been released by General Motors. In effect, Souter was asking the group to clarify what it wanted the Court to do. He wondered whether Citizens United was suggesting that all corporations be allowed to spend money during elections, or whether the group's position was that there was something about the film itself that warranted exemption. Olson's answers suggested the latter. He said that since the film "informs and educates" over the course of its 90 minutes, it was not the sort of material that Congress had intended to ban in the BCRA. Indeed, Olson's position was that *Hillary: The Movie* was precisely the sort of communication that the Court had exempted in the *WRTL* decision.

Justice Ginsburg appeared to disagree with that premise, noting that the Court in *WRTL* had in fact exempted *issue* ads, and not those geared toward campaign advocacy. Though it was 90 minutes long, and in the opinion of Justice Breyer likely "more intelligent" and an example of "better electioneering" in comparison, the early questioning from the justices suggested that they saw *Hillary: The Movie* as effectively a 90-minute campaign commercial, little different from the familiar ones of the 30-second variety. It might therefore have appeared early on in the argument that the Court was unlikely to find that Citizens United was due an exemption. As Justice Kennedy—the presumed swing vote among the justices—noted,

> If we concede . . . that a short, 30-second, 1-minute campaign ad can be regulated, you want me to write an opinion and say, "well, if it's 90 minutes, then that's different." It seems to me that you can make the argument that . . . 90 minutes is much more powerful in support or in opposition to a candidate.

Olson disagreed, however, stating that the Court had previously found that broadcast materials whose purpose was to "inform and educate," in *addition* to mere persuasion, were "on the line of being permissible." As a documentary film, Olson argued that *Hillary: The Movie* held greater potential than the typical 30-second campaign commercial to educate viewers. Justice Souter did not appear to be persuaded, saying,

> [The film is] not a musical comedy. I think we have no choice, really, but to say this is not issue advocacy; this is express advocacy saying "don't

vote for this person." And if that is a fair characterization, the difference between 90 minutes and 1 minute, either for statutory purposes or constitutional purposes, is a distinction that I just cannot follow.

Souter's question suggested that his position was that neither the length of the film nor its general level of information was relevant to whether Citizens United could legally broadcast it. Because it was (to Souter, presumably) a totally one-sided description of why Hillary Clinton was unfit for the White House, the movie amounted to electioneering of the sort proscribed by the BCRA.

Olson, however, pressed his point that *Hillary: The Movie* should be protected speech precisely because it was *different* than the traditional broadcast media that the BCRA targets. He noted more than once that had Citizens United released the same material in a different format—on the Internet or in a book, for instance—there would be no constitutional issue, as Congress had only banned corporate electioneering for broadcast media. Justice Scalia appeared to agree, and offered some thoughts that seemed to aid Olson's position:

It may well be that the kind of speech that is reflected in a serious 90-minute documentary is entitled to greater constitutional protection. And it may well be that the kind of speech that is not only offered but invited by the listener is entitled to heightened First Amendment scrutiny, which is what this is since you have pay for view.

Scalia's was an important distinction, if one accepted the premise that Congress had sought to ban electioneering communications with the understanding that the voting public could find corporate-funded advertising persuasive, and also that people would have little choice with regard to the advertisements that they saw during a given telecast. Because people were in effect paying to watch *Hillary: The Movie* at their leisure (via television on-demand), Scalia was suggesting that perhaps it was difficult to argue that they were being forcibly influenced.

This opening allowed Scalia and his fellow conservative members of the Court, namely Chief Justice John Roberts and Justice Samuel Alito, to question whether the true difference between Citizens United's film and a 30-second campaign commercial was not its length, but the fact that it was broadcast in such a way that consumers would view it *by choice*. If that were the case, then the film might be no different than a book or an Internet site, which Congress had not subjected to the electioneering restrictions in the BCRA. Malcolm Stewart, Deputy Solicitor General of the United States (and the government's advocate in the case), quickly found himself on the defensive as the justices pursued this line of argument.

Throughout his argument, Stewart was adamant that because it was a corporate-funded, prolonged attack of Clinton's capacity for office, and that it was intended to air on television, *Hillary: The Movie* was subject to the ban on electioneering communications. Since candidates had previously elected to air extended "infomercial" ads in the past (most notably, Ross Perot in 1992 and 1996), the government's position was that a communication expressly advocating the defeat of a candidate was certainly electioneering, regardless of how long it lasted. Stewart said,

> It may be rare to find a 90-minute film that is so unrelenting in its praise or criticism of a particular candidate that it will be subject to no reasonable interpretation other than to vote for or against that person, but when you have that, as I think we do here, there's no constitutional distinction between the 90-minute film and the 60-second advertisement.

The government's rationale was that the film clearly met the definition of "express advocacy" that the Court had outlined in *WRTL*, since the only reasonable interpretation of the film was that it was encouraging viewers not to support Senator Clinton. This assertion was part of a crucial exchange in the argument. To Stewart's claim that an ad and the film were functionally equivalent, Justice Kennedy was quick to respond that "If we think that . . . this film is protected, and you say there's no difference between the film and the ad, then the whole statute must be declared" unconstitutional.

Kennedy's question proved clairvoyant, though not quite as it was originally intended. During Stewart's argument, the justices began laying the groundwork for an expanded scope of argument in the case. Justice Scalia once again suggested that the "on-demand" nature of the film's availability made the constitutional question more complicated. Of Stewart, he asked,

> Unlike over-the-air television you have a situation where . . . this message would only air if somebody elects to hear it. So you really have two interested people, the speaker and the listener who wants to get this. Isn't that a somewhat heightened First Amendment interest than just over-the-air broadcasting of advertising which probably most listeners don't want to hear?

Justice Alito sharpened this point, asking Stewart,

> Do you think the Constitution required Congress to draw the line where it did, limiting this to broadcast and cable and so forth? What's your answer to Mr. Olson's point that there isn't any constitutional difference between the distribution of this movie on video demand and providing access on the Internet, providing DVDs, either through a commercial service or maybe in a public library, providing the same thing in a book? Would the Constitution permit the restriction of all of those as well?

Stewart's answer was that had Congress seen fit, it would have been consti-tutionally permissible for that body to apply the BCRA electioneering regu-lations to additional forms of media beyond broadcast advertising. Alito's response was sharp, and began a crucial exchange:

ALITO: "That's pretty incredible. You think that if a book was published, a campaign biography that was the functional equivalent of express advocacy, that could be banned?"

STEWART: "I'm not saying it could be banned. I'm saying that Con-gress could prohibit the use of corporate treasury funds and could require a corporation to publish it using its—"

ALITO: "Well, most publishers are corporations. And a publisher that is a corporation could be prohibited from selling a book?"

STEWART: "Well, of course the statute contains its own media exemption or media—"

ALITO: "I'm not asking what the statute says. The government's position is that the First Amendment allows the banning of a book if it's published by a corporation?"

At this point in the argument, Justice Kennedy and Chief Justice Roberts began asking questions designed to clarify under what conditions Stewart believed that the BCRA provisions could prevent the publication of a book. Justice Roberts ultimately posed a hypothetical question to Stewart: If a 500-page book was ostensibly about some issue, but contained a single sen-tence of express advocacy—that is, the last sentence said to vote for a can-didate—could that book be banned? Stewart responded that the publication of such a book could indeed be prohibited if its production was paid for via a corporation's general funds, and not from a PAC. In so doing, Stewart noted that the challenged material in the *MCFL* case had been a newsletter, which established a constitutional basis for prohibiting express advocacy—regardless of medium—funded by corporate treasuries.

Justices Alito, Kennedy, and Chief Justice Roberts had effectively backed Stewart into a corner. In admitting that the BCRA could potentially enable the government to ban the publication of a corporate-funded book for a single line of express advocacy out of 500 pages, the justices had greatly expanded the scope of the case. Was it, as it had appeared during much of the argument, a narrow case about the permissibility of corporate funding for on-demand videos? Or had Stewart's suggestion that the government was empowered to go beyond broadcast media in regulating corporate-funded electioneering opened the door to a much broader conversation about the corporate speech rights in American elections? In the weeks following the argument, it became clear that the government's defense of the BCRA was far from over.

ROUND TWO AT THE COURT

Citizens United v. FEC had at first appeared to be a fairly narrow question on an esoteric area of campaign finance regulation. Indeed, at the conclusion of arguments that March, the justices appeared to be considering two questions, neither of which held the potential to change much of note about the conduct of American elections. The first was whether *Hillary: The Movie* should be considered "express advocacy," that is, a communication whose sole purpose was to attack Clinton's capacity for office, or whether it was more akin to the issue ads that the Court had protected in *FEC v. Wisconsin Right to Life.* The government had argued that the film was indistinguishable from a traditional campaign advertisement in that its major message was to criticize a candidate by name. Citizens United's position was that due to its length and the extent to which it explored various elements of her biography, *Hillary: The Movie* could be reasonably interpreted as something else: an informational documentary whose primary purpose was to educate.

The second question was whether airing the film on-demand was the sort of broadcast communication that the BCRA sought to regulate, or whether on-demand broadcasting was more akin to the less-regulated media of books and Internet communications. The government's position was that *Hillary: The Movie* met the definition of broadcast media express advocacy, and could therefore be legally prohibited. Citizens United, on the other hand, saw on-demand as a fundamentally different form of media, exempt from the electioneering restrictions in federal campaign finance law.

In tandem, the questions about the legality of on-demand distribution of the film were hardly earth shattering, even in the world of campaign finance. However, there was a basis in the first argument—namely, the conversation between Malcolm Stewart, the government's advocate, and a number of justices—for expanding the scope of the case. Specifically, it seemed that several justices were now wondering whether, if on-demand videos could be banned by the BCRA, other forms of communication such as books or DVDs might also one day be subject to prohibition. Stewart had suggested that this was a possibility in at least some instances. Stewart's admission evidently sparked a conversation among the justices about whether the questions put before them in the first argument were too narrow, or whether there was in fact a larger First Amendment issue in the case. Put another way, if the government could ban books under existing campaign finance law, then perhaps the constitutionality of that law should be re-examined.

In June, the Supreme Court informed the parties that it wanted to hear new arguments in the case. The parties were instructed to argue a new question: "For the proper disposition of this case, should the Court overrule either or both *Austin v. Michigan Chamber of Commerce* and the part of *McConnell v. FEC* which addresses the facial validity of the Bipartisan Campaign Reform Act of 2002?"[11] The order to reargue was a clear signal that the Supreme Court was willing to consider whether those decisions—which held that corporate spending during elections could be banned in most conditions—could stand against the First Amendment. And if that were the case, then it was entirely possible that the Court could, for the first time, answer the question of whether corporations possess speech rights akin to those of individual citizens.

* * *

The parties returned to the Court on September 9, 2009. The flow of the second argument reflected an understanding among the justices and advocates alike that the Court was facing two possible courses of action: A *narrow* decision in which the Court would determine whether *Hillary: The Movie* (and similar on-demand broadcasting) was an electioneering communication subject to BCRA limitations, or a *broad* opinion that addressed the question of whether any corporate spending could be banned, presumably on the grounds that doing so violates the speech rights of corporations. If the Court chose to rule broadly—assumedly in favor of Citizens United—the opinion would effectively grant First Amendment speech rights to all corporations, regardless of their nonprofit status or involvement in business enterprise, allowing them to spend freely in American elections.

The new tone of argument was evident immediately. Both Theodore Olson, who once again represented Citizens United, and Floyd Abrams, arguing as an ally to Citizens United on behalf of Senator Mitch McConnell (R-KY), who had joined the case, did their best to drive the point that the case should be decided in as broad a fashion as possible. Considering the manner in which the Court had previously evaluated cases of corporate independent expenditure, the opening exchange between Justice Ginsburg and Olson—and the tone that it conveyed—carried great importance in setting the terms of the ensuing argument. In *Buckley,* the Court had held that while individual citizens' contributions could be limited in the interest of preventing the appearance of something akin to a quid pro quo exchange between contributor and candidate, the spending of neither individuals nor candidates could be constitutionally limited. If corporations were entitled to the same First Amendment protections as individuals, as Olson asserted, then their spending could therefore not be constitutionally limited and the corporate electioneering ban in the BCRA would have to be struck down.

Olson's opening statement at once broadened the scope of the debate and harkened to the government's waffling on the permissibility of banning books during the first oral argument of *Citizens United*:

> The government claims it may [prohibit corporate expenditure] based upon the *Austin* decision that corporate speech is by its nature corrosive and distorting because it might not reflect actual public support for the views expressed by the corporation. The government admits that that radical concept of requiring public support for the speech before you can speak would even authorize it to criminalize books and signs.

Justice Ginsburg asked the first question, and wasted no time in getting to the heart of the matter. Ginsburg asked,

> Mr. Olson, are you taking the position that there is no difference in the First Amendment rights of an individual? A corporation, after all, is not endowed by its creator with inalienable rights. So is there any distinction that Congress could draw between corporations and natural human beings for purposes of campaign finance?

Mr. Olson's reply—which made a claim on speech rights of all corporations—was a marked departure from the first argument, and set the stage for all that followed: "What the Court has said in the First Amendment context . . . over and over again, is that corporations are persons entitled to protection under the First Amendment."

Floyd Abrams also framed the case broadly. He began by noting the Supreme Court's traditional role of protecting First Amendment rights, and argued that it therefore had a responsibility to quell continual campaign finance litigation. This argument was consistent with one that Olson had made on behalf of Citizens United. If the Court were to rule narrowly, he had argued, then any conceivable standard or test that the Court might create for permissible corporate spending could keep the door open for sustained litigation. No matter where the Court put the line, it would likely be tested based on any number of unforeseen circumstances, and anyone who wished to do so would face the threat of punishment. As Olson had noted,

> The movie might be shorter, it might be video on demand, it might be a broadcast, it might have a different tone with respect to a candidate. Every one of those lines puts the speaker at peril that he will go to jail or be prosecuted or there will be litigation, all of which chills speech.

Abrams echoed this sentiment in his initial comments. He cited the Court's opinion in *New York Times v. Sullivan* (376 U.S. 254 (1964)) in which it had effectively nationalized libel law in an effort to preclude lawsuits brought by citizens of Southern states against media outlets during the Civil Rights Movement, absent demonstrated damages. Abrams argued that the Court decided *Sullivan* in the broadest possible terms because doing so was the most efficient way of protecting a free press reporting on a controversial issue. In short, Abrams felt that the Court "had come to the conclusion that the degree of First Amendment danger by the sort of lawsuits which were occurring in Alabama and elsewhere was something that had to be faced up to by the Court now." To Abrams, the issue in *Citizens United* was similar: Either recognize that corporations have speech rights, or force the courts to define the scope of legal corporate spending on a case-by-case basis.

As she had with Olson's statement, Ginsburg was the first justice to question Mr. Abrams, noting that unlike in *Sullivan*, there was a great deal of precedent upholding restrictions on corporate spending in elections. This sparked a lengthy debate on both the legislative and judicial history of the regulation of political money, during which Abrams—as Olson before him had been—was careful to distinguish between limits on contributions and limits on expenditures. Indeed, throughout the argument of both advocates for Citizens United, the questions from the liberal bloc of Justices—Breyer, Ginsburg, Sotomayor, and Stevens—focused on whether there was in fact a practical distinction between the corrupting potential of corporate contributions to candidates—which had been illegal since 1907 and were not being challenged—and the purchase of advertising that a candidate would surely notice and appreciate. If there was in fact no difference, precedent would seem to suggest that corporate spending could be restricted to advance the government's interest in preventing corruption, as the Court had held in *Buckley*. However, Abrams pointed out that the precedents in *Austin* and *McConnell* were not all that old (at 19 and 6 years, respectively), so if the Court held that expenditure was a different act than contribution, a ruling for Citizens United did not necessarily have to overturn well-established precedents.

The discussion of precedent culminated in a question from Justice Sotomayor, who was on the bench for her first oral argument as an Associate Justice, having replaced David Souter after the first argument in *Citizens United*. Justice Sotomayor began by noting that on the question of precedent,

> The one thing that is very interesting about this area of law for the last 100 years is the active involvement of both state and federal legislatures in trying to find that balance between the interest of protecting in their views how the electoral process should proceed and the interests of the First Amendment. And so my question to you is, once we say they can't, except on the basis of a compelling government interest narrowly tailored, are we cutting off or would we be cutting off that future democratic process? Because what you are suggesting is that the courts who created corporations as persons, gave birth to corporations as persons, and there could be an argument made that that was the Court's error to start with, not *Austin* or *McConnell*, but the fact that the Court imbued a creature of State law with human characteristics.

Abrams, however, appeared to believe that a broad ruling was inevitable. His answer to Sotomayor's question insinuated a belief that the government was by then desperately trying to limit its losses because it recognized that a majority of justices on the Court was thinking about the question in terms of rights—not just for Citizens United, but for *all* corporations. In picking the types of groups who were allowed to speak concurrent with elections,

Abrams argued that the government was creating an unreasonable burden on political speech. He did not miss the opportunity to communicate both points:

> I think that, reading [the government's] brief[s] . . . some of them at least come pretty close to saying that there must be a way for Citizens United to win this case other than a broad way. In my view the principles at stake here are the same. Citizens United happens to be sort of the paradigmatic example of the sort of group speaking no less about who to vote for or not who to vote for or what to think about a potential ongoing candidate for President of the United States. But in lots of other situations day by day there is a blotch to public discourse caused as a result of this Congressional legislation.

* * *

Given that the justices themselves had requested a broadening of the argument, Abrams appeared to be correct in his belief that the government's effort to limit the ruling to a narrow scope was on the ropes. However, throughout her argument on behalf of the government, Solicitor General Elena Kagan did her best to keep the focus not only on the narrow advocacy focus of Citizens United, but also on the government interest in preventing corruption. She began by invoking the consistency with which the Court had upheld restrictions on political money out of the interest of preventing corruption. Very early in her remarks, Kagan said, "For 100 years this Court, faced with many opportunities to do so, left standing the legislation that is at issue in this case—first the contribution limits, then the expenditure limits . . . and then of course in *Austin* specifically approved those limits."

To Kagan's position that the government's anti-corruption interest allowed it to restrict the flow of political money—and specifically, corporate independent expenditures—Justice Alito asked,

> What is your answer to the argument that more than half the States, including California and Oregon, Virginia, Washington State, Delaware, Maryland, a great many others, permit independent corporate expenditures for just these purposes? Now have they all been overwhelmed by corruption? A lot of money is spent on elections in California. Is there a record that the corporations have corrupted the political process there?

Alito's point was clear: If the government felt that barring groups like Citizens United from electioneering was reducing instances of corruption in federal politics, it should be willing to offer proof. Yet, Kagan was adamant in her insistence that congressional judgment supersedes such empirical claims. In response to Alito, she said, "I think the experience of some half the States cannot be more important than the 100-year old judgment of Congress that these expenditures would corrupt the Federal system."

Justice Kennedy appeared to take issue with the claim that the history of congressional action in the relevant area was 100 years old, saying that Kagan's assertion to that effect was "correct if you look at contributions, but this is an expenditure case." Kennedy's comment spoke to the heart of the matter in the minds of several justices: Whether corporations possessed a right to "speech" in the political arena, realized mainly via the direct expenditure of money for electioneering purposes, analogous to the First Amendment rights of an individual citizen. If such rights existed for corporations, then the burden of proof of corruption resulting from corporate independent expenditures would fall on the government. The tone of Kennedy's question was similar to that of several other more conservative justices, namely Alito, Scalia, and Chief Justice Roberts. In contrast to their liberal colleagues who had questioned the necessity of a broad ruling, the conservative bloc pressed Kagan on whether the Court's previous rulings in light of the BCRA were sufficient to guarantee that political speech would not be stifled, and whether corporate spending would indeed result in corruption.

Kagan noted that corporations may express themselves outside of the context of an election, and can both disseminate information and advocate favored policies via the standard lobbying process. She drew a distinction between lobbying and election expenditure, saying, "Of course corporations can lobby members of Congress in the same way that they could before this legislation. What this legislation is designed to do, because of its anticorruption interest, is to make sure that that lobbying is just persuasion and it's not coercion." The problem with corporate spending, according to Kagan, is the unidimensionality of corporate interest. "Few individuals," she said, have "only our economic interests. We have beliefs, we have convictions; we have likes and dislikes. Corporations engage the political process in an entirely different way and this is what makes them so much more damaging."

Chief Justice Roberts took issue with Kagan's characterization of corporate interests, arguing that, "a large corporation, just like an individual, has many diverse interests . . . The idea that corporations are different than individuals in that respect, I just don't think holds up." Justice Scalia attacked the premise from a different direction, noting that many for-profit corporations are very small, and are indeed only one person. To Scalia this meant that

> Most corporations are indistinguishable from the individual who owns them, the local hairdresser, the . . . auto dealer who has just lost his dealership and who wants to oppose whatever Congressman he thinks was responsible for this happening or whatever Congressman won't try to patch it up. . . . There is no distinction between the individual interest and the corporate interest. And that is true for the vast majority of corporations.

Scalia's point linked the speech rights of individuals with those of corporations, and made clear that there was a strong contingent of justices on the Court that favored deciding the case broadly. Indeed, for much of Kagan's argument the writing appeared to be on the wall. She consistently tried to maintain a narrow focus, and appeared to fight to the end for a minimally bad outcome. The government had argued in its briefs that since Citizens United—like the Michigan Chamber of Commerce in *Austin*—was funded with corporate contributions, it failed the MCFL Test. During the argument, Kagan deviated somewhat from that position. That resulted in an exchange between Kagan and Chief Justice John Roberts that proved telling:

> *KAGAN:* "This is an anomalous case in part because this is an atypical plaintiff. And the reason this is an atypical plaintiff is because this plaintiff is an ideological nonprofit and—"
>
> *ROBERTS:* "So you are giving up the distinction from MCFL that you defended in your opening brief? There you said this doesn't qualify as a different kind of corporation because it takes corporate funds, and now you are changing that position?"
>
> *KAGAN:* "No, I don't think we are changing it. MCFL is the law, and the FEC has always tried to implement MCFL faithfully. And that's what the FEC has tried to do."
>
> *ROBERTS:* "Do you think MCFL applies in this case even though the corporation takes corporate funds from for-profit corporations?"
>
> *KAGAN:* "I don't think *MCFL* as written applies in this case, but I think that the Court could, as lower courts have done, adjust *MCFL* potentially to make it apply in this case, although I think that would require a remand. What lower courts have done . . . *MCFL* was set up, it was written in a very strict kind of way so that the organization had to have a policy of accepting no corporate funds whatsoever. Some of the lower courts, including the D.C. Circuit, which, of course, sees a lot of these cases, have suggested that *MCFL* is too strict."
>
> *ROBERTS:* "Do you think it's too strict?"
>
> *KAGAN:* "The FEC has no objection to *MCFL* being adjusted in order . . . to give it some flexibility."
>
> *ROBERTS:* "So you want to give up this case, change your position, and basically say you lose solely because of the questioning that we have directed on reargument?"
>
> *KAGAN:* "No, I don't think that that is fair. We continue to think that the judgment below should be affirmed. If you are asking me, Mr. Chief Justice, as to whether the government has a preference as to the way in which it loses, if it has to lose, the answer is yes."

THE DECISION

The opinion, written by Justice Anthony Kennedy, was released in January 2010. Kennedy and his colleagues in the majority wrote that the case could not be resolved based on Citizens United's initial argument that on-demand television should be exempted from the electioneering provisions of the BCRA. The majority's rationale for this finding was that doing so would ignore a larger issue: That the rules banning corporate electioneering chilled the political speech of Citizens United and its funders. As such, the Court held, it must decide the case broadly, and decide the much larger question of whether corporations like Citizens United have a right to speech that the BCRA violated. In short, the majority found that such a right did exist.

The opinion of the Court addressed two main questions. The first was whether the electioneering rules in the BCRA as written covered *Hillary: The Movie*. The court determined that since more than 30 million households could have conceivably seen the film (well more than the 50,000 threshold set for a legal definition of an electioneering communication), the movie— even though it was offered in an on-demand setting, was an electioneering material as defined by law. Second, the Court also held that *Hillary: The Movie* certainly met the established definition of express advocacy, as it would be "understood by most viewers to be an extended criticism of Senator Clinton's qualifications and fitness for office." Given these findings (and previous opinions of the Court), the film could reasonably be prohibited.

But that was the end of the good news for the government. The Court went on to hold that the BCRA "beyond doubt discloses serious First Amendment flaws," and hinted that it would have to go well beyond Citizens United's initial request to exempt nonprofit corporate expenditures from the federal spending ban. The series of cases, beginning with *MCFL*, and moving through *Austin* and *McConnell*, had required the federal courts to judge the permissibility of corporate spending on a case-by-case basis. The Court noted that while such litigation was pending, speech was chilled as parties awaited judicial opinions. In *Citizens United*, the Supreme Court drew the line and decided that in order to ensure the protection of constitutional speech, it must eschew a framework that mandated such piecemeal action. Indeed, the majority likened the FEC's silencing of corporate groups to "prior restraint," when the government acts to prevent publication of material before it is ever made public. A broad opinion from the Court was necessary, Kennedy wrote, "especially if we are convinced that, in the end, this corporation has a constitutional right to speak on this subject."

The majority was indeed convinced. The Court in *Citizens United* overruled its decision in *Austin* and the parts of its opinion in *McConnell* that had upheld the ban on corporate spending. Corporations, it determined, were free to spend in elections however they liked (short of contributing to candidates). The Court's decision in *Citizens United* broke from previous opinions that tolerated the regulation of corporate spending on the basis of preventing corruption. Such an interest, wrote Kennedy, was minimal in comparison to the necessity of protecting the freedom of speech, including that of corporate organizations. In short, the justices determined that corporations—regardless of their structure or purpose—had First Amendment speech rights akin to those of private citizens. They deemed the BCRA's "prohibition on corporate independent expenditures . . . an outright ban on speech, backed by criminal sanctions . . . notwithstanding the fact that a PAC created by a corporation can still speak, for a PAC is a separate association from the corporation. Because speech is an essential mechanism of democracy—it is the means to hold officials accountable to the people—political speech must prevail against laws that would suppress it by design or inadvertence."

Indeed, the majority held that not even the historical rationale for regulating political money—reducing instances of corruption—could stand against what it saw as a violation of speech rights that occurred when corporate spending was prohibited. As Kennedy wrote,

> The *Buckley* Court upheld limits on direct contributions to candidates . . . recognizing a governmental interest in preventing quid pro quo corruption. However, the Court invalidated [the FECA's] expenditure ban, which applied to individuals, corporations, and unions, because it "fail[ed] to serve any substantial governmental interest in stemming the reality or appearance of corruption in the electoral process." While *Buckley* did not consider a separate ban on corporate and union independent expenditures found in [the FECA], had that provision been challenged in *Buckley's* wake, it could not have been squared with the precedent's reasoning and analysis.

As appeared likely in the second argument, the Supreme Court had ruled broadly. Kennedy further wrote that the majority in *Citizens United*

> now concludes that independent expenditures, including those made by corporations, do not give rise to corruption or the appearance of corruption. That speakers may have influence over or access to elected officials does not mean that those officials are corrupt. And the appearance of influence or access will not cause the electorate to lose faith in this democracy.

Speech rights, he wrote, must prevail, as "all speakers, including individuals and the media, use money amassed from the economic marketplace to fund their speech, and the First Amendment protects the resulting speech." Moreover, given the rapid rate with which technology changes the manner in which political speech can be delivered, the Court could not be assured that any tests it would establish in *Citizens United*, short of allowing *all* corporate speech, could prevent the unlawful prohibition of *some* corporate speech.

In sum, because the Supreme Court in *Citizens United* determined that the First Amendment would prevail over legislative efforts to curb corporate expenditures, corporate spending in American politics could thereafter not be stopped by any act of Congress, short of a constitutional amendment. In reaching this opinion, the Court had taken the unconventional step of asking for a reargument so that the parties could argue on broader terms than were originally proposed. Ultimately, the Supreme Court overturned its precedents in *Austin* and *McConnell*, and held that speech rights, regardless of the corporate structure of the entity purchasing political advertising, outweighed concerns stemming from the (small, in the Court's estimation) possibility of creating untoward relationships between corporations and candidates. In 2010 and beyond, American politics would certainly be different, but the character and importance of that difference remained to be seen.

* * *

Reaction to *Citizens United* was swift. Immediately following the release of the opinion, Fred Wertheimer, president of reform advocacy organization Democracy 21, called the decision a "disaster for the American people and a dark day for the Supreme Court" (Wertheimer 2010). Wertheimer was especially concerned with the "abandonment of precedent established by cases decided in 1990, 2003 and 2007, without any changed circumstances to justify these abrupt reversals" (ibid.). Longtime Court-watcher and journalist Jeffrey Toobin criticized the Court's "bad judgment" and "judicial activism" in the *New Yorker*, predicting that the decision would benefit Republican candidates and would be particularly harmful in state-level judicial elections (Toobin 2010). Reform-minded interest groups and think tanks such as Common Cause and the Brennan Center have taken strong positions against the *Citizens United* decision; the former initiated an "Amend 2012" campaign to restore limits and disclosure, while the latter hosted a conference in 2011 during which the key question was whether government would remain accountable to citizens under the new rules.

Others hailed the Court's opinion, which they saw as an expansion of speech rights in American elections. Bill Maurer, executive director of the Washington Chapter of the Institute for Justice, wrote in a guest column for the *Seattle Times*, "This is America. We do not ban books. We do not make it a crime to speak because the speech may be too influential. With this decision, Americans will get more information, hear more debate, and learn more about their elections" (Maurer 2010). Conservative columnist George Will noted in the *Washington Post* that the decision would simplify the regulations governing political speech, and argued that Americans could be trusted to weigh candidates on their merits instead of being swayed by advertising that would buy elections (Will 2010).

As the dust settled following the release of the opinion in *Citizens United v. FEC*, it was clear that the case had come a long way from its humble origins. The opinion had greatly expanded the scope of permissible spending concurrent with American elections, and had provoked strong reactions from both sides. That conversation continued into the 2010 midterm elections and beyond, as government officials, pundits, and the public alike tried to determine just what the practical effects would be. Before the new regulatory landscape was clear, however, the federal courts had more work to do.

NOTES

1. Americans for Campaign Reform. "Money in Politics: Who Gives." Accessed September 26, 2013 from: www.acrreform.org/research/money-in-politics-who-gives/.
2. Technically, the *Citizens United* decision reversed two decades of law, stemming largely from *Austin v. Michigan Chamber of Commerce* (494 U.S. 652 (1990)), the Bipartisan Campaign Reform Act of 2002, and a case that challenged it: *McConnell v. FEC* (540 U.S. 93 (2003)).
3. Citizens United. "Who We Are." Accessed September 28, 2013 from: www.citizensunited.org/who-we-are.aspx.
4. Financial information obtained from the website of the Center for Responsive Politics: www.opensecrets.org/pacs/lookup2.php?strID=C00295527&cycle=2008.
5. Citizens United. "Online Store." Accessed February 1, 2013 from: https://secure.donationreport.com/productlist.html?key=1QSEBUQ9MLSW.
6. Interested readers will find trailers for the movie at: www.hillarythemovie.com/trailer.html.
7. FEC Complaint. MUR 5467.
8. Box Office Mojo. "Documentary." Accessed September 26, 2013 from: www.boxofficemojo.com/genres/chart/?id=documentary.htm.
9. FEC Advisory Opinion 2004–30.
10. Outside groups often pushed the envelope in this area however, releasing ads that were quite negative in tone without expressly advocating the election or defeat of a candidate (see: Franz et al. 2006).
11. Supreme Court of the United States. "No. 08–205." Accessed September 26, 2013 from: www.supremecourt.gov/Search.aspx?FileName=/docketfiles/08-205.htm.

2   Rise of the Super PAC

Two years after the decision in *Citizens United*, during the South Carolina Republican Presidential Primary in early 2012, Republican presidential candidate Mitt Romney was accused of being a serial killer. The accusation rested on the fact that Bain Capital, the financial company with which Romney had been associated since the mid-1980s, had overseen the breakup and sale of a number of corporations over its roughly thirty years of operations. The claim was based on Romney's own characterization of corporations during a testy conversation about tax rates with some hecklers at the 2011 Iowa State Fair. In that exchange, Romney had justified his support of low corporate tax rates by arguing that "corporations are people," a claim which had been widely reported and which was generally considered to be an early campaign gaffe (Rucker 2011).

Romney had been trying to argue that corporate earnings ultimately support jobs and shareholder earnings, and his position was generally consistent with the Supreme Court's rationale in *Citizens United*. Still, comedian Stephen Colbert seized the opportunity to make a satirical point during the Republican primary in his home state. If corporations are people, Colbert reasoned, liquidating them was tantamount to murder. Moreover, since Bain—under Romney's direction—had shuttered a number of corporations, Romney was worthy of a new moniker: "Mitt the Ripper," a play on "Jack the Ripper," the London serial killer who famously eluded capture in the 1880s. Thus, Romney was depicted in Victorian garb as a dollar-wielding killer on South Carolina television, and voters were told, "If you believe corporations are people, do your duty and protect them" by voting against Romney.[1]

The comedic lampooning of a politician is nothing new in American politics—one needs only to tune in to NBC's *Saturday Night Live* during campaign season for countless examples—but Colbert's activity in the 2012 election broke new ground. The "Mitt the Ripper" joke was part of a prepared, one-minute television gag. Yet despite the fact that Colbert's popular Comedy Central pseudo-news show *The Colbert Report* typically draws about 1.5 million nightly viewers, "Mitt the Ripper" did not initially appear there, and neither Colbert's image nor his voice appeared in the video.[2] It might seem strange that a man so well prepared for large-scale political satire would choose an avenue other than his own show to disseminate a lighthearted video. However, Colbert was on a mission to demonstrate firsthand the new possibilities for independent expenditures. Colbert's "serial killer" allegations in the video were certainly intended to be lighthearted and frivolous, but given the profound changes that the federal courts had brought to campaign finance regulations in elections to all levels of American government, his broader effort was anything but.

"Mitt the Ripper" was in fact a campaign ad, styled like the classic attack ads that become all too familiar to Americans in even-numbered years. This one happened to appear on the television screens of South Carolinians in mid-January, sandwiched between others supporting or attacking Romney and the other Republican presidential candidates. There could be little doubt that Colbert's group was behind "Mitt the Ripper," because as the ad was concluding, a crucial bit of text appeared underneath a doctored image of Romney giddily running corporate logos through a wood chipper: "Paid for by Americans for a Better Tomorrow, Tomorrow, Which is Responsible for the Content of This Advertising. Not Authorized by any Candidate or Candidate's Committee."

Americans for a Better Tomorrow, Tomorrow (ABTT) was among a new type of player in American politics. It was not a corporate advocacy group like Citizens United, nor was it a for-profit corporation. Rather, ABTT was a "super PAC" that Colbert had created in an effort to further a national conversation about the newly expanded ability of groups to influence the political process with unlimited—and sometimes anonymous—contributions. Colbert's super PAC, like hundreds of others functioning during the 2012 election, was able to solicit contributions of any size from individuals, corporations, and labor unions, so long as it only used the funds for political advertising, and so long as it did not "coordinate" its activities with any political campaign or committee. Although they did have to disclose their donors, super PACs therefore provided a vehicle for people to directly finance political advertising, no matter how sizable their financial contribution. In theory, the emergence of super PACs meant that a small group of people could parlay large donations in order to make their voice heard.

Citizens United is often cited as the genesis of the super PAC (see Wendy Kaminer's [2012] critique in *The Atlantic* of *New York Times* coverage of the *Citizens United* decision and its aftermath), and super PACs are frequently characterized as contributing to an explosion of campaign spending, beginning in the 2010 elections and continuing during the 2012 presidential race. Both of these claims require some qualifications, however. The *Citizens United* finding certainly laid the groundwork for the emergence of super PACs, but the first event did not by itself lead to the other. Moreover, in both organizational form and objective, super PACs are similar to groups that had been participating in politics long before *Citizens United* made *Hillary: The Movie*. To fully understand the impact of super PACs and other groups on American politics in 2012 and beyond, it is therefore necessary to consider the groups in existence before the Court decided *Citizens United*, how lower federal courts applied the precedent from that case, and how groups have responded to the new rules.

HOW BIG OF A DEAL WAS *CITIZENS UNITED*?

As noted in Chapter 1, the *Citizens United* decision expanded the scope of permissible spending, and allowed corporations and unions to spend money for express advocacy at any point during an election. That alone is a significant change in campaign finance regulations. However, in considering its singular effects on permissible players in American elections at large, it is important to keep *Citizens United* in perspective. Indeed, considering both the regulatory environment in place before the decision and subsequent federal court decisions based on it, *Citizens United* itself might best be characterized as a decision that made an incremental (if significant) change to permissible spending, which in turn supported further developments (Levitt 2010). As such, it seems worthwhile to consider the campaign finance environment at work before *Citizens United*, and how courts and outside groups alike responded to that decision.

Prior to 2010, the Court's holding in *Buckley v. Valeo* (424 U.S. 1 (1976))—in which it equated spending to political speech—meant that individuals were free to spend unlimited sums on their own, even for "express advocacy" of the election or defeat of a named candidate. Individuals funding communications in this way were (and are) subject to only one constraint: They had to identify themselves on/in the material, generally with a "paid for by" disclosure statement. However, individuals seeking to pool their resources with others were subject to significantly more regulations. This was true even if only two people desired to jointly fund an ad, as the Federal Election Campaign Act (FECA) defined a political committee as "any committee, club, association, or other group of persons which receives contributions aggregating in excess of $1,000 during a calendar year or which makes expenditures aggregating in excess of $1,000 during a calendar year; or in order to add their funds to those of like-minded individuals for the purpose of amplifying the message" (2 U.S.C. § 431). In sum, the letter of the law was fairly clear: Once a group as small as two people crossed the $1,000 spending threshold in federal elections, contributions to it could be regulated, and its donors had to be disclosed. The option to spend unlimited sums for the direct purchase of ads therefore narrowed substantially if individuals decided to channel their money through most types of political groups first.

Nonetheless, the concept of a group bundling small contributions into larger sums is hardly a foreign concept in American politics. Indeed, political action committees (PACs) have been part of American politics since 1947. That year, the Congress of Industrial Organizations (CIO), a federation of industrial labor unions, responded to the Taft-Hartley Act—which had banned direct contributions by unions to candidates—by forming a PAC. Congress had banned contributions from the union treasury largely on the basis that the dues of a given member might be used to fund candidates that the member would not have chosen to support. The CIO therefore reasoned that it could legally circumvent the ban on contributions from its treasury by forming a committee that would be affiliated with the union for the purposes of supporting political candidates, but that would only accept voluntary contributions from members.

PACs therefore afford the benefit of legal compliance; a corporation or union can channel voluntary contributions from employees or members through a PAC without running afoul of federal law. But PACs also come with the advantage of bundling; that is, they can combine many small contributions from members of an organization into a larger one that is more likely to garner attention from a politician. For donors looking to "invest" in candidates who would look after their interests in Washington (see: Francia et al. 2003), the appeal of a PAC is clear: In bundling their funds with those of like-minded individuals and passing them on to candidates, PAC contributors helped to ensure that legislators would notice where their money was coming from, providing an attractive option for donors who may not have otherwise been able to afford a stake in the express advocacy game.

Before long, PACs were a rising force in American politics, as the CIO's approach was copied not just by other unions and corporations, but also by trade groups, interest organizations, ideologically motivated associations, and politicians. Congress formalized the rules regarding PACs in the FECA, passed and amended in the early/mid 1970s. Thus there are today three types of PACs: The first is "separate segregated funds" (SSFs) that are attached to corporations and unions, and which may solicit contributions only from employees, stockholders, owners, or members. Major corporations such as Ebay and Microsoft, as well as large unions like the AFL-CIO typically have SSFs. The second is "non-connected" PACs that are not affiliated with a corporate or labor interest, and that solicit contributions from the public at large in support of a common value. For example, EMILY's List, whose name is an acronym for "Early Money Is Like Yeast," helps women candidates "rise" by providing them with funding to jumpstart their campaigns. EMILY's List may accept contributions from anyone willing to donate to the cause. Finally, "leadership PACs" are established by federal officeholders to help other candidates get elected. When members of Congress do not face a strong challenge in their own reelection campaigns, for instance, they can channel part of their war chest to other candidates via a Leadership PAC.

Figure 2.1 underscores the increased prominence of PACs over time, breaking out the type of organization with which PACs are affiliated. As Figure 2.1 demonstrates, corporations have traditionally been the most prominent player in the PAC game. During the 1970s, the number of registered corporate PACs rose sharply, peaking in the early 1980s. That number decreased somewhat throughout the 1990s (the peak years of "soft money") before rising slightly with the passage of the BCRA. The number of "trade, member, or health" PACs also exploded in the 1970s, and grew steadily thereafter. Those PACs are connected to existing trade groups that are neither corporations nor unions, such as the National Association of Realtors. In contrast to the growth of corporate and member PACs over time, the number of PACs affiliated with labor unions has been fairly flat, probably due to the small number of unions nationwide relative to corporations and interest groups, which offers little growth potential. Finally, Figure 2.1 shows that non-connected PACs like EMILY's List became the second-most numerous type of PAC in the early 1980s, and have maintained that position ever since. In 2008, there were 1,300 of them registered—only 300 fewer than the number of corporate PACs that year.

In total, between 1990 and 2008—the last election before the *Citizens United* decision—there were roughly 4,000 registered PACs in any given year, making them a significant political player as donors communicated their preferences via bundled contributions. There is a possible downside for some prospective PAC donors, however: Unlike the direct purchase of advertising or other campaign materials, money contributed by individuals to PACs for the purpose of redistribution to candidates is subject to some limitation. Under the BCRA, donors could contribute $5,000 to a PAC, which was more than twice their legal contribution limit to candidates.

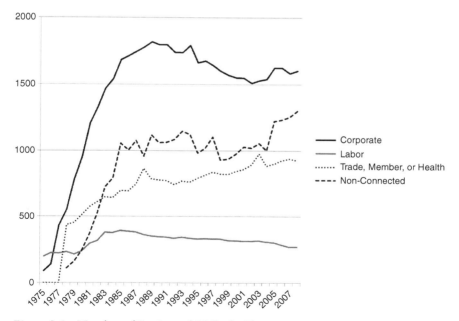

Figure 2.1 Number of Registered PACs, by Type
Source: Federal Election Commission

Even so, individuals with the means to fund their own advertisements might find themselves constrained by PAC contribution limitations.

Prior to *Citizens United*, PACs therefore might not always have been the optimal conduit for individuals looking to donate large sums. As noted in the previous chapter, under the FECA, nearly anyone—including corporations and unions—could make unlimited contributions to political parties, outside of normal contribution limits, for the purpose of "party building." The courts and the FEC eventually came to allow such "soft money" contributions to fund get-out-the-vote campaigns on behalf of candidates, as well as advertising that did not rise to the bar of "express advocacy." As such, unregulated soft money eventually became a major source of funding for both parties, and each effectively circumvented FECA contribution limits (Gill and Lipsmeyer 2005). Outside groups took full advantage of the opportunity to contribute large sums that soft money presented: In the 2000 presidential elections, soft money donations from groups including corporations and unions amounted to more than half of all unregulated money in the political system.[3]

Soft money was banned in the BCRA, removing the ability of groups (and wealthy individuals) to give unlimited sums to parties (see: La Raja 2008, Chapter 4). In the period between the BCRA and *Citizens United*, so-called 527 organizations emerged to fill the gap.[4] These groups were named for the section of the federal Internal Revenue Code (26 U.S.C. §527) that allows political organizations a tax-exempt status. To some extent, a regulatory gray area was presented by 527 groups; they were by the FEC's definition "political committees" that had to disclose their donors, so technically, all PACs are also 527 groups. But even before *Citizens United*, political committees were subject to neither contribution nor spending limitations so long as they did not fund express advocacy. As such, 527s prior to 2010 tended to focus on issue advocacy ads rather than donations to candidates. Of roughly $365 million spent by 527 organizations (on activities other than transfers to other groups) in the 2004 election, the vast majority paid for direct political activities such as media costs, campaign consultants, and get-out-the-vote efforts, with only about 15 percent of 527 spending going to candidates in the form of contributions.[5] In 2008, about 30 percent of the roughly $230 million in non-transfer expenditures of 527s was spent on contributions.[6]

Though their political efforts were ostensibly devoted to issue ads that were not supposed to explicitly name a candidate, the activities of 527s have been noticeable in federal elections. Perhaps the most famous instance of a 527 group exerting influence in an election was Swift Vets and POWs for Truth, which spent nearly $23 million during the 2004 presidential campaign.[7] That group, whose intent was to cast doubts about Democratic presidential nominee John Kerry's military service record, purchased four television ads that aired in key battleground states during the spring and summer of 2004. The ads featured testimony from men who claimed to have served with Kerry during the Vietnam War, and portrayed him as an opportunist, exaggerator, or as the title of one ad suggested, a "sellout."

The veracity of the claims made in the group's ads was widely questioned during the campaign (see: Lehigh 2004). Indeed, the ad campaign sponsored by Swift Vets and POWs for Truth led to a new term in the political lexicon: "swift-boating," which has come to mean an attack made against an opponent based on dubious facts. To say the least, in directly impugning Kerry's record, the ads pushed the envelope on permissible "issue advocacy" funded by unlimited contributions. In the wake of the swift boat attack ads, even Kerry's opponent, President George W. Bush, came out against spending by outside groups. In late August 2004, he told media covering the campaign, "I don't think we ought to have 527s. I can't be more plain about it and I . . . hope my opponents join me in . . . condemning these activities of 527s. I think they are bad for the system."[8]

However, *Citizens United* effectively removed the distinction between issue and express advocacy altogether, making it much easier for outside groups to fund political advertising naming a candidate. If independent expenditures for express advocacy were, as the Supreme Court had determined, not a corrupting influence, then conceivably any group could spend unlimited sums for that purpose. Moreover, if a group's sole purpose was to make independent expenditures, then the group would be, by the definitions set forth in the Supreme Court's various opinions, simply a conduit for political speech. As such, the federal courts had one more question to answer: If a 527 organization wanted only to make independent expenditures (as opposed to candidate donations), could the FEC impose contribution limits on its donors? *Citizens United* did not itself address that question, but it set the stage for another case that would render "527 groups" as the media had understood them functionally obsolete, giving rise to a new political buzzword: "super PAC."

SPEECHNOW.ORG V. FEC

Although it may not be as well-known as the seminal action in *Citizens United v. FEC*, there was another federal court case decided in 2010 that also proved to be an important factor in loosening restrictions on independent expenditures. That case was brought by a group called Speechnow.org (SpeechNow), which unlike Citizens United, was not a corporate entity. Rather, it was a nonprofit 527 "political organization" dedicated to advocating for the First Amendment rights of speech and assembly. SpeechNow accepted donations only from individuals, and its bylaws prohibited it from contributing funds to candidates for office.

Though SpeechNow had not begun political activity when it initiated the federal lawsuit in February 2008 (well before the outcome of *Citizens United* was known), its stated intention was to accept donations from private donors, aggregate them, and spend those funds solely on independent expenditures. Importantly, however, SpeechNow also wanted to pursue express advocacy promoting the election of certain candidates who it hoped would advocate for the First Amendment when they reached office. Speech-Now was therefore effectively asking the federal judiciary to carve out rules for a new type of political group. Unlike standard PACs, SpeechNow was not interested in contributing to candidates, and unlike 527s, it wanted to purchase express advocacy advertising.

In the wake of the *Citizens United* decision, there appeared to be very little that would prevent the courts from allowing it to do so. If corporations were freely able to spend in elections—so long as they did not contribute money to candidates directly—then it stood to reason that private citizens and/or corporations should be able to pool their resources for the same purpose, even if they were not an incorporated group. SpeechNow challenged existing federal law that defined it as a political committee subject to hard-money contribution limits under the FECA and the BCRA the moment it spent more than $1,000 that came from more than one person. For the Institute for Justice, a civil liberties law firm that represented SpeechNow in its challenge to the FEC, the restrictions on political committees were too onerous. The Institute claimed that the $1,000 expenditure threshold was "barely enough to put up a website and register a post office box before government regulation kicks in."[9] Given the substantially higher costs associated with purchasing election communications, the Institute argued that the regulations effective in 2008 imposed a substantial burden on the speech rights of people who wished to express an opinion about federal candidates—people like those who donated to SpeechNow.

In early 2008, the FEC issued an advisory opinion that classified SpeechNow as a political committee subject to federal contribution limitations—$5,000 from any single individual in a year—once it spent more than $1,000 for political purposes. While the FEC's opinion was not binding due to its lack of a quorum, it provided little comfort to SpeechNow, which was looking for assurance that it would not be subject to fines and penalties should it accept contributions over $5,000. As such, the organization challenged the FEC in federal court on First Amendment grounds, arguing that the regulations it would be subjected to as a political committee amounted to an unconstitutional infringement on its donors' speech rights. SpeechNow also asked the federal courts to prohibit the FEC from enforcing contribution limits while the litigation was pending. The U.S. District Court for the District of Columbia sent the constitutional question directly to the United States Court of Appeals for the District of Columbia Circuit (as required by law). It also denied Speech-Now's request for an injunction on contribution limits. The group appealed that denial, and the Court of Appeals heard the case on January 27, 2010—six days after the Supreme Court released its opinion in *Citizens United*.

The timing of the case was important, because *Citizens United* provided a guiding precedent for the Court of Appeals. In *SpeechNow.org v. FEC*

(599 F.3d 686 (D.C. Cir. 2010)), the D.C. Court of Appeals effectively considered two questions: The first was whether the application of contribution limits akin to those binding a standard PAC would violate the constitutional rights of either SpeechNow or its donors. This question applied not only to the $5,000 individual contribution limit to a single group planning to make independent expenditures, but also to the aggregate limitation that restricted an individual's biennial total to roughly $70,000 to any combination of political committees. The second question was whether SpeechNow could be constitutionally required to keep records of its donors and to file quarterly disclosure reports with the FEC listing all donors who contributed more than $200, as PACs were required to do.

With regard to whether individuals could be legally subjected to contribution limits if SpeechNow or other groups had no intention of contributing to candidates for office, the Court of Appeals looked to *Citizens United*. There, the Appeals Court justices found a clear answer. "Because of the Supreme Court's recent decision in *Citizens United v. FEC*," they wrote, "the analysis is straightforward. [In *Citizens United*], the Court held that the government has no anti-corruption interest in limiting independent expenditures" (10). Given that the only legitimate rationale the Supreme Court had traditionally recognized for regulating political money was the government's anticorruption interest, and because its opinion in *Citizens United* held that independent expenditures (regardless of size) are not inherently corrupting absent coordination between a group and a candidate, the Appeals Court determined that SpeechNow was free to accept contributions of any size. The majority put it rather succinctly: "No matter which standard of review governs contribution limits, the limits on contributions to SpeechNow cannot stand" (16).

With regard to SpeechNow's claim that it should not be forced to register as a political committee with the FEC—thus avoiding the reporting and disclosure requirements that have traditionally affected standard PACs—the Appeals Court noted that disclosure requirements impose a much lower burden on speech than contribution limits, and provide the benefit of easier detection of campaign finance violations. Moreover, the majority held that "the public has an interest in knowing who is speaking about a candidate and who is funding that speech, no matter whether the contributions were made towards administrative expenses or independent expenditures" (20). In short, the Appeals Court determined that SpeechNow would have to register as a political committee, and would have to disclose its donors—consistent with the Supreme Court's reasoning in *Citizens United* that disclosure allows citizens to "see whether elected officials are 'in the pocket' of so-called moneyed interests" (*Citizens United v. Federal Election Commission*, 130 S.Ct. 876, 916 (2010)). However, as long as it only spent money on independent expenditures, the Appeals Court held that the size of individual contributions to SpeechNow could not be limited.

The opinion in *SpeechNow.org v. FEC* was released in March of 2010, and reaction to it hardly matched the intensity garnered by *Citizens United*.

Whether because the effects of *SpeechNow* were seen as less monumental, or because the media was fatigued after discussing campaign finance regulations so intently after *Citizens United*, *SpeechNow* failed to provoke mass outrage. Nevertheless, while the Supreme Court's decision in *Citizens United* clearly paved the way for the D.C. Court of Appeals' ruling in *SpeechNow*, the latter case had far-reaching implications. Indeed, in greatly expanding the ability of private citizens to collectively spend money to influence the outcome of campaigns at all levels of government, *SpeechNow* was an important case in shaping American elections in its own right.

Effectively, *SpeechNow* lifted contribution limits on PACs if they neither contributed money to candidates or parties nor coordinated their activities with them. Indeed, the FEC moved quickly to clarify the new rules in advisory opinions issued shortly thereafter, which clearly stated not only that corporations could form "independent expenditure-only committees," but that those committees could accept unlimited contributions from individuals, corporations, and unions.[10] The new rules meant that PACs intending to allocate their funds only to independent expenditures—absent guidance from a party or candidate committee—could not be subject to the limitations faced by traditional, donation-focused committees. Individuals were free to donate as much as they wanted to such organizations, which quickly came to be known as "super PACs." Coupled with the holding in *Citizens United* that corporations and unions could sponsor express advocacy at any point in the election, super PACs were free to take unlimited contributions from individuals and corporations alike, and to spend freely to either support or oppose federal candidates, so long as such activity was conducted absent coordination with candidates and/or parties.

The ability to raise and spend unlimited sums in an era of mass-media campaigning imparts real potential for independent expenditure groups to make a difference in the outcome of elections, which is presumably among the central goals of such organizations. As the 2010 campaigns loomed, it was difficult to argue that the new, looser restrictions would not eventually lead to more money, contributed in larger amounts, funding a higher number of political advertisements. Still, there were remaining gray areas, particularly for existing committees that wanted to make independent expenditures under the "super PAC" rules. In the wake of the 2010 election, some of those groups sought to determine just how loose the new rules were.

HYBRID PACS AND "DARK MONEY"

Since the decision in *SpeechNow*, a number of campaign finance cases have made their way through the system, and most have sought to chip away further at the regulatory framework. Perhaps the most notable of such cases decided to date is *Carey v. FEC*. At issue in *Carey* was a natural second question in light of the holding in *SpeechNow*: If super PACs could form for the sole purpose of channeling unlimited money from donors to mass communications, were there circumstances in which traditional PACs could do the same? By 2010, traditional PACs had been making both independent expenditures and donations to federal candidates for more than sixty years. However, under the FECA and the BCRA, donations to PACs were limited, just as they were for candidates, and PACs, in turn, could only give candidates $5,000 per election cycle. These donations were certainly useful for candidates, but for PACs looking to invest, the ability to make unlimited independent expenditures surely posed an attractive option as well.

Simply, the *SpeechNow* decision dramatically changed the calculus for existing PACs. If, some groups reasoned, they maintained a separate account that would fund only communications (and not donations to candidates), then surely they could accept unlimited contributions to that account. The federal courts had held that contributions posed some risk for increasing the appearance of corruption, and so any contributions made to PACs for the purpose of bundling into larger ones destined for campaign coffers would be subject to hard-money limitations. But if donations to groups who promised to make no contributions to candidates could not be limited, then established PACs saw an opportunity to be both a contribution bundler and a super PAC. By keeping the contributory and independent expenditure functions separate, PACs could use regulated, limited donations to fund their traditional activities such as donating to candidates, while money in separate, "dedicated independent expenditure" accounts could fund communications exclusively. Such a "hybrid PAC" could be a significant player in a given election, and in the wake of *SpeechNow*, there appeared to be little to stand in the way of a group that desired to be both contributor of regulated funds and spender of unlimited money.

It was only a matter of time before a traditional PAC challenged the FEC with this goal in mind. In late January 2011, the National Defense PAC (NDPAC) did just that, filing a federal suit that would have compelled the FEC to allow it to raise unlimited contributions for the purpose of making independent expenditures. The NDPAC was a non-connected PAC, unaffiliated with a corporation, union, or interest group. Chaired by retired Navy Rear Admiral James J. Carey, the NDPAC sought to support congressional candidates with military experience "dedicated to promoting the Free Enterprise System that created the greatest economic engine in the history of Planet Earth."[11] NDPAC had in the previous year asked the FEC for an advisory opinion on whether it could permissibly use unlimited contributions so long as those funds were utilized solely for making independent expenditures. Although such activities were clearly permissible given *SpeechNow* and subsequent FEC action, the NDPAC was clear that it also intended to carry on its more traditional PAC activities; namely, raising limited contributions which would be redirected to the candidates it supported.

When the FEC could not reach a decision before the 2010 election, the NDPAC sought relief from the federal courts, challenging the contribution limits in the BCRA that would traditionally bind a "standard" political action committee focused mainly on candidate contributions. The NDPAC asserted that if super PACs could legally accept money from corporate and labor groups, then it should be able to as well, so long as the money was spent on independent expenditures alone. The NDPAC's position was that limitations on its ability to solicit corporate and union money were unconstitutional *if and only if* the PAC created a separate account for the purpose of segregating money bound for candidates from donations intended to fund communications. In other words, the NDPAC argued that the law required more nuance in light of *Citizens United* and *SpeechNow*. In acknowledging that it desired to pursue political activities in two coexisting regulatory environments, the NDPAC desired to become a "hybrid PAC" that would follow applicable rules depending upon the ultimate purpose of the monies it handled. Given that the Court had long upheld contribution limits to candidates and PACs—despite loosening rules on groups making independent expenditures—the NDPAC's claim seemed reasonable.

In June 2011, the FEC and NDPAC reached an agreement in the case (*Carey v. FEC*, No. 11–259-RMC D.D.C. 2011). The D.C. District Court subsequently issued a stipulated order to halt the FEC from enforcing contribution limitations on PACs when money is contributed to an account that exists solely to hold money destined for independent expenditures. In a memorandum opinion issued two months earlier, the district court had found that the FEC's probability of successfully defending contribution regulations for a dedicated independent expenditure account would be quite low. The district court's reasoning was that the FEC had failed to communicate how the NDPAC's proposed organizational structure would function differently than one in which it divided itself into two separate committees—one a super PAC, and the other a traditional one.[12]

That is, the court recognized that the NDPAC could in theory comply with the law by dividing itself into two separate organizations with singular goals. Given recent precedent that was highly hostile to contribution limits on super PACs, it seemed that forcing NDPAC to divide its organizational structure in this way would be overly restrictive on its speech rights. Thus, so long as the independent expenditure account was kept separately, and its finances regarding independent expenditures were both reported to the FEC and conducted in line with the laws governing super PAC contributions, the FEC could not punish the NDPAC. As such, the court held that the NDPAC could not be proscribed from accepting corporate contributions to its independent expenditure account (in line with the *Citizens United* ruling), and contributions to that account could not be limited either (consistent with *SpeechNow*). In October of 2011, per the terms outlined in the district court's order, the FEC issued a statement announcing that it would no longer enforce restrictions on contributions to non-connected PACs like the NDPAC, so long as such groups maintained separate accounts for donations and independent expenditures.[13] This announcement marked the birth of the "hybrid PAC," which can make contributions to federal candidates using regulated, limited contributions, and can make independent expenditures using unlimited contributions, including those from corporate and union sources.

Carey has clarified the permissibility of independent expenditures from nonaffiliated PACs. Yet, nothing in that or any other case in recent years has suggested that even unlimited contributions destined for independent expenditure accounts should escape disclosure. In other words, money contributed to super PACs and other "political committees" (per FEC definitions) must always be disclosed, and those committees' financial supporters are a matter of public record. However, there were other groups in 2012 that sought to avoid disclosure requirements. Perhaps the most widely discussed in that year—both before and after the election—were so-called 501(c)(4) groups, named for the section of the Internal Revenue Code (26 U.S.C. § 501(c)) that defines them.

All organizations covered in Section 501(c) are not-for-profit groups that are entitled by law to some kind of tax exemption. Indeed, there are nearly thirty varieties of nonprofit established in the revenue code. Groups falling in the fourth category (thus the designation 501(c)(4)) are defined by law as:

> civic leagues or organizations not organized for profit but operated exclusively for the promotion of social welfare, or local associations of employees, the membership of which is limited to the employees of a designated person or persons in a particular municipality, and the net earnings of which are devoted exclusively to charitable, educational, or recreational purposes.[14]

It is the term "social welfare" that allows some leeway for groups who might be inclined to participate in federal politics, as it can be argued that political advocacy falls within the broad umbrella of promoting the common good. The 501(c)(4) designation therefore allows groups to conduct political activities, but it also affords an additional benefit: 501(c)(4) groups are not required to disclose their donors to the FEC.

This latter point became particularly important in the wake of *Citizens United*. The 527 organizations that began gaining notoriety for their activities in 2004 had long been allowed to pursue political activities exclusively, and had been required to disclose their donors even before passage of the BCRA. Although the BCRA limitations on "express advocacy" constrained the 527s somewhat, the rules did provide an outlet for unlimited—albeit disclosed—contributions for issue advertising prior to 2010. There was effectively no benefit of seeking 501(c)(4) tax status during this period, however. Since the IRS prior to 2010 employed a broad definition of political activities prohibited for 501(c) groups, there was little reason to risk running afoul of the tax code. Groups with a primarily political purpose could achieve tax-free status and avoid IRS scrutiny by organizing as a 527 group and disclosing their donors.[15]

In expanding permissible election-related activity however, the *Citizens United* decision immediately made 501(c)(4)s a more attractive option for groups looking to make independent expenditures. Importantly, because they are primarily defined as nonprofit "social welfare" organizations as opposed to political committees, 501(c)(4)s are not allowed to make or sponsor advertisements naming a candidate their primary activity, meaning that they must constrain their election-related spending to half of their overall expenditures. Yet, if corporations and other groups could not be stopped from spending money in elections—even for express advocacy—in the wake of *Citizens United*, it was considerably more difficult for the IRS to stop a 501(c) group from doing so either. After *Citizens United*, 501(c)(4)s therefore differed little from 527s either in the type of activities they could legally spend money on or the size of the contributions they could receive.

However, the lack of a disclosure requirement for 501(c)(4)s provides a considerable advantage compared to 527s. Seeking 501(c)(4) status in the post–*Citizens United* world therefore seems like a prudent move for groups wanting to accept unlimited contributions, but who might not be inclined to publicize their donor lists: At present, 501(c)(4)s can pursue electioneering activities using anonymous unlimited funders so long as their activities can plausibly be defended as contributing to the social welfare (broadly defined) and so long as political spending does not constitute their "primary" expenditure (Luo 2010). In practice, the IRS/FEC has taken "primary" to mean more than half of a group's overall expenditures.

Electioneering among nonprofit, supposedly charitable organizations does create a regulatory problem however. Simply, it can be very difficult to determine where "social welfare" ends and campaign politics begin. It is unclear whether the Federal Election Commission or the Internal Revenue Service should be primarily responsible for making that call, and so both agencies have a role in oversight of politically active 501(c) groups. Specifically, it is the IRS's job to determine if a group is entitled to tax-exempt status as a "social welfare" organization, while groups who name a candidate with ads they fund must file independent expenditure reports with the FEC. Regardless of the agency in charge, because the law does not compel the financial backers of 501(c)(4)-funded ads to be named—501(c)s are required to disclose their donors to the IRS, but this information is confidential and not made public (see 26 U.S.C. § 6104)—the main problem for reformers is that while the government may know where social welfare groups are spending their money, the source of those funds often remains a mystery.[16]

Nonetheless, the newfound ability to funnel unlimited contributions to electioneering ads without disclosing donor identity is obviously attractive for many groups and donors alike; and it stands to reason that 501(c)(4)s will only become a more popular mechanism for channeling political money. Indeed, according to an audit report from the United States Treasury Inspector General, the IRS saw a sharp increase in 501(c)(4) status applications after the *Citizens United* decision, with requests rising from about 1,700 in 2009 and 2010, to 2,265 and 3,357 in 2011 and 2012, respectively.[17] Since their funding is far less transparent than FEC-regulated political committees like super PACs, reform-minded watchdog groups such as the Sunlight Foundation have classified politically active 501(c)(4)s among "dark money" organizations, which do not disclose their donors. According to the Sunlight Foundation, such groups made nearly $300 million in independent expenditures during the 2012 federal campaigns, and social welfare organizations comprised 15 of the top 50 "dark money" spenders.[18]

As 501(c)(4)s have grown in both number and money spent, the federal government has struggled to keep meaningful regulations in place. Most visibly, in the spring of 2013, the IRS provoked a political firestorm after admitting that it had applied extra scrutiny to 501(c)(4) applications that contained political words or missions. An audit of the IRS by the Treasury Inspector General determined that "the IRS used inappropriate criteria that identified for review Tea Party and other organizations applying for tax-exempt status based upon their names or policy positions instead of indications of potential political campaign intervention."[19] The unfortunate result for the agency was that, for several reasons, applications from conservative groups (and Tea Party groups in particular) appear to have been more likely to receive additional scrutiny, though it is also worth noting that many such groups were plainly engaging in political activities (see: Confessore and Luo 2013). At this writing, it remains to be seen whether there were truly political motivations at play in targeting political groups, or whether the IRS merely succumbed to poor management and a glut of cases in employing shortcuts for evaluation. Nonetheless, the events surrounding the IRS in 2013 underscore the difficulties associated with asking a revenue agency to regulate political behavior. That proposition was but one of several new questions about what was, practically speaking, a new regulatory environment in the 2012 elections.

THE RULES IN 2012

Considering the developments in 2010 and 2011, it is safe to say that the regulatory landscape was quite different at the dawn of the 2012 election than in any other presidential election year before it. Indeed, as the lower half of Table 2.1 indicates, there was a considerable expansion in 2012 in the number of groups able to name candidates in advertising. The foremost change was the decision in *Citizens United* that greatly expanded corporations' and unions' ability to make independent expenditures. Although those groups had been barred from electioneering in 2008, just four years later their spending capacity was limited only by the money in their coffers. *SpeechNow* and *Carey* had given rise to super PACs in 2010 and hybrid PACs in 2012, respectively, both of which could make unlimited independent expenditures. The combined capability of these PACs to raise and spend

Table 2.1 Key Contribution and Expenditure Rules in 2012

	Contributions							
	Individuals	PACs	Super PACs	Hybrid* PACs	National Parties	Corporations	Unions	501(c)(4)
Can donate directly to candidates	Yes	Yes	No	Yes	Yes	No	No	No
Contribution limit to federal candidates, per election	$2,500	$5,000	N/A	$5,000	$5,000	N/A	N/A	N/A

	Expenditures for "Express Advocacy"							
	Individuals	Standard PACs	Super PACs	Hybrid* PACs	National Parties	Corporations	Unions	501(c)(4)
Can purchase ads naming candidates near an election	Yes	Yes	Yes**	Yes**	Yes	Yes**	Yes**	Yes**
Limitation on express advocacy	No	No	No	No	No	No	No	Yes***

*Hybrid PACs, like traditional PACs, can make contributions to federal candidates using regulated, limited contributions. So long as the hybrid PAC maintains a separate account, it can also make independent expenditures using unlimited contributions for express advocacy, like a super PAC.

**Was legal in 2012, but not 2008.

***There is no statutory dollar limitation on political activities of 501(c)(4) groups, but they are constrained to spending 50% of their budget on such activities.

unlimited sums for political communication was unprecedented at the commencement of the 2012 federal elections. Finally, 501(c)(4) groups were on the rise, seeking to cash in on the ability to spend unlimited sums without disclosure.

Considering the panoply of new groups able to raise and spend limitless funds to purchase ads naming federal candidates in 2012, it is difficult to overstate just how unique that year was relative to previous elections. Yet, there was plenty in 2012 that remained unchanged from previous years. For instance, contribution limitations had survived every legal challenge since the implementation of the FECA (most notably in *Buckley v. Valeo*), and as Table 2.1 indicates, the BCRA's limitations remained intact without expansion to new groups during the 2012 race.[20] In 2012, individuals could donate $2,500 to a federal candidate or $5,000 to a PAC or party per election—that is, during the primary, and then again in the general election.[21] PACs and parties were allowed to contribute twice that amount. Candidates retained the ability to contribute unlimited sums to their own campaigns. There were also biennial limitations on the amount that individuals could contribute to candidates and/or PACs and parties in total during the two-year election cycle: $46,200 to the former and $70,800 to the latter. So while there were immense changes in the ability of outside groups to fund ads naming candidates in 2012 relative to 2008, in the world of contributions, little was different.

CONCLUSION

It is hard to know prima facie what to make of the further loosening/ challenging of regulations delivered via *SpeechNow*, *Carey*, and the growth of 501(c)(4)s. One interpretation is that the emergence of super PACs, coupled with the ability of corporations to either back them or to spend their own money, opened the door to much more money in American politics. While the courts had spoken with regard to political money vis-à-vis the First Amendment, the practical ramifications of the judiciary's decision remained to be seen before the 2012 polls opened. One obvious possibility is that elections would be hijacked by those with the deepest pockets. Indeed, upon receiving FEC approval to form his super PAC—and well before running "Mitt the Ripper" in South Carolina—Stephen Colbert had hinted that his satirical aim was to expose the new campaign finance environment as being practically dominated by unlimited money. On the steps of the FEC building in June of 2011, he said his new super PAC's aim would be to "raise unlimited monies and use the monies to determine the winners of the 2012 election." Later in the same address, Colbert satirically linked spending to his own civil liberties, saying, "I do not accept limits on my free speech. I don't know about you, but I do not accept the status quo. But I do accept Visa, MasterCard and American Express."[22]

Yet despite claims from critics that the newfound ability of outside groups to spend money would lead to an explosion of campaign cash that would distort American democracy, there has been little in-depth study of the extent to which super PACs alter either the conduct or the outcome of American campaigns. Nor do we know much about whether super PACs change knowledge and/or participation among voters. As noted, soft money before passage of the BCRA and the rise of 527s thereafter had long allowed unlimited contributions to flow into the system. It could be that super PACs simply provided the newest avenue for large donors to spend their money, and so voters would not notice many changes; or, even if they do notice, they simply do not care. Alternatively, the newfound ability of outside groups to fund "express advocacy" could have large effects. For instance, if outside groups are more likely to spend their money on attack ads, then the media environment might be a more negative place with the advent of super PACs. Suffice it to say that much remains unknown about the broad effects, if any, of the federal court decisions that opened the door to spending by corporations and super PACs.

NOTES

1. ABC News. "Colbert's PAC Ad: 'Mitt the Ripper'." Accessed September 26, 2013 from: http://abcnews.go.com/ThisWeek/video/stephen-colberts-super-pac-ad-mitt-ripper-15371195.
2. Figures on Colbert's viewership taken from: Borrelli, Christopher. 2011 (July 20). "Who Benefits Most from the Colbert Bump?" *Chicago Tribune.* Accessed September 24, 2013 from: http://articles.chicagotribune.com/2011-07-20/entertainment/ct-ent-0720-colbert-as-political-forc20110720_1_colbert-nation-colbert-report-dutch-bank-dsb.
3. Center for Responsive Politics. "Soft Money Backgrounder." Accessed September 26, 2013 from: www.opensecrets.org/parties/softsource.php.
4. Donations to 527s do not appear to have totally replaced the void left by soft money in the 2004 election (Weissman and Hassan 2006).
5. Center for Responsive Politics. "Expenditure Breakdown: Federally Focused Organizations." Accessed September 26, 2013 from: www.opensecrets.org/527s/527cmtes.php?level=E&cycle=2004.
6. Ibid.
7. Center for Responsive Politics. "527 Organizations Affiliated with Swift Vets and POWs for Truth." Accessed September 26, 2013 from: www.opensecrets.org/527s/527cmtes2.php?ein=&cycle=2004&tname=Swift+Vets+%26+POWs+for+Truth.
8. "Transcript: Bush in Crawford, Texas." *Washington Post.* Accessed December 22, 2013 from: www.washingtonpost.com/wp-dyn/articles/A26648-2004Aug23_2.html.
9. Accessed June 11, 2013 from: www.ij.org/speechnoworg-background.
10. See: FEC Advisory Opinions 2010–09 and 2010–11.
11. Accessed September 10, 2013 from: http://nationaldefensepac.org/?page_id=78.
12. See: www.fec.gov/law/litigation/carey.shtml.
13. See: www.fec.gov/press/Press2011/20111006postcarey.shtml.

14. See: www.law.cornell.edu/uscode/text/26/501.
15. See: "Political Law Briefing." www.politicallawbriefing.com/my-blog/2013/06/501c4s-why-all-the-fuss.html.
16. Technically, according to a 2007 FEC explanation of its rules, 501(c) groups running election ads do have to disclose those contributions specifically designated for election ads (see 11 CFR 109.10(e)), but no one is compelled to designate their donations specifically for election ads. See Torres-Spelliscy (2011) and Aprill (2011) for extensive discussions of the various ways in which donors have been able to remain anonymous.
17. See: www.treasury.gov/tigta/auditreports/2013reports/201310053fr.html.
18. See: http://sunlightfoundation.com/blog/2013/05/21/the-political-spending-of-501c4-nonprofits-in-the-2012-election/.
19. See: www.treasury.gov/tigta/auditreports/2013reports/201310053fr.html.
20. At this writing, the U.S. Supreme Court awaits arguments in *McCutcheon v. FEC*, which poses a challenge to the biannual individual overall limit—that is, the total amount of money a single individual can give to federal committees combined over a 2-year election period ($123,200 in 2013–14), but not the limitation on contributions to single candidates ($2,600 per primary and general election in 2013–14).
21. See: www.fec.gov/info/contriblimits1112.pdf.
22. Public Radio East. October 9, 2012. "Colbert 'Re-Becoming' the Nation We Always Were." Accessed April 15, 2013 from http://publicradioeast.org/post/colbert-re-becoming-nation-we-always-were.

3   Money in Elections

After the federal court rulings in *Citizens United* and *SpeechNow* in early 2010, it seemed all but certain that federal elections thereafter would feature more spending by a larger number of citizens and groups. Because the federal courts had long equated monetary expenditure with political speech, in the view of the Supreme Court and many supporters of the *Citizens United* decision, the removal of bans on corporate and union contributions (and the subsequent creation of super PACs) would therefore likely lead to a boon for political speech. For reform-minded advocacy groups, this was precisely the problem. Many critics assumed that due to the superior financial position of corporations and unions relative to most private citizens, those groups could effectively diminish the importance of traditional funding sources, such as contributions from individual citizens, by spending large sums in a given race. Moreover, the creation of super PACs meant that political campaigns might very well lose their place as the dominant source of political information during elections. The worst-case scenario was one in which campaigns would take a back seat to moneyed elites, and elections would be sold to the highest bidder. For instance, a February 2010 editorial in the magazine *The Nation* characterized the *Citizens United* decision as "an assault on American democracy," suggesting that elections "could become little more than Super Bowl games, with corporations spending whatever it takes to sell their products, er, candidates."[1]

Concerns about money in American politics are hardly new; indeed, corporate contributions to federal candidates have been banned since 1907. Although regulations of various reach have been passed in the interceding years, money has always found a new path into the political system. This has in turn necessitated further activity on the part of reform-minded people and groups, and the process has repeated. Indeed, concerns remained after the passage of the large-scale reforms in the Bipartisan Campaign Reform Act of 2002—even among members of Congress. For instance, in the wake of the 2004 presidential election, which featured the rise of 527 organizations (including the "swift boat" ads), Senator Charles Schumer (D-NY) advocated a bill that would have subjected 527s to the same limitations as PACs. On February 2, 2005, Schumer said, "We are not saying that 527s should be abolished, simply that they should be bound by the same laws everyone else is bound by."[2] Senator Schumer's rationale for this statement was the potentially corrosive effect of unregulated 527 spending. Even after the legal proscription of so-called soft money, Schumer said that it "will find its way and seep into the political system and corrode it, unless we plug every hole. The biggest hole is the one dug out by the 527s. . . . On this Groundhog Day, we might wait all day for Puxatawny Phil to come out of his hole, but we can't afford to wait for the 527s to come out and come clean."[3]

Senator Schumer also disagreed strongly with the subsequent federal court decisions in *Citizens United* and *SpeechNow*. Indeed, Schumer was one of a number of senators to publicly advocate a constitutional amendment in 2012 that would have overturned the core holdings in those decisions, eliminating the legality of corporate and union contributions. At a press conference that the amendment's supporters held in April of that year, a number of reform-minded groups also expressed support for the amendment, which would have ended constitutional protections for corporate campaign spending. Senator Bernie Sanders (I-VT), another of the amendment's chief proponents, summed up the key position of the measure's advocates, saying it would help to ensure that "America does not become an oligarchy where people with unlimited sums of money control the political process and the economic process."[4] Although that amendment made little progress in the Senate, subsequent attempts have been made in both chambers. For instance, Senator John Tester (D-MT) and Congressman Tom Udall (D-NM) introduced constitutional amendments that would end "corporate personhood" during the summer of 2013 (MacNeal 2013).

Unsurprisingly, those amendments gained little steam in Congress. Constitutional amendments require a two-thirds vote to pass, which is a high hurdle in any situation. But the 112th Congress—which met for the two years after the *Citizens United* decision in 2011 and 2012—was the least productive in history (Dinan 2013). The polarized environment in Congress is likely to frustrate most major, contentious bills (McCarty, Poole, and Rosenthal 2006; Theriault 2008), not to mention a constitutional amendment requiring a super-majority to pass. Since the Supreme Court's position on the constitutionality of corporate spending was made quite clear in the *Citizens United* opinion, absent significant changes in congressional efficacy, the new, looser regulations on independent expenditures appear to be here to stay.

Accordingly, reformers have sought policies that would diminish any nefarious effects of outside money in American politics. The so-called DISCLOSE Act has probably been the most notable of these. The act, whose name is an acronym for "Democracy Is Strengthened by Casting Light On Spending in Elections," was first introduced in the U.S. House in April 2010 (during the 111th Congress), three months after the *Citizens United* decision was released. The bill was sponsored by Congressman Chris Van Hollen (D-MD), and Charles Schumer subsequently introduced one in the Senate—two years before attending the press conference to advocate a constitutional amendment to end corporate contributions. The fact that Schumer was still fighting *Citizens United* two years later is indicative of the DISCLOSE Act's ultimate success: The bill passed the House (219–206), but failed to overcome a Republican-led filibuster in the Senate, and died in that chamber.[5]

Unlike the constitutional amendment proposed two years later, the DISCLOSE Act would have done little to threaten the permissibility of most corporate and/or super PAC expenditures. However, it did contain several regulations intended to diminish what its supporters viewed as some of the more nefarious possibilities in the new campaign finance environment. For instance, the DISCLOSE Act would have banned corporations with significant (i.e., more than 20 percent) foreign ownership from making independent expenditures. Corporations with a majority of foreign nationals on their board or those in which a foreign citizen had significant control of a U.S. subsidiary would also have been prohibited from spending in elections. Furthermore, the bill would have banned government contractors (with contracts in excess of $50,000) from making independent expenditures,[6] and would have done the same for corporations that had received government funding via the TARP "bailout" program until taxpayer funds had been repaid.

Most notably given the legislation's catchy name, the DISCLOSE Act would have required all organizations—corporate, labor, nonprofit, or otherwise—making independent expenditures in excess of $10,000 to report to the FEC the identities of donors who had contributed $1,000 or more during the calendar year. This measure was intended to prevent 501(c) organizations from making independent expenditures funded by anonymous donors. The bill also required the highest-ranking official of the organization to record a statement appearing in the ad in which he/she expressed approval of the message—akin to that mandated in the BCRA for candidate advertising now so familiar to Americans—and made the same requirement of the advertising's top donor.[7] The DISCLOSE Act was clearly intended to foster greater transparency in the new Wild West of independent expenditures, and its "stand by your ad" provisions likely would have made many donors and/or corporate CEOs think twice about whether they wanted to appear on television supporting or opposing a candidate. The Supreme Court likely would have upheld many of the DISCLOSE Act's provisions, as even in its *Citizens United* ruling the Court had upheld disclosure (of donors) and disclaimer (of ad sponsors) requirements. As Justice Kennedy had reasoned, donor disclosure permits citizens to "see whether elected officials are 'in the pocket' of so-called moneyed interests," suggesting there is a clear anti-corruption rationale underpinning such laws.[8] In proposing at minimum greater regulatory oversight of independent expenditures, the DISCLOSE Act and subsequent proposed constitutional amendments attempted to curb what their advocates saw as possible negative ramifications of the *Citizens United* opinion.

Yet for all the attention that *Citizens United* and subsequent developments have garnered from elected officials and the political media, it is not immediately clear whether the more dire predictions of reform-minded actors have come to pass. It certainly seemed safe to expect in 2010 that the first federal elections conducted in the new environment would take on a different feel, with considerably broader contribution opportunities for corporations and advocacy groups. However, it is important to note that despite the emergence of super PACs and other groups, actors that have traditionally participated in American campaign politics—namely, candidates, parties, and traditional PACs—remain part of the electoral system. Thus, the emergence of new participants in the electoral process leads to several interesting questions about how *all* players have adapted. Among the most obvious is whether the presence of corporations, super PACs, and 501(c) groups has changed the flow of campaign money, and how those groups behave relative to other, more traditional players in the political marketplace.

THE BIG PICTURE: MONEY IN FEDERAL ELECTIONS

As noted, in the wake of the *Citizens United* and *SpeechNow* decisions critics asserted that the infusion of unregulated money would result in more expensive elections on average. This is a commonsense claim. Given that the federal courts had allowed both corporate spending and unlimited contributions to groups such as super PACs and 501(c)s for the purpose of making independent expenditures, 2010 presented an opportunity for an infusion of money that may not have found its way into the political system had it been subject to limitation. Indeed, the years since *Citizens United* have seen an explosion in the number of independent expenditure–only committees (super PACs) registered with the FEC. Approximately eighty such organizations existed during the 2010 election, spending roughly $90 million during that cycle (Garrett 2013). At the dawn of the 2012 election cycle in July 2011, 108 super PACs had registered with the FEC.[9] As of September 2013, that number has risen to 726.[10] Meanwhile, a similar trend has occurred with so-called "hybrid PACs" that could accept and spend unlimited contributions via noncontribution accounts consistent with *Carey v. FEC*. Between the FEC's August 2011 opinion in *Carey* and the end of that year, thirteen hybrid PACs formed; another ten followed in the first six weeks of 2012 (Levinthal 2012). Ultimately, forty-seven such organizations registered with the FEC during the 2012 campaign.[11]

It is hard to ignore the potential import of so many new groups able to raise and spend unlimited sums. Considering the addition of these new players, it seems worthwhile to further examine the big picture in American campaign finance. The first step is to determine how aggregate campaign spending might have changed since 2010. Despite the fact that federal candidates have, since the mid-1970s, been subject to relatively strict reporting requirements, this task is not necessarily as straightforward as it seems. A true measure of aggregate campaign cost must account for the spending not only of candidates, but also of all other individuals and groups spending money to influence election outcomes—and these figures are not as easy to come by as those for the candidates and parties. Luckily, the nonpartisan Center for Responsive Politics (CRP) has calculated the total cost of elections since 1998—the height of the "soft money" era of federal campaign finance—summing the spending of all federal candidates, parties, and outside groups (including super PACs, corporations, and unions), plus PAC overhead and the cost of hosting national party conventions.

The CRP's tabulations are depicted in Figure 3.1.[12] The black line in Figure 3.1 displays the total cost of federal elections (presidential race, when applicable, plus spending in all congressional races); the gray line displays the total cost of all congressional races. Therefore, the gap between the two lines in presidential election years represents spending in the presidential race alone—e.g., more than $2 billion in 2012. That data suggest that elections have in fact become more costly since *Citizens United*. Indeed, from 2006 (the last midterm election before the federal court decisions) to 2010 (the first midterm election thereafter), total spending in federal elections rose from $2.8 billion to $3.6 billion. Comparing presidential election years, total

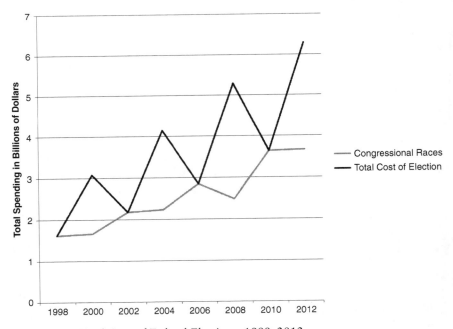

Figure 3.1   Total Cost of Federal Elections, 1998–2012

Source: Adapted from Center for Responsive Politics data at www.opensecrets.org/bigpicture/index.php

spending climbed roughly $1 billion between 2008 and 2012, topping $6.2 billion in 2012.[13] After adjusting for inflation (examining all figures in 2012 dollars), the CRP numbers suggest that total spending in the 2010 midterm was about 17 percent higher than in 2006.

Although that might seem to provide some ammunition to critics who argued that super PACs and corporations would drive up spending in 2010, the rate of growth observable in that year is comparable to that in elections past. For instance, in 2006, total spending was 16 percent higher than in 2002, when it was 22 percent higher than in 1998. Comparing presidential years, the inflation-adjusted CRP data suggest that spending in all federal elections combined in 2012 was 11 percent higher than in 2008, when it was in turn 11 percent higher than in 2004. Moreover, the CRP data suggest that spending actually *decreased* by about 12.5 percent in the 2012 presidential election between Barack Obama and Mitt Romney relative to 2008's contest between Obama and John McCain, breaking a pattern of about 25 percent spending growth in the 2008 and 2004 presidential elections. In congressional races, however, the inflation-adjusted CRP data suggest that spending was about 38 percent higher in 2012 than in 2008. So with regard to an explosion in spending after *Citizens United*, the CRP's data offers mixed evidence at best.

Regardless, it is hard to deny that super PACs were a major player in the 2012 federal campaigns. Figure 3.2 depicts total inflows and outflows to committees registered with the FEC in 2012. The term "committee" effectively denotes any organization that must report its financial activity to the FEC. Figure 3.2 includes 2012 financial data from the campaign organizations for House, Senate, and presidential candidates, as well as party organizations and standard, hybrid, and super PACs. Three transaction types are depicted: total receipts that the committees collected, total money that the committees reported spending, and the amount that committees spent on independent expenditures.

The totals in Figure 3.2 reveal some interesting patterns. First, there are few surprises in the financial activities of federal candidates, at least in terms of who controls the most money. Candidates in the national, high-visibility presidential contest raised and spent more total cash than House candidates, who raised and spent more than Senate candidates. This is intuitive because while the statewide constituencies of U.S. senators make their races more expensive on average, there are only about 33 such elections in a given cycle (there were exactly 33 in 2012), compared to 435 races for the U.S. House. Second, both parties and traditional PACs—which can contribute to federal candidates, and which are subject to federal contribution limitations—were significant factors in 2012. Indeed, parties and PACs spent more than $2 billion each in the 2012 elections. The roughly $2.3 billion spent by PACs is approximately twice the combined spending of all House candidates, but it is important to note that much PAC spending was likely funneled directly to House candidates via contributions.

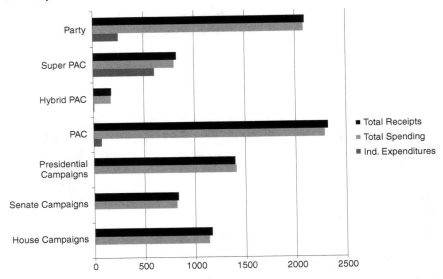

Figure 3.2   Total Committee Financial Activity (in Millions of Dollars), 2012 Federal Elections
Source: Federal Election Commission Summary Data File

Third, although the $179 million spent by hybrid PACs is hardly inconsequential, the spending of those organizations paled in comparison to super PACs. The latter spent $800 million in total during the 2012 federal elections. Of that sum, more than $600 million was spent on independent expenditures. Given that making independent expenditures is the sole political purpose for the existence of super PACs, it is hardly surprising that they directed 75 percent of their funds to that purpose. Super PACs' independent expenditures are far and away the leader in that category, and amount to about half of the total spending of House candidates in 2012. It remains to be seen what the future holds for hybrid PACs, but it seems safe to conclude that super PACs in 2012 were key players with a capacity for mass communication rivaling that of most federal candidates. As such, it is worthwhile to explore more deeply where money comes from as it makes its way to political committees, where it goes, and when. For the most part, we will focus our attention on elections to the U.S. House, which provide many more data points than either senatorial or presidential contests.

INFLOWS OF MONEY IN HOUSE ELECTIONS

Money is spent to influence voters during federal elections in two major ways: Either campaigns spend money they raised, or outside groups make coordinated (in the case of parties) or independent (in the case of all other noncandidate committees) expenditures. Individual citizens have traditionally provided the majority of direct funding to most candidates for federal office, including those for the U.S. House.[14] That trend is true of presidential campaigns as well. For instance, the FEC data on aggregate committee expenditures (depicted in Figure 3.2 above) suggest that individual contributions amounted to nearly 77 percent of presidential campaigns' total receipts during the 2012 election. According to the CRP, in the 2008 election (before the emergence of super PACs and corporate spending), individual contributions comprised nearly 90 percent of then-Senator Barack Obama's campaign funds, while Senator John McCain collected 54 percent of his total campaign money from individuals in that race—even though, unlike Obama, he participated in the federal public funding program that granted him a lump sum of $84.1 million.[15]

A similar pattern holds in congressional elections, where watchdog groups have long monitored candidates' funding sources. For example, an analysis of aggregate money flowing into congressional elections conducted by the nonpartisan Campaign Finance Institute (CFI) has found that in no election between 2000 and 2012 did individual sources fail to comprise a majority of all money raised by candidates.[16] Individuals are particularly important to challengers, whose contributions from individuals typically comprise about two-thirds of all receipts, according to the CFI's analysis. Challengers also tend to rely more on small donors than do incumbents.[17] In 2012, for example, about 14 percent of challenger funding came from small donors, and small-donor funding in turn comprised nearly 22 percent of all individual contributions. The CFI's data also show that incumbents raised 9 percent of their overall funding from small donors, and 16 percent of their contributions from individuals came from sub-$200 contributors.

The Center for Responsive Politics tabulates data at the candidate level, which allows for analysis of a typical candidate's funding profile. The CRP data from the 2004–2012 congressional elections underscore the importance of private citizens as a significant source of campaign cash in U.S. House races, particularly for nonincumbents. Figure 3.3 depicts the inflation-adjusted receipts of U.S. House campaigns (in 2012 dollars) in those years, calculated separately for incumbents (black bars), challengers with (light gray bars) or without (white bars) previous elected experience, and open seat candidates (dark gray bars).[18] Total receipts (top panel), mean contributions from PACs (middle panel), and candidate self-financing (bottom panel) are tabulated separately.

Several trends are worth noting. First, incumbents and open seat candidates raise large sums of money, which should not be particularly surprising given the institutional advantages enjoyed by the former (see: Cain, Ferejohn, and Fiorina 1987; Goodliffe 2005; Jacobson 2009; Prior 2006) and the high-visibility races contested by the latter (Jacobson 2009; Sorauf 1988). In the majority of elections since 2004, the CRP data indicate that incumbents topped $1.5 million in funding, on average. Open seat elections—which

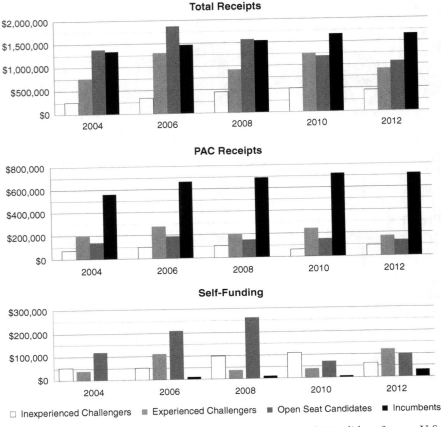

Figure 3.3   Mean Receipts (2012 Dollars), by Source and Candidate Status, U.S. House General Election Candidates

Sources: Financial data from the Center for Responsive Politics; candidate data from Professor Gary C. Jacobson

often represent a party's best chance at gaining a seat in Congress—also attract large amounts of money, with candidates in those races generally exceeding $1 million in fundraising. Indeed, from 2004 to 2008, mean fundraising among open seat candidates exceeded that of incumbents, on average.

Figure 3.3 also shows that relative to incumbents and open seat candidates, challengers typically face a more difficult fundraising challenge. Once again, this is not a controversial finding given that challengers tend to face long odds against incumbents and often confront difficulties in attracting funding from donors looking to support a likely winner. However, there is a clear distinction in total receipts between challengers who have previously won election to a lower office and those who have not. Political science researchers typically refer to the former as "high quality" challengers out of recognition that winning a campaign for lower office leaves one better equipped to seek higher offices (see: Bond, Covington, and Fleisher 1985; Green and Krasno 1988; Jacobson and Kernell 1983; Krasno and Green 1988). Presumably, a candidate who has previously waged a successful campaign will have an established base of donors and supporters, and will take valuable lessons from the experience to subsequent campaigns. Figure 3.3 is consistent with that narrative. Challengers with previous elected experience tend to raise more than twice the mean receipts of political neophytes. In 2004, the latter raised about $250,000 on average (in 2012 dollars), more than $1 million less than the incumbents they were challenging. While inexperienced challengers fared better in subsequent elections—raising nearly $500,000 in 2012—the seven-figure funding gap between them and incumbents appears to be a fairly standard feature of the campaign finance landscape.

Incumbents also demonstrate considerable success raising money from PACs. Incumbent members of the House have on average exceeded $600,000 (in 2012 dollars) of PAC funding in every election since 2006. Typically, about 40 percent of incumbents' funding comes from PACs. Moreover, House incumbents appear to have increased their average PAC receipts by about $150,000 between 2004 and 2012, even after adjusting for inflation. In contrast, mean PAC funding of nonincumbents remained relatively stable during that period, though challengers who had previously been elected to another political office (such as state legislator) demonstrated considerably more success than their inexperienced colleagues. Whereas the gap in PAC receipts between challengers and incumbents is typically several hundred thousand dollars, experienced challengers often raise twice as much PAC money as candidates who have never been elected to a lower office. Without a doubt, convincing policy-minded PACs to invest in their campaigns seems to be a difficult task for political neophytes, who rarely topped $100,000 in PAC receipts on average. In 2012, the gap in mean PAC funding between incumbents and inexperienced challengers was more than $600,000, almost three times more than the latter raised for their entire campaign. Open seat candidates generally fared a bit worse than experienced challengers at attracting PAC money, though they typically exceed $100,000.

Figure 3.3 also suggests that nonincumbents are more likely to make up for the lack of PAC investment by spending their own funds, self-financing their campaigns to a greater extent than incumbents on average. It should be noted however that the concept of "average" self-funding can be a bit misleading. The bars in Figure 3.3 represent means. Some candidates spend large sums from their personal wealth to get elected, but many others spend nothing at all. The median self-funding amount—that is, the amount at which an equal number of self-funders lie above and below—is therefore typically much smaller than the means in Figure 3.3. For example, median self-funding for open seat candidates in a given year is often less than $1,000. Indeed, the apparent spike for open seat candidates in 2008 comes largely from the activities of one candidate, Jared Polis, who spent nearly $6 million of his own money in Colorado's 2nd District. In contrast, twelve of the thirty-five open seat Democratic candidates in 2008—and fifteen of the thirty-three Republicans—spent nothing from their own personal wealth. So, readers should take self-funding means presented in Figure 3.3 with a grain of salt. Still, for both challengers and open seat candidates, mean self-funding typically accounts for about 10 percent of overall receipts, whereas incumbents tend to spend very little of their personal money on their own races.

By definition, PACs have fewer possible funding sources than political campaigns. Unlike candidates, for instance, there is no way for a group of more than one person to self-fund. Rather, PACs of all types rely on contributions. As with campaigns, FEC data reveal that contributions from individuals were the largest source of funding for all types of PACs, comprising over 94, 89, and 85 percent of standard, hybrid, and super PAC funding, respectively. Of course, with no statutory contribution limit, it seems reasonable to expect the average size of donations to super PACs and hybrid PACs to exceed that of standard PACs, which in 2012 were limited to accepting $5,000 from individuals per election cycle, and campaigns, which were bound by a $2,500 limit.

HOW IS MONEY SPENT?

Federal law requires federal campaigns to keep track of every dime leaving their coffers; even the purchase of a $0.99 box of paper clips must be reported. The standard reporting guidelines require each campaign to identify the purpose of every expenditure using a twelve-part coding system. An analysis of the expenditures contained in candidates' FEC reports therefore yields a remarkably complete picture of the manner in which campaigns spend their money. By extension, given that campaigns presumably spend money to further their core objectives, analyzing spending data allows us to get a sense of what federal candidates *do*.

To that end, we collected data from the FEC on every expenditure made by a U.S. House candidate in the 2012 election cycle. These data, which do not include independent expenditures, included more than half a million individual transactions, ranging from a one-penny "direct deposit enrollment fee" paid by Tim D'Annunzio's campaign in North Carolina's 4th Congressional District to a $1.3 million television ad purchase made by Bill Bloomfield's campaign in California's 33rd Congressional District.[19] Not every expenditure was coded within the FEC's twelve-part system on the reports filed by the campaigns; however, in nearly all cases the line item did contain a description of purpose that allowed the transaction to be properly retro-coded.[20] Once we categorized the expenditures, we were able to tabulate all spending in the 2012 House elections by purpose.

Table 3.1 contains the total amount spent by U.S. House candidates during the 2012 election cycle in each of the twelve FEC categories, using all data for which we were able to discern a clear expenditure purpose. The table is sorted from the smallest to the largest amount of spending by category. Some of the categories comprise a relatively trivial percentage of House candidates' overall spending, which may come as a surprise to the casual political observer. For instance, although many people might think of a campaign as consisting mainly of a series of events where the candidate gives a stump speech and shakes hands with the crowd, less than 3 percent of House candidates' money was spent on such events ("event expenses"), and only about 1.5 percent was devoted to travel. Likewise, the most visible elements of the "ground campaign," such as signs, stickers, and buttons, amounted to 6.5 percent of campaign spending in 2012 ("campaign materials"), and polling costs amounted to less than 2 percent of expenditures. That said, it is important to note that because our data contain more than $1 billion in transactions, the dollar amounts in each category can be quite large—even when the percentages of overall spending are small. For instance, U.S. House candidates exceeded $20 million in aggregate spending on both events and polling, and $70.5 million was expended on campaign materials.

Other common expenses are much less visible. For example, candidates made nearly $5 million in charitable donations, and spent $8.3 million to refund contributions, either by request or necessity.[21] Candidates were also

Table 3.1 Purpose of Expenditures Made by U.S. House Candidates in 2012

Purpose	Amount	Percentage of Total
Donations	$4,982,351.00	0.47%
Refunds	$8,356,003.00	0.78%
Travel	$16,300,000.00	1.52%
Loan Repayments	$18,515,640.70	1.73%
Polling	$20,300,000.00	1.90%
Event Expenses	$29,000,000.00	2.71%
Transfers	$29,600,000.00	2.76%
Campaign Materials	$70,500,000.00	6.58%
Contributions	$74,200,000.00	6.93%
Fundraising	$97,100,000.00	9.07%
Advertising	$316,000,000.00	29.51%
Salary/Overhead/Admin.	$386,000,000.00	36.05%
Totals	$1,070,853,995.00	100.01%*

Source: Federal Election Commission
*Percentage exceeds 100 due to rounding.

quite generous to other candidates, parties, and committees: House campaigns contributed more than $74 million of their own campaign money to other organizations on the same "team," presumably in the interest of winning more seats in Congress (or the presidency). House candidates also made nearly $30 million in "transfers" (which often reflects money moved among various accounts associated with a candidate) and repaid about $18.5 million in funds that they or others had lent to the campaign.[22] Finally, campaigns spent over 9 percent of their funds—more than $97 million—to raise more funds.

There are two categories in Table 3.1 that vastly exceed the others in cost to House campaigns. The first is advertising expenses. House campaigns spent $316 million on advertising in the 2012 election; this figure includes both the cost of manufacturing an ad for radio, television, print, or the Internet and the price for paying a media company to run it. That campaigns spent so much on advertising should come as no surprise. It is practically impossible to watch television during the fall of an election year without encountering a constant barrage of advertising as campaigns broadcast their message, and advertising—particularly on television—can be an expensive proposition. Still, campaigns need to broadcast their message, and the FEC reports yield considerable evidence that ad buys remain a core component of campaigns' communications strategy.

Finally, the leading expenditure category consists of the "back-office" expenses of running the campaign: Wages, payroll taxes, employee benefits, consulting fees, office rentals, equipment, and the like. Campaigns need at least one physical location and have a relatively large need for communication capacity so that they can maintain a presence in their districts, both online and on the ground. House campaigns therefore spend a great deal of money on telephone and IT infrastructure, as well as on physical space for volunteers and staff to work. The costs of phone and Internet bills, office supplies, and bank fees add up quickly: At $386 million, House campaigns' administrative expenses exceeded advertising costs by $70 million in 2012, and accounted for more than one-third of total campaign spending.

In short, candidates invest heavily in back-office infrastructure, and much of their money is spent on activities that will go undetected by most voters (such as contributions to other campaigns). Nevertheless, House campaigns also focus heavily on targeting and disseminating their campaign message: Nearly 30 percent of campaign spending goes to advertising. In addition, House campaigns topped $210 billion in combined expenses for fundraising, polling, events, travel, and campaign materials. Taken together, these activities plus advertising accounted for half of the money spent by candidate committees in the 2012 elections for U.S. House. So although overhead and salaries do place constraints on campaign budgets, on average campaigns successfully devote a majority of their funds to spreading their political message.

Money in Elections 67

INDEPENDENT EXPENDITURES

Compared to campaigns, PACs and related groups are less directly accountable to voters. With no clear mechanism for punishing a group that never stands for election, it seems reasonable to surmise that independent expenditures might be more likely to fund attacks on candidates with whom the group disagrees. Given the apparent deluge of independent expenditures made by outside groups beginning in 2010, it is therefore worthwhile to consider whether the tone or purpose of such expenditures also changed after *Citizens United*. One relatively simple way of answering this question is to analyze the stated intent of independent expenditures on groups' FEC reports. Generally, groups spend money during elections to either support a federal candidate or to oppose one, and the reports they file with the FEC contain this information. As such, it is possible to determine whether groups are more likely to spend money in order "to oppose" a federal candidate since *Citizens United* was decided.

Data from previous years are consistent with the notion of a growing proportion of independent expenditures spent to oppose—rather than support—candidates in federal elections. The CRP maintains summary records of independent expenditures made for every federal candidate, and Figure 3.4 depicts the percentage of independent expenditures made

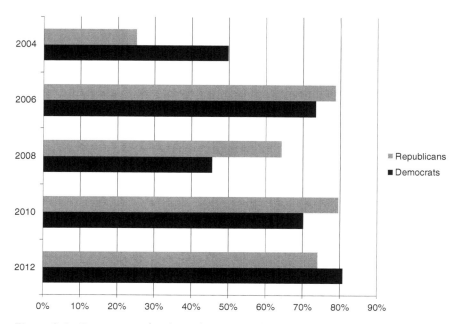

Figure 3.4 Percentage of Independent Expenditures Made to "Oppose" General Election Candidates for U.S. House, 2004–2012
Source: Authors' analysis of data obtained from the Center for Responsive Politics website

"in opposition" to candidates for election cycles going back to 2004.[23] Data are included for expenditures made during the entirety of an election cycle for candidates who ran through the general election.

There are some patterns in Figure 3.4 worth noting. First, independent expenditures made in U.S. House races in the post–*Citizens United* era are overwhelmingly negative. More than 70 percent of independent expenditures in both 2010 and 2012 were made to oppose a candidate. This rate is much higher than that in 2004—the first federal election conducted under the BCRA rules—in which about half of independent expenditures referencing Democrats were made in opposition and only about a quarter of independent expenditures referencing Republicans opposed their candidacies. A considerably higher percentage of independent expenditures opposed Republicans in 2008, but even the 64 percent rate of opposing spending that year is smaller than either 2010 or 2012. Compared to 2004 or 2008, spending to oppose Democrats is much higher post–*Citizens United* and *SpeechNow*. Indeed, the rates of opposition spending against Democrats in those years are 70 percent and 80 percent, respectively.

The anomaly in Figure 3.4 is the 2006 election, which (compared to the other two pre–*Citizens United* elections) saw a considerably higher percentage of independent expenditures made to oppose candidates of both parties. Considering the short timeline for analysis—there were only three cycles under the BCRA before the federal courts loosened restrictions on groups seeking to make independent expenditures—it is unclear in Figure 3.4 whether *Citizens United* led to a chain of events that ended with a higher proportion of negative ads. It is possible that 2006 was an uncharacteristically negative election, and that the data from 2004 and 2008 represent a more "typical" tone for the earlier, pre–*Citizens United* period. Rather than saying that post–*Citizens United* elections are more negative than those that have come before (proportionally speaking), we believe that the safest conclusion is simply that most of the money spent by outside groups in 2010 and 2012 was intended to inflict damage on a candidate, rather than to build one up.

Of course, the percentage of negative ads in a given election may be less important than the amount of money spent on attack ads. On that point, another arguably superior measure of the tone of independent expenditures is the *average amount spent* to support or oppose candidates in a given congressional contest. Voters are more likely to notice and internalize ads when they are encountered frequently (Gerber et al. 2011), and so the volume of ads is probably more meaningful in assessing the extent to which independent expenditures have changed the practical tone of an election. Put another way, if the proportion of attack ads (out of the total number of ads) is the same in two separate elections, with $100,000 being spent on one and $1 million in the other (implying a greater number of total ads), voters are probably more likely to notice the tone of the latter.

Figure 3.5 depicts the mean inflation-adjusted amounts spent to support or oppose House candidates of various types (inexperienced challengers,

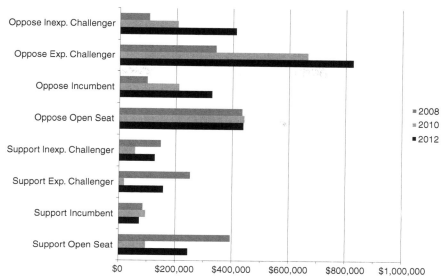

Figure 3.5 Mean Independent Expenditures 2008–2012 (in 2012 Dollars), by Candidate Status, in U.S. House Races Where Expenditures Were Made

Sources: Financial data from the Center for Responsive Politics; candidate data from Professor Gary C. Jacobson

experienced challengers, incumbents, and open seat candidates) from 2008 to 2012. Although expenditures in support of candidates (bottom half of the figure) were lower in 2010 relative to both 2008 and 2012, the fact that they rebounded somewhat for the 2012 election provides little confidence in the premise that supporting expenditures have dipped since *Citizens United*. There is, however, a clear trend in independent expenditures made to oppose House candidates (top half of the figure). Regardless of whether they possessed previous political experience, independent expenditures made to oppose challengers rose steadily from 2008 to 2012. Indeed, Figure 3.5 shows that average outside spending to oppose inexperienced challengers more than tripled from about $98,500 in 2008 to roughly $329,000 in 2012. Mean expenditures made against experienced challengers increased by nearly the same factor over the same four-year period, rising from $341,000 to $847,000. The growth in opposing expenditures is even larger for incumbents, who saw average outside spending against them rise steadily from $98,500 in 2008 to $329,000 in 2012—an increase by a factor of nearly four.

Although there is little change in mean spending to oppose open seat candidates across the three cycles depicted in Figure 3.5 (the three bars are almost identical), it seems safe to conclude that in districts where incumbents met a general election challenger, voters were exposed to more outside-funded attack advertising in the two elections conducted after the *Citizens United* decision than they were in 2008. On average, a race featuring an incumbent facing a so-called high quality challenger with previous elected experience saw about $716,000 more (in 2012 dollars) in spending to oppose the candidacies of one candidate or the other in 2012 than in 2008. That figure is sufficient to fund a meaningful communications effort in all but the most unique circumstances. So while the *proportion* of independent expenditures to oppose incumbents and challengers has remained fairly steady (or maybe increased a little) since 2008 (see Figure 3.4), the *volume* of outside-funded negative communications has risen significantly (see Figure 3.5), as did outside groups' overall spending and share of total advertising (Franz 2012).

What did independent expenditures buy in 2012? The CRP's data are not conducive to examining aggregate spending for/against a given candidate: Sometimes groups make a lump-sum expenditure (for example, on television advertising in several markets at once) that mentions a number of candidates. This makes it especially difficult to pinpoint the amount that went to support or oppose a given candidate. Examining outside spending using the transaction (not the candidate) as the unit of analysis is therefore a useful strategy to decipher group behavior. Fortunately, the FEC maintains comprehensive data on spending of outside groups, recording even the smallest of transactions. To gain greater insight into the scope and intent of outside spending in the 2012 election, we therefore examined independent expenditures using FEC records from that year.[24] We analyze data from all federal races, but given the sheer number of expenditures made, we restrict our focus to those that occurred in calendar year 2012.

The FEC data show nearly 100,000 separate monetary expenditures made in calendar year 2012 to oppose or support candidates running for the U.S. House, Senate, or the presidency, totaling more than $1.2 billion (the average expenditure amount was about $13,000). Again, one of the most striking trends in the FEC data is the negative tone of outside spending. Overall, more than 80 percent of transactions—amounting to just over $1 billion—were made to oppose a candidate rather than offer support. Moreover, the mean amount spent on a given transaction to oppose a federal candidate in 2012 was about $22,000, which was more than four times the amount spent to support a candidate in a single transaction, on average. Considering these figures, the growth in spending by outside groups since 2010 is suggestive that their enhanced role may be increasing the negativity of federal campaigns. Given that ads to oppose a candidacy are by definition negative in tone, the FEC data suggest that outside groups infused an extra $1 billion of negativity into the 2012 federal campaign.[25]

The FEC data can answer yet another important question: What do outside groups spend their money on? Table 3.2 contains summary information about independent expenditures made by nonparty committees during the 2012 calendar year across all federal races.[26] We might assume that the bulk of these expenditures were made to buy advertising—since that is the most visible sort of communication for most voters—and an examination

Table 3.2   Purpose of Independent Expenditures Made to Support/Oppose Federal Candidates in 2012

Activity	Number of Expenditures	Total Expenditures	Mean Expenditure	Percentage of Total Expended
Printing Costs	668	$749,496	$1,122	0.06%
Events	185	$937,950	$5,070	0.07%
Newspaper/Print Ads	434	$1,461,278	$3,367	0.12%
Travel/Meals	12,967	$1,543,073	$119	0.12%
Polling	223	$3,631,778	$16,286	0.29%
Other	3,273	$3,767,223	$1,151	0.30%
Campaign Materials	588	$5,448,408	$9,266	0.43%
Wages	58,472	$8,069,136	$138	0.64%
Field Canvassing	2,906	$30,620,522	$10,537	2.41%
Phoning	3,981	$32,461,074	$8,154	2.56%
Radio Ads	1,186	$35,511,212	$29,942	2.80%
Online Activity	3,577	$59,946,943	$16,759	4.73%
Direct Mail	3,180	$72,275,040	$22,728	5.70%
Television Ads	2,432	$502,487,680	$206,615	39.63%
Unspecified Advertising Expense	3,706	$509,096,926	$137,371	40.15%

Source: Federal Election Commission

of the data supports such an assumption. Relative to campaign expenditures (displayed in Table 3.1 for House candidates), spending by outside groups skews on average much more heavily to communication activities. In total, more than 87 percent of independent expenditures in 2012 were spent on advertising via television, radio, the Internet, and in print (i.e., combining the radio ads, online activity, direct mail, television ads, and unspecified advertising expense categories), running a total bill of more than $1.1 billion. Of the advertising expenditures that could be assigned to media categories, television advertising expenses clearly lead the way, with over $500 million in expenditures. Other media were less prominent compared to television, but were still widely utilized by outside groups. For instance, nearly twice as much money was spent on Internet and social networking activities as was spent on radio advertising. Even so, 2012 saw more than $35 million in outside group spending on radio ads, which underscores the large amounts of money being spent on advertising in federal elections. Groups spent large sums on other forms of political communication as well: More than $72 million was spent on direct mail campaigns, and more than $30 million on field canvassing activities. While those sums are meaningful, there is no doubt that advertising was the chief purchase of independent expenditures in 2012.

With all that money spent on ads, it is worthwhile to consider how outside spending compares to campaigns, particularly with regard to advertising. This is true both in terms of how much each type of organization spent, but also *when* expenditures were made during the election cycle. As noted above, the 2012 election saw unprecedented levels of outside spending, and much of the new money funded activities to oppose (rather than support) campaigns. One remaining question though is whether aggregate independent expenditures on ads rose to—or exceeded—the level of campaign advertising spending during any point of the election. The combined independent expenditures of outside groups amounted to more than half of the total spending of House candidates. We also note above that House candidates on average spent around half of their money on message dissemination. With fewer back-office expenses than campaigns (which have to maintain an office and communications infrastructure in the district) PACs might be able to wait until the end of the election before spending their money. If that is the case, then it stands to reason that particularly as Election Day nears, campaigns may cede the advertising field to well-funded, opportunistic outside groups.

We examine this possibility using data from 2012 House elections obtained from FEC expenditure data. Figure 3.6 portrays the daily total spent on advertising by both House campaigns and nonparty outside groups, from January 1, 2012, through Election Day. Depicted in this fashion, the data allow the flow of advertising spending to be observed throughout the 2012 congressional campaign. Perhaps the most important point to make about Figure 3.6 is that the vertical axes of the two panes employ a different scale, and readers should therefore judge the relationships accordingly. That said, Figure 3.6 is revealing with regard to the similarities and differences between House campaign spending on advertising and that of outside groups in House races. For instance, Figure 3.6 shows that there was considerably more variation in daily advertising expenditures among campaigns than outside groups, at least before mid-September. Indeed, although there were (both practically and relatively) almost no independent ad expenditures before that point, the pattern for House candidates is dual-peaked. The first peak occurs in late April and early May—primary season in many states. Average daily campaign ad spending then diminishes until June, when the pattern rises in what appears to be a pattern akin to exponential growth. Indeed, the most money spent by House candidates for advertising on any single day was $10.7 million, which occurred on October 26, eleven days before the election. On most other days in late October and early November, it was typical for House campaigns to combine for spending between four and eight million dollars on ads.

Although substantial sums in their own right, House candidates' ad spending paled in comparison to that of outside groups, at least near the end of the election. Though they were dormant for most of the year, outside groups awoke in the late summer, outspending candidates on many days as the election loomed. As the campaign entered September, the size of

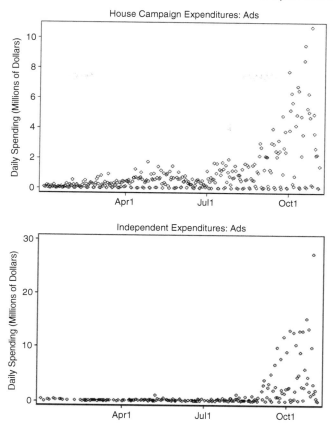

Figure 3.6 Daily Advertising Expenditures by Campaigns and Outside Groups, 2012 U.S. House Elections

Source: Federal Election Commission Candidate Disbursements and Independent Expenditures Data Files

daily independent ad expenditures in House races increased dramatically. While there were many days in October during which the ad expenditures of outside groups were essentially on par with those of campaigns, Figure 3.6 also shows that there were eight days in which outside groups exceeded the highest day of campaign spending for ads. Indeed, the most expensive day for outside group ads—exactly one week before Election Day on October 30—saw more than $27 million in spending. Moreover, outside groups combining for ad spending between five and ten million dollars a day was not an oddity late in the election. Perhaps most telling are the mean of daily ad spending for candidates and outside groups before and after September 1. Campaigns averaged $450,000 worth of ad buys on each day before that date, and $1.5 million thereafter. Groups purchasing ads via independent expenditures averaged $142,000 of daily purchases before September 1, after which they averaged $4 million in advertising purchases every day.

CONCLUSION

There is no doubt that the kinds of political committees born from the *Citizens United* decision—namely, super and hybrid PACs—are significant players in federal elections. With more than a billion dollars spent in 2012 alone, it is hard to deny the potential impact of outside spending in the post–*Citizens United* era. Indeed, outside groups funded ads at a rate generally exceeding that of campaigns late in the election, when advertising is likely to be most effective (Gerber et al. 2011; Hill et al. 2013). With regard to the question of whether outside spending is at least a force to be considered on par with campaigns in its ability to disseminate a political message during elections, the answer is clearly in the affirmative.

Yet, the revelations about the scope and scale of outside spending in 2012 also raise several new questions. For instance, the data presented in this chapter suggest that roughly $800 million was spent on negative advertising against House candidates alone in 2012. It seems safe to conclude then that the practical result of *Citizens United* and subsequent events has been to unleash a torrent of attack ads, and that not all of those ads would necessarily have appeared without the new ability of donors to fund some groups with unlimited contributions (also see Farrar-Myers et al. 2012; Fowler and Ridout 2012; Franz 2012). It could very well be that the emergence of super PACs and related groups has changed the general tone of federal elections—or at least, the manner in which that tone is perceived by voters. Put another way, the new era of campaign finance might have slanted the tone of political discourse in a decidedly negative direction.

It could also be that the money spent by outside groups is affecting election outcomes. One possibility here is that voters come to judge candidates more negatively when outside groups spend large sums against them. This scenario would be consistent with the one described at the outset of this chapter, in which elections are effectively purchased by the group willing to make the most independent expenditures. Alternatively, voters could sympathize with candidates who bear the brunt of negative advertising, punishing the attacker instead. Or, given the overwhelmingly negative tone of outside groups' ads, voters might simply give up and check out of the political process altogether. In these cases, it is unclear whether voters differentiate between PAC-funded and candidate-funded advertising, or whether they simply identify players working for the same general "team."

Of course, it is also possible that despite the large amounts being spent by outside groups on advertising that is quite likely to skew toward the negative, there is little practical effect in elections themselves. Voters might make up their mind early on, ignoring the subsequent advertising, or perhaps the strength of voters' partisan affiliations is sufficient to resist the appeals made in ads funded by outside groups. Suffice it to say that for all the money being spent, it remains unclear whether voters notice or care. Untangling these questions requires considerable attention to the manner in which people respond to external stimuli in post–*Citizens United* elections. In short, having established in this chapter that independent expenditures are fueling considerable, likely negative advertising activities, we now turn to the manner in which the presence of those groups and their political spending affects voters and elections more generally.

NOTES

1. "Democracy, Inc." *The Nation*. February 15, 2010. Accessed September 3, 2013 from: www.thenation.com/article/democracy-inc#axzz2api1UqsS.
2. Senate Press Release. "Schumer: Eliminate The Soft Money Honey Pot Before Next Election." Accessed September 3, 2013 from: www.schumer.senate.gov/Newsroom/record.cfm?id=260882&&year=2005&.
3. Ibid.
4. Senator Bernie Sanders News. April 19, 2012. Accessed September 3, 2013 from: www.sanders.senate.gov/newsroom/news/?id=46d0ee80-3fd8-43ac-80bb-ea4572446d45.
5. A narrower version of the bill was introduced in the 112th Congress, by Senator Sheldon Whitehouse (D-RI) but met a similar fate; it too died in the Senate.
6. Contractors are already banned from contributing to candidates.
7. For a legislative summary, see: http://electionlawblog.org/archives/DISCLOSE%20Act_Sec-by-Sec.pdf.
8. *Citizens United v. Federal Election Commission*, 130 S.Ct. 876, 916 (2010).
9. Accessed September 3, 2013 from: www.opensecrets.org/news/2011/06/super-pac-registrations-accelerate.html.
10. Accessed September 3, 2013 from: www.fec.gov/press/press2011/ieoc_alpha.shtml.
11. Accessed September 3, 2013 from: www.fec.gov/press/press2011/2012 PoliticalCommitteeswithNon-ContributionAccounts.shtml.
12. Accessed August 3, 2013 from: www.opensecrets.org/bigpicture/index.php.
13. We compare spending in presidential years and midterm years separately. Presidential elections draw considerable attention from media, and are generally seen as more high-salience affairs among voters and donors alike. Consequently, even congressional candidates can expect their elections to be more expensive in presidential years.
14. Campaign Finance Institute. "Campaign Funding Sources for House and Senate Candidates, 1984–2012." Accessed September 28, 2013 from: www.cfinst.org/pdf/vital/VitalStats_t8.pdf.
15. See: www.opensecrets.org/pres08/index.php.
16. Campaign Finance Institute. 2013. "House Receipts from Individuals, PACs, and Other, All General Election Candidates, 1999–2012."
17. The CFI employs a fairly conventional definition of "small donor" as one who gives less than $200 over the course of a campaign.

18. We obtained information on candidates' previous elected experience from Gary C. Jacobson, who maintains a comprehensive database of congressional candidates.
19. There are several thousand "negative expenditures" in the FEC data. These usually result from occurrences such as contributions returned by candidates or committees, lost or voided checks, and accounting errors. Since we are concerned mainly about initial purchasing decisions, we analyze only "positive expenditures"; that is, money paid by the campaign to another person or entity.
20. We used a combination of machine and hand coding for this purpose; slightly more than 20 percent of the original data were categorized in this manner. We were able to assign categories to all but about 2,000 transactions.
21. Candidates must return contributions from corporate entities, or those that exceed the mandatory limits imposed by federal law.
22. By far, the leading lender to House candidates is the candidate him/herself.
23. See, for instance: www.opensecrets.org/outsidespending/summ.php?cycle=2012&disp=C&type=H.
24. If anything, FEC records on independent expenditures are too thorough. The Commission reports independent expenditures in real time, which sometimes creates the opportunity for transactions to be entered more than once. In fact, there are numerous duplicate transactions in the FEC database of independent expenditures. We scrubbed the FEC data of duplicates before analysis.
25. Negative ads attack one candidate either without explicitly mentioning/promoting the other or while promoting the other; the former are commonly referred to as "attack" ads, while the latter are typically labeled "contrast" ads. When compared to advertising by candidates and parties, outside group advertising appears to have been particularly negative in tone in 2012. Under the direction of Professors Erika Franklin Fowler (Wesleyan University), Michael Franz (Bowdoin College), and Travis Ridout (Washington State University), the Wesleyan Media Project (http://mediaproject.wesleyan.edu/) tracks advertising in federal and state elections using data obtained from Kantar Media/Campaign Media Analysis Group (see Fowler and Ridout 2012 for more details). As of this writing, the data on congressional races is not yet available, but Fowler and Ridout (2012, Table 8) report that, of all the presidential advertisements to air between June 1, 2012 and Election Day, 85 percent of the ads aired by outside groups were attack ads, whereas only 54 percent of candidate and 51 percent of party/coordinated ads were attack ads. Granted, there were very few solely positive ads—i.e., ads promoting one candidate and not mentioning the other—but the candidates (19 percent of their ads) and parties (11 percent of their ads) tended to sponsor those, not groups (only 5 percent of all ads sponsored by groups were positive).
26. The report contains a description of the expenditure's purpose. Since there is no standard classification scheme for an independent expenditure—unlike campaign (candidate and party) expenditures—we assigned each expenditure to basic categories, given the committee's description.

4 Does It Matter Where Money Comes From?

Forbes Magazine hardly has an anti-business reputation. On Election Day 2012, however, it ran an opinion piece in its online blog section by Russell Glass, CEO of the marketing firm Bizo. Glass's piece was decidedly opposed to both the *Citizens United* ruling and corporate spending in American elections. "Self-governance," Glass wrote, "is being replaced by corporate-governance, and your freedom is being sapped in the process. Actually, it is our votes that are being bought. But our vote is our freedom, and so our freedom is being bought. Corporate financing of elections has allowed corporations and the wealthy to openly buy our freedom" (Glass 2012).

Glass was hardly alone in his suspicion of corporate money, as opposition to *Citizens United* also came from more predictable sources. In a speech on the House floor supporting a Constitutional amendment to overturn *Citizens United* in January 2012, Rep. Dennis Kucinich (D-OH) said,

> One of the biggest stumbling blocks to America's economic recovery is corporations can legally buy elections and then influence policies which move millions of jobs out of America, which escape taxation by off shoring profits, which cash in on wars, which press military industrial spending through the roof . . . While we pledge allegiance to the Red, White, and Blue, corporations, whose only allegiance is to green, are selling out America and they are becoming ever more powerful because of a Supreme Court decision in *Citizens United* which effectively turns this government into an auction where policies may go to the highest bidder. (Dolan 2012)

Despite the widespread concern about corporate money "buying" elections, it remains to be seen whether objections to outside spending are justified. Put another way, even if corporations, super PACs, 501(c)(4)s, and other groups infused hundreds of millions of dollars into federal elections in an effort to swing the results, did their efforts matter?

There are several ways in which money may have influenced election outcomes in 2012. The most obvious, given the tone of popular discussion, is that more outside money being spent by one side is likely to positively impact that side's vote totals. This narrative is consistent with outside groups "buying" an election; in other words, more money leads to more votes. The mechanism for this narrative, given the findings in the previous chapter, is primarily advertising. In this story, outside groups purchase advertising, which persuades voters to vote (or vote differently than they would have otherwise). There are some possible alternatives, however. For one, money might not buy votes in the first place (Brown 2013). Second, voters may pay attention to the sources of candidate funds and update their preferences accordingly. For instance, voters may be more or less likely to support a candidate who is heavily supported by interest groups, or who spends more of his or her own money in the race. Such voters may be turned off by the notion of a candidate apparently beholden to interest groups, or one who is out of touch with the needs of average people. Thus, heavy spending by outside groups—or even by the candidate him/herself—might push some voters away.

MONEY AND VOTES IN 2012

The relationship between campaign spending and electoral outcomes is a much-studied one, but there is no firm consensus on whether more money spent leads to vote gains for a candidate. At least one previous study has determined that spending matters very little in congressional elections (Levitt 1994), while others have found that both incumbents and challengers realize vote gains from higher spending (Green and Krasno 1988; Gerber 1998). To date, however, the majority of studies have found that only congressional challengers win more votes with their campaign spending, while incumbents' spending does little to increase their vote share (e.g., Jacobson 1978; 1980; 1990; Ansolabehere and Gerber 1994). Jacobson (1990) offers a theoretical explanation for this difference: Incumbents are relatively well-known to the electorate before a campaign even begins; in most cases they have won election in the district before, and can utilize the resources of their office to inform voters about their accomplishments and service work during their term. Because they therefore start from a more established position, Jacobson argues, incumbents' campaigning does not yield large gains.

Even if challengers do receive a greater benefit from spending than incumbents, they still face a difficult task. Incumbents enjoy a clear electoral advantage over their competition in both federal and state elections (Carey et al. 2000; Cox and Katz 1996; Erikson 1971; Ferejohn 1977; Mayhew 1974). Part of this advantage is certainly monetary: Whereas incumbents can easily raise funds as needed to combat a strong challenge—and therefore generally control more money than their competition at all phases of an election—challengers who fail to raise funds early rarely exhibit success later (Krasno et al. 1994). Challengers' ability to raise money is at least partially constrained by prospective donors' assessments of their viability, as they must often confront the paradoxical reality that donors are less likely to contribute to them due to concerns about their likelihood of winning, but they cannot win without money.

In theory at least, there is somewhat more potential fluidity with regard to independent expenditures, which can be made at any time by anyone. Challengers who had difficulty raising money—or who have run out of money to spend on their own ads—could conceivably benefit from a sympathetic outside group that views an incumbent as beatable. However, practically speaking, it is reasonable to assume that PACs, super PACs, corporations, and other groups are likely to spend money where it is expected to affect the outcome of a race. Because challengers are unlikely to win if they cannot raise much money, outside groups are probably not keen to invest in cash-poor challengers either.

To examine the effect of both candidate and independent expenditures on election outcomes, we combined financial data on both candidate and group spending obtained from the Center for Responsive Politics website with election data from each House district.[1] We obtained data from the CRP for elections from 2008–2012, and utilize incumbent-contested elections as the unit of analysis.[2] We follow the modeling approach utilized in Jacobson (1990), employing a multivariate regression model that allows us to gauge the effect of spending while controlling for other relevant factors. The dependent variable in our analysis is the challenger's share of the two-party general election vote. The independent variables are the logged campaign spending (in thousands) of incumbents and challengers, as well as the logged net spending (in thousands) of nonparty outside groups on behalf of incumbents and challengers. We log these amounts to account for the likelihood that the benefits from spending diminish as more money is spent; that is, the effect of the first thousand dollars in campaign spending is likely greater than the last thousand (see: Jacobson 1990). By "net" independent expenditures, we mean the total money spent to support a candidate and/or to oppose his or her opponent. So for challengers, net independent expenditures are calculated as those recorded with the FEC to support that challenger plus those to oppose the incumbent. Given that the dependent variable is the *challenger's* vote share, if spending by either campaigns or groups leads to increased vote margins, we would expect that the coefficients for challenger spending would be positive (increasing the challenger's vote share) and those for incumbent spending would be negative (decreasing the challenger's vote share).

Because spending is not the only reasonable factor that would determine the challenger's electoral success, we include several control variables in the model. The first is the challenger's party strength in the district, measured as the percentage of the two-party vote that the candidate from his/her party received in the previous House election. Presumably, if a Republican challenger does well in Election 0, it stands to reason that the subsequent Republican challenger will be a strong performer in Election 1. We also control for the challenger's party with a dichotomous variable coded 1 for Democrats (0 for Republicans), and another for challenger experience coded 1 if the challenger had previously won election to a lower office (0 if not). Challengers who have been previously elected to lower offices should be able to leverage that experience and name recognition to greater success than political neophytes (Green and Krasno 1988); as such, we would expect the coefficient for an experienced challenger to be positive, indicating that so-called "high-quality" challengers perform better.

The results of two multivariate regression models are summarized in Table 4.1. Since there is little substantive difference between the model that

Table 4.1 Challenger's Vote Share as a Function of Challenger and Incumbent Spending, 2008–2012 U.S. House Elections

	(1)	(2)
	Challenger's Share of the Two-Party Vote	
Log challenger spending	1.36*	1.41*
	(0.19)	(0.18)
Log challenger independent expenditures	0.31*	0.32*
	(0.06)	(0.06)
Log incumbent spending	0.93*	0.99*
	(0.47)	(0.46)
Log incumbent independent expenditures	0.31*	0.29*
	(0.07)	(0.07)
Challenger party strength	0.29*	0.29*
	(0.03)	(0.03)
Democratic challenger (1 = yes)	1.51*	1.26*
	(0.41)	(0.40)
Experienced challenger (1 = yes)	1.32*	1.27*
	(0.50)	(0.50)
Constant	12.30*	12.00*
	(3.35)	(3.30)
Year fixed effects	Yes	No
Observations	816	816
R-squared	0.65	0.65

Note: OLS regression coefficients with robust standard errors in parentheses. Unit of analysis is U.S. House elections in which an incumbent was running (i.e., open seats are excluded from the analysis). $*p < 0.05$.

Source: Financial data from the Center for Responsive Politics; candidate data from Professor Gary C. Jacobson

holds effects of each individual election year constant (year fixed effects in column 1) and the one that does not (column 2), we focus our discussion on the former. Column (1) displays the coefficients and corresponding robust standard errors for each independent variable in the model, and the asterisk (*) denotes coefficients that are statistically significant at the 95 percent confidence level (i.e., $p < .05$). As expected, the challenger's vote share is significantly (and positively) correlated with the success of the challenger's party candidate in the previous election. As also expected, experienced challengers performed better than their inexperienced counterparts. In addition, Democratic challengers received a higher percentage of the vote than Republican challengers from 2008–2012.

Of most interest to us, however, are the coefficients on the four spending independent variables—challenger and incumbent spending and independent expenditures for/against the challenger and incumbent. Some interesting findings emerge when these variables are considered. First, both challeng-ers' campaign spending and net independent expenditures on their behalf are positively correlated with their vote total. That is, the more challengers spend—or the more that is spent by outside groups to support their campaign—the higher their expected share of the general election vote. Notably, the effect of spending from the campaign is more than four times higher than the effect of independent expenditures, which is a statistically significant difference.[3] Both campaign spending and independent expenditures appear to help challengers, but the former delivers more bang for the buck.

The models also indicate that incumbents appear to win *fewer* votes as their campaigns spend more money. Furthermore, independent expenditures for incumbents are a significant determinant of vote share, but in *a direction opposite of expectation*. That is, the results suggest that holding all other variables in the model constant, more money spent for incumbents was associated with higher *challenger* vote share, regardless of whether it was spent by the incumbent's campaign or on his/her behalf by outside groups. In contrast with the stronger apparent effect of challenger campaign spending vis-à-vis independent expenditures on their behalf, there is no such statistical difference apparent in the effect of incumbent campaign spending versus incumbent independent expenditures.[4]

In sum, our statistical models indicate that challengers receive vote gains from their own campaign spending, as well as independent expenditures on their behalf, but that the positive effect of the former on their vote share is more than four times that of the latter. Challengers also earn a higher percentage of the vote when incumbent campaigns spend more money. The same is true for spending by outside groups on behalf of incumbents, which is correlated with a higher percentage of the vote received by the *challenger*.

The apparent differential effect of incumbent and challenger spending is not without precedent (Jacobson 1990), and it is worth noting that there is an inherent theoretical complexity in the relationship between incumbent spending and vote share. Put another way, there is a well-known maxim in the social sciences that "correlation does not prove causation." It could be that incumbent campaigns and sympathetic outside groups spend money when the incumbent is perceived to be in danger of losing his/her reelection campaign. If this were the case, the conventional wisdom about money and votes (more money leads to more votes) could actually flow in the opposite direction, as strong challengers (or weak incumbents) attract funding. Indeed, it seems reasonable to expect that incumbents whose challengers are destined to win a greater share of the vote for some reason, such as scandal, poor party conditions in the district, etc., will receive more money. They will in other words be pre-identified as likely to win fewer votes, and both donors and outside groups likely spend in an effort to aid them. Given the results of our model, that is certainly a possibility in the 2008–2012 elections.

In Figure 4.1, the challenger's share of the two-party vote is plotted against both the log of incumbent independent expenditures and incumbent campaign spending. To be clear, the plots in Figure 4.1 show how incumbent spending (by both outside groups and the incumbent's own campaign) changed with incumbents' vote share.[5] The pattern observable in Figure 4.1 is consistent with the notion of both incumbent campaigns and outside groups spending to aid incumbents when they are faced with a strong challenge. The bottom pane of Figure 4.1 shows a clearly positive relationship between (logged) incumbent spending and the challenger's ultimate vote share.[6] Incumbents appear to have spent more when they were facing a strong challenge, as evidenced by the slight upward slope of the data points. That is, incumbents who were in close elections spent more than those who won handily; many of the incumbents who spent the most lost their elections, as evidenced by the fact that the points lie to the right of the vertical line, which indicates the point at which the challenger won the election. That is not wholly surprising given the results from the models above, which showed that incumbent spending is positively associated with challengers' vote totals when controlling for other factors.

There is a similar pattern when we plot independent expenditures for incumbents against challenger vote share. As is evident in the top pane of Figure 4.1, with very few exceptions the highest amounts of independent expenditures for incumbents were clustered around the vertical line, which again denotes the point at which the challenger would have defeated the incumbent. Indeed, nearly all of the highest totals lie between challenger vote receipts of 40 and 60 points. Another noticeable trend in the top pane is the string of data points lying in a horizontal line at the bottom of the plane. These points indicate races in which no independent expenditures were made, and underscore that outside money does not flow to all races. It is worth noting, however, that there were fewer than ten races in which no independent expenditures were made, but in which the challenger received more than 40 percent of the two-party vote. Outside money apparently flowed to incumbents in close elections, where the result could conceivably have gone either way.

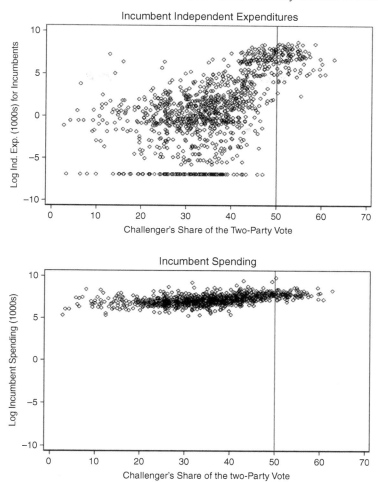

Figure 4.1 Independent Expenditures and Campaign Spending for Incumbents and Challenger's Ultimate Share of the Two-Party Vote, 2008–2012

Source: Financial data from the Center for Responsive Politics; candidate data from Professor Gary C. Jacobson

Although elections in which more outside money is spent appear to be close, that is not to say that either campaign spending or independent expenditures alone make them so. More likely, in our view, both campaigns and outside groups recognize well ahead of the election that an incumbent is in trouble, and spend money to help keep him or her in office. This account certainly helps to explain the results in the models above, as well as in Figure 4.1, but there are other possible explanations as well. For instance, it could be that voters form judgments about incumbents (or other candidates) benefiting from heavy outside spending, those who receive large amounts of their money from interest groups, or even candidates who spend a large amount of their own personal money on their campaign. If they pay attention to the sources of campaign funding, voters might use information about funding sources to form opinions, rewarding or punishing candidates based on where their money came from.

DO FUNDING SOURCES MATTER TO VOTERS?

The results above—in tandem with existing studies (e.g., Abramowitz 1991; Gerber 2004; Jacobson 1990; 2006; Krasno and Green 1988)—suggest that challengers in particular realize vote returns when they spend money. Luckily for many candidates, there are plenty of people and groups all too happy to put money into the political system, as evidenced by the consistent growth in both campaign spending since the 1970s (Gross and Goidel 2003; Jacobson 2009, Ch. 3; Lott 2000) and independent expenditures since 2010 (as described in Chapter 3).[7] Conventional wisdom holds that candidates use their political skills or exploit national or local competitive conditions to raise money.[8] Once raised, this money is spent with the aim of delivering returns in the form of higher vote totals. Within this framework, the percentage of a candidate's overall funding portfolio that is composed of any single source (for federal candidates: individual contributions, PAC donations, party support, or self-financing) should not be correlated with that candidate's vote percentage. Moreover, one would naïvely expect little difference in the gains from campaign spending and those from independent expenditures. In other words, if money is a fungible commodity in terms of its ability to persuade voters, then it should deliver the same benefit to the campaign regardless of the source from which it was obtained or the account from which it was spent.[9]

With this dominant framework in mind, it should not be too surprising that higher-spending challengers do better at the polls, but our analysis above leaves some open questions with regard to the relationship between money and the decisions that voters make. First, the fact that challengers' campaign spending appears to have won more votes than outside spending on their behalf is at odds with the notion of fungible money: If all spending is equal, we would not expect challengers to receive a larger vote gain from their own spending than from outside group expenditures supporting them. Second, the seemingly counterintuitive result regarding both incumbent spending and independent expenditures on their behalf—namely, that they appear to benefit challengers—suggests that the path from spending to votes may not be the tidy, linear story it is sometimes made out to be. As noted, we believe this finding is likely explained in part by the strategic behavior of donors and outside groups coming to the aid of incumbents who were already going to do relatively poorly, but the data above cannot rule out another possibility: Voters incorporate information about campaigns' financial backers into their judgments about candidates.

If this is true, then any number of factors surrounding campaign money might form the basis for voters' decisions. For instance, considering that a substantial majority of the American public perceives a link between campaign finance and corruption (Persily and Lammie 2004), and that funding sources or independent expenditures—particularly for candidates who either spend large sums of their own money or have it spent on their behalf—are often reported in the media, it seems prudent to examine whether the source of a candidate's money is associated with the likelihood that voters will support him/her. If it is, then it is possible that money from different contribution sources—and money spent from outside groups versus that spent by the campaign—may not impart equal benefits in terms of votes.

Existing research has detected correlations between the percentage of a candidate's funding derived from certain sources and that candidate's ultimate electoral success. Such studies have generally found a positive association between election outcomes and PAC donations, but that self-financing has at best (from the perspective of those spending the money) a small positive association with a candidate's vote share. For instance, Alexander's (2005) study of open seat House candidates from 1996 to 2002 found that candidates who relied more heavily on self-financing performed worse, but those who accepted more PAC funding did better. Steen (2006, 106) found a very small (relative to other contribution sources) positive correlation between self-funding and electoral success for open seat House candidates from 1992 to 2000 in "potentially competitive" contests. In a study of gubernatorial elections from 1998 to 2008, Brown (2013) found that unlike funding from other sources, levels of self-funding did not significantly correlate with electoral success. These findings are inconsistent with the notion that money is a fungible resource, and suggest that the sources from which a candidate raises his/her money matter for his/her electoral prospects.

There are at least two explanations for the apparent association between funding sources and electoral success. The first is that funding sources are a proxy for a candidate's political talents, attractiveness, and policy positions, and money is simply an observed correlate of unobserved (by the researcher) candidate traits. Consistent with this explanation, Brown (2013) argues that external funding correlates with electoral success because good candidates attract donors and voters alike. One possible explanation for the lack of a strong positive association between self-funding and candidate success is therefore that candidates are compelled to spend their own money because external donors have failed to provide the necessary resources. In short, a self-funded candidate may feel compelled to spend his/her own money because he/she is viewed by donors as a lower-quality candidate, and thus lacks other funding options. The same attributes—or lack thereof—that inhibit fundraising would also frustrate efforts to win votes.

Likewise, candidates who draw a higher percentage of contributions from interest organizations, or those who attract more outside spending, may be inherently stronger. The strategic decision making of PACs has received substantial attention in both federal and state elections, where previous research has consistently found that incumbents, leadership, and powerful members of the rank and file benefit disproportionately from PAC donations (Cassie and Thompson 1998; Herrnson 1992; Herrnson and Curtis 2011; Snyder 1990; Stratmann 1992; Thielemann and Dixon 1994; Thompson et al. 1994). These studies suggest that candidates who finish well on Election Day may have received PAC contributions precisely because they were expected to do so. This stands in contrast to the behavior of outside groups making independent expenditures for weak incumbents (as we describe above), underscoring that the strategy of contributing to candidates likely differs from the calculations that go into spending money on their behalf. Nonetheless, if PACs invest in winners, candidates who raise a clear majority of the PAC money in a given election are likely able to do so because strategically-minded interest organizations viewed them as the safer bet.

We find the above framework to be compelling and likely true in part for both self-funded and PAC-supported candidates. However, it is also worth considering whether the manner in which candidates fund their campaigns communicates a message to voters on its own, providing information that voters use when evaluating candidates. Given that most people pay little attention to campaign finance regulations (Primo 2002), it might seem unreasonable to expect funding source cues to function well in many elections. Yet, information about candidate funding sources—or at least, intimations about those sources—is often reported by media and reform-minded interest organizations who disseminate summary financial information for mass consumption, particularly as part of "horse-race" coverage to describe which candidate has raised more money at each quarterly deadline. Media stories about the candidate or the campaign may also include information about a candidate's financial sources, particularly in the case of those who rely heavily on their own funds. For instance, Meg Whitman and Jeff Greene were often described as "billionaires" during the 2010 California gubernatorial and Florida U.S. Senate elections, respectively.[10] Whitman's self-contribution of more than $140 million was also widely reported during her 2010 California gubernatorial campaign, ultimately becoming a component of the overarching campaign narrative.

It is possible that such media coverage could spell trouble for self-funded candidates, who risk a backlash from a public that sees them as trying to "buy the election" or as out of touch with average people. By the same token, candidates who benefit from heavy spending by outside groups may face scrutiny from voters. Perhaps those with more apparent ties to outside groups will face a backlash effect as voters perceive them to be more corrupt. On the other hand, voters may look favorably upon self-funded candidates. If they are not accepting money from interest organizations, candidates might be seen as less likely to engage in shadowy deals in the proverbial "smoke-filled room."[11] Given that many voters have a less-than-optimistic assessment of candidates in this area generally (e.g., Persily and Lammie 2004), it may benefit candidates to credibly claim that they are not entangled with self-interested contributors.

Previous research in psychology provides some empirical basis for the potential existence of voters who view self-financing in a negative light. In lab experimental settings, psychologists typically find an effect of "affluence cues" on evaluations of others, where greater affluence is found to be associated with perceptions that an individual is less likely to help others (Christopher et al. 2005) and generally "not nice" (e.g., less kind and honest, see Christopher and Schlenker 2000). Notably, this work finds that people also respond to the *source* of greater affluence, where income acquired from an inheritance (or even an inheritance plus some other source, such as a job) is typically viewed less favorably than income obtained through work (Christopher et al. 2005; Kirby 1999).

Information about PAC contributions or outside spending may also directly affect voters' perceptions of candidates. Descriptions of candidates as heavily reliant on PAC funding or independent expenditures might create an image of them as susceptible to corruption, risking a rebuke from an American electorate that has previously been shown to react negatively to perceptions of graft (Bowler and Karp 2004). Alternatively, it is possible that voters view information about PAC donations favorably, taking cues from the behavior of strategically minded elites who form judgments with more complete information. Or, perhaps voters pay attention to none of these things, and the narrative of PAC contributions or outside money flowing to strong candidates while weak(er) ones self-fund is correct.

We know of no existing work that addresses how voters process information about either candidates' funding sources or the groups spending on their behalf. As noted above, existing studies relying on observational (i.e., non-experimental) election data suggest that levels of PAC- and self-funding are significant predictors of candidate vote share, but these data allow neither randomization of funding status nor the ability to assess voters' motivation for supporting a given candidate. As such, although prior analyses have established that there are linkages between funding sources and votes, it does not show the causal direction of these relationships, and so the underlying causal mechanism for these relationships remains unclear. If candidates who accept money from PACs tend to do better in elections, it is not known whether this is because they are stronger candidates or because (or in spite) of how people treat this information when making voting decisions. The same can be said for candidates benefitting from (or being attacked by) independent expenditures. Given that researchers cannot manipulate candidate funding sources or independent expenditures in the field, it is difficult to address such questions using observational election data (but see: Feigenbaum and Shelton 2013).

Experimental methods therefore hold great promise to illuminate the directional nature of the relationships between funding sources and candidate success. With that in mind, we ran a series of survey experiments designed to further assess the relationship between candidate funding sources and electoral success; these experiments are described in greater detail in the appendix.[12] In a survey experiment, respondents take what appears (to them) to be a normal survey. Researchers may randomly manipulate the questions or information to which the participant is exposed, however, to measure how their responses change as a result of various informational "treatments" (for more on survey experiments, see: Mutz 2011; Sniderman 2011). To analyze how people respond to information about candidate funding sources and independent expenditures, we therefore had participants read brief vignettes describing a fictitious candidate for Congress, and manipulated various aspects of the candidate's political biography, his primary source of funding during the election, and, in some cases, the extent to which super PACs supported him.

The first experiment was included on the 2010 Cooperative Congressional Election Study (CCES), a national public opinion survey that was fielded the month leading up to the 2010 midterm election. The CCES was administered by YouGov/Polimetrix over the Internet, where respondents opt-in to participate. Our experiment on the CCES (further described in the appendix) was completed by roughly 800 participants.[13] The experiment consisted of a brief vignette that provided a short biography of a fictitious candidate running for an open seat in the United States House of Representatives or Senate (randomly assigned with equal probability) whose party affiliation was randomly assigned with equal probability to be either Democratic or Republican, or left blank (i.e., no party).[14] The primary manipulation of interest was the candidate's source of funding. There were four funding source treatments, each assigned with equal probability. Respondents were told that the candidate was "financing his campaign primarily with . . ." (1) "money he made in the private sector," (2) "money he inherited," (3) "contributions from individual citizens and interest groups," or (4) "contributions from individual citizens." This design permits us to test whether and to what extent citizens respond to funding sources when evaluating candidates for office.

We also asked several candidate evaluation questions. First, on the same page as the vignette, respondents were asked, "Based on what you know about this candidate, how likely do you think you would be to vote for him in the upcoming (November 2010) election?" Responses to this item (*Vote Intent*) were recorded on a scale ranging from 0 to 100, where 0 was labeled "not very likely" and 100 was labeled "very likely." Respondents were then presented with a grid on the next page with the header text,

"And to what extent do you agree with each of the following statements?"[15] The statements (i.e., rows of the grid, the order of which was randomized) were designed to obtain more specific evaluations of the candidate. Among other things, we asked respondents whether they thought the candidate "has the experience and skills necessary to represent me in Congress" and "would focus on serving special interests."

We conducted two additional survey experiments using online samples we recruited through Amazon.com's Mechanical Turk (MTurk) service; we refer to these below as MTurk 1 and MTurk 2. MTurk is an online platform on which people ("requesters") can recruit and pay subjects ("workers") to perform tasks. Each of these experiments is further described in the appendix, but their general format is consistent with the one conducted on the CCES— and we note key differences below. In each case, we showed participants a short biographical vignette about a candidate and randomly manipulated particular aspects of a candidate's financial backers. In total, the experiments are designed to clarify the manner in which voters assess candidates who accept a large proportion of their overall money from "interest groups," those who spend a large amount of their own money, and those who are heavily supported by independent expenditures.

EXPERIMENT RESULTS

We begin by reporting the results from the CCES experiment, in which participants saw treatments describing the primary source of a candidate's funds: his own money made in the private sector, his own inherited money, "contributions from individual citizens and interest groups," or "contributions from individual citizens." We restrict this analysis to the 756 respondents who provided responses to all of the questions used in the analysis presented below. Our analysis has three outcome measures of interest: *Vote Intent* (whether the respondent is more or less likely to vote for the candidate), *Candidate Evaluation Index* (an index of our outcomes that assesses participants' general evaluation of the candidate), and *Candidate would NOT serve special interests* (a measure of whether participants believe the candidate would be independent from the influence of interest organizations).[16] Our analysis includes indicator variables for each of the three funding source treatments, with the "contributions from individual citizens" condition serving as the excluded category. Columns (1)–(3) of Table 4.2 display the results of these multivariate regression models.

Column (1) of Table 4.2 displays the results for *Vote Intent*, which ranges from 0 ("not very likely" to vote for the candidate) to 100 ("very likely" to vote for the candidate). Compared to a candidate described as using funds from contributions primarily from individuals to fund his campaign (the omitted condition), the candidates described in the other three treatment groups rate more negatively on vote intent. For two of the treatment groups, the

Table 4.2 Effect of Funding Source Treatments on Candidate Evaluations

	(1) Vote intent (0 = Not very likely; 100 = Very likely)	(2) Candidate Evaluation Index (M = 0, SD = 1; negative-positive)	(3) Candidate would NOT serve special interests (−3 = Disagree strongly; 3 = Agree strongly)
Contributions from individuals and interest groups condition (1 = yes)	−7.270 [2.553]**	−0.186 [0.091]*	−0.392 [0.173]*
Inherited money condition (1 = yes)	−6.091 [2.686]*	−0.240 [0.090]**	−0.243 [0.174]
Money made in the private sector condition (1 = yes)	−2.494 [2.686]	0.002 [0.089]	−0.147 [0.173]
Democratic candidate condition (1 = yes)	−11.123 [2.250]**	−0.406 [0.077]**	−0.422 [0.141]**
Republican candidate condition (1 = yes)	0.937 [2.223]	0.002 [0.076]	−0.266 [0.142]
Respondent's PID (−3 = Str. Rep.; 3 = Str. Dem.) × No party condition	−3.348 [0.762]**	−0.118 [0.028]**	−0.140 [0.045]**
Respondent's PID (−3 = Str. Rep.; 3 = Str. Dem.) × Dem. condition	7.377 [0.708]**	0.222 [0.026]**	0.072 [0.051]
Respondent's PID (−3 = Str. Rep.; 3 = Str. Dem.) × Rep. condition	−9.014 [0.699]**	−0.287 [0.025]**	−0.265 [0.051]**
Office treatment (U.S. Senate = 0; U.S. House of Representatives = 1)	−0.648 [1.821]	−0.009 [0.064]	−0.011 [0.121]
Constant	47.874 [11.146]**	0.070 [0.356]	0.835 [0.614]
Observations	756	756	756
R-squared	0.313	0.286	0.087

Note: OLS regression coefficients with robust standard errors in brackets. The omitted funding source treatment condition is "contributions from individual citizens" and the omitted party treatment condition is no party. Controls included, but suppressed from table: female (1 = yes), age (years), age-squared/100, race (indicators for Black, Hispanic, and Other), education (linear), income (linear), and income missing (1 = yes). $*p < 0.05$; $**p < 0.01$.
Source: 2010 CCES

differences are statistically significant. A candidate that primarily finances his campaign with contributions from individuals and interest groups is about 7 points (on the 100-point scale or 1/4 of a standard deviation) less likely to be voted for, whereas a candidate that primarily uses money he inherited to finance his campaign is about 6 points (or 1/5 of a standard deviation) less likely to be voted for.[17] However, there is no statistically identifiable difference between a candidate who primarily uses money he made in the private sector to finance his campaign and a candidate who is primarily financing his campaign with contributions from individuals.[18]

Column (2) of Table 4.2 presents the results for the *Candidate Evaluation Index* constructed from five of the specific candidate evaluation items (see the appendix for details).[19] The results are quite similar to those presented in column (1) for *Vote Intent*. Once again, a candidate that primarily finances his campaign with either contributions from individuals and interest groups or money he inherited is viewed less favorably than a candidate who primarily finances his campaign with contributions from individuals, whereas a candidate who finances his campaign primarily with money he made in the private sector is viewed no differently.

The coefficient of –.240 for the inherited money condition is statistically distinguishable from both the (omitted) contributions from individual citizens condition and the money made in the private sector condition.[20] In addition, the –.186 effect of the contributions from individuals and interest groups condition is also statistically distinguishable from both the (omitted) contributions from individual citizens condition and the money made in the private sector condition.[21] The inherited money and contributions from individuals and interest group conditions are not statistically distinguishable from one another. In short, when it comes to overall evaluations of candidates (e.g., doing a good job, understanding issues, and representing constituents effectively), candidates who the vignette suggested had taken money primarily from individuals and interest groups and candidates who the vignette suggested spent inherited money fared worse than the other two funding descriptions.

Analysis of perceptions of whether the candidate would serve special interests, which ranges from –3 (strongly disagree that the candidate would NOT serve special interests) to +3 (strongly agree that the candidate would NOT serve special interests), is presented in column (3) of Table 4.2. We find that the individuals/interest group treatment has a rather large effect on perceptions that the candidate would serve special interests compared to the (omitted) contributions from individuals treatment. This effect is not statistically distinguishable from the effects of the other funding source treatment coefficients, however. Still, compared to candidates described as using contributions primarily from individuals, those who were described as using contributions primarily from individuals and interest groups were much more likely to be viewed as prone to serve special interests.

* * *

The first experiment we conducted using the Mechanical Turk service (MTurk 1), described in detail in Panel B of Appendix Table 4.1, was completed by about 1,600 participants in spring 2012. The main goal of this follow-up experiment was to ascertain whether the results from the CCES experiment would hold with a more complex informational treatment. Like the CCES experiment, MTurk 1 provided participants with a fictional vignette about a candidate for an open congressional seat. As before, we randomly assign the candidate's partisan affiliation (Democratic or Republican) and various funding conditions. However, we make three changes to the design framework employed in the CCES experiment.

First, we provided participants with a specific amount of money raised ($700,000) from a randomly assigned source out of a total of $1.3 million for his campaign.[22] The funding source treatment conditions were either that the candidate raised $700,000 from one of three possible sources (his own funds, interest groups, or individual contributions) or that his "campaign is funded with a mixture of individual contributions, contributions from interest groups, and his own money." Providing participants with dollar figures (as opposed to informing them directly about the "primary" source of the candidate's funding as in the CCES experiment) requires them to make their own judgments about the extent to which various funding sources were important in the candidate's funding portfolio, and is therefore a less overt expression of the candidate's status as a "self-funded" or "interest-backed" politician. Second, we include an "extra information" condition in which participants read additional biographical material about the candidate, including his background as a business owner, status as a college graduate, and focus on growing the economy. Supplying this information at the end of the vignette more closely mimics the sort of background provided in a news story that a voter might encounter during a real-world election, once again likely making the information about funding sources more difficult for participants to pick out. In tandem, these first two changes should, if anything, blunt the effect of the funding source treatments. In other words, these changes should make it less likely to find an effect of funding sources on candidate evaluations.

Third, the design of MTurk 1 includes a control condition that is not present in the CCES experiment. Participants assigned to the control condition saw only the biographical information about the candidate (or the biographical information plus "extra information"), and received no information about the candidate's funding sources. In providing no information about campaign funding, the control condition is likely to reflect the lack of knowledge that many voters might have of a typical candidate's campaign finance sources, thereby providing a logical point of reference in the experimental design.

We restrict analysis of MTurk 1 to the 1,463 respondents who provided responses to all of the questions used in the analysis presented below. We again analyze our results using a regression model, reported in columns

(1)–(3) of Table 4.3. Before proceeding, we note that the excluded category for funding source indicators is the control condition in which no information about funding sources was provided, so the treatment indicator coefficients for the respective funding source variables compare the effect of participants receiving that information to that of receiving none. There are several findings worth describing. First, receiving a large proportion of contributions from interest groups ($700,000 of $1.3 million) appears to send a strong negative signal to voters. Compared to the control group that received no information about the candidate's funding portfolio, participants assigned to the interest groups condition rate the candidate less favorably, are significantly less likely to vote for the candidate, and are significantly more likely to feel he will serve special interests.[23] It is also worth noting, however, that simply indicating that a candidate receives a "mixture" of contributions, including contributions from interest groups, sends a negative signal to voters compared to receiving no information about funding sources at all.[24] Yet, a candidate who self-finances or receives most of his money from individual contributions is viewed no differently than the same candidate who is described without any mention of his funding portfolio: Each of the coefficients for these two treatment conditions in columns (1)–(3) of Table 4.3 are positive, but fall short of conventional levels of statistical significance.[25] In sum then, it appears that interest group funding sends a negative signal (compared to receiving no information about candidate funding), whereas contributions from individuals and self-financing send, if anything, small positive signals.

Presenting participants with monetary amounts should mitigate the effect of the funding source treatments by leaving it up to them whether $700,000 was a substantial enough proportion of the candidate's total money raised ($1.3 million) to warrant shifting their opinion of him. Despite this change, we find similar results using the MTurk 1 design to those in the CCES experiment. If we compare the equality of the funding source treatment condition coefficients ascertained from the regression analysis we find, as was the case in the CCES experiment, that the interest groups condition is significantly different from the contributions from individuals condition for each of the three outcome measures. Moreover, the substantive effect of this difference is also similar to those found in the CCES experiment.[26]

Last, we turn to the difference in results between giving participants extra information (presented in columns [7]–[9] of Table 4.3) and not giving participants that information (presented in columns [4]–[6] of Table 4.3). Including extra information should diminish the effect of the funding source treatments. Yet, the results presented in columns (7)–(9) are consistent with those presented in columns (4)–(6) and, by extension, those presented in the CCES experiment where we also did not include such extra information about the fictitious candidate. When the extra information is presented to the respondents, not only is the effect of receiving $700,000 (out of $1.3 million) from interest groups significantly different from the

Table 4.3 Effect of Funding Source Treatments on Candidate Evaluations, for Full Sample and by Extra Information Conditions

	(1)	(2)	(3)	(4)	(5)	(6)	(7)	(8)	(9)
	Full Sample			No Extra Information			Extra Information		
	Vote Intent (−3 = very unlikely; +3 = very likely)	Candidate Evaluation Index (M = 0, SD = 1; negative-positive)	Candidate would NOT serve special interests (−3 = Disagree strongly; 3 = Agree strongly)	Vote Intent (−3 = very unlikely; +3 = very likely)	Candidate Evaluation Index (M = 0, SD = 1; negative-positive)	Candidate would NOT serve special interests (−3 = Disagree strongly; 3 = Agree strongly)	Vote Intent (−3 = very unlikely; +3 = very likely)	Candidate Evaluation Index (M = 0, SD = 1; negative-positive)	Candidate would NOT serve special interests (−3 = Disagree strongly; 3 = Agree strongly)
Contributions from individuals condition (1 = yes)	0.082 [0.106]	0.011 [0.078]	0.115 [0.111]	0.321 [0.159]*	0.220 [0.109]*	0.107 [0.159]	−0.159 [0.141]	−0.174 [0.112]	0.124 [0.159]
Contributions from interest groups condition (1 = yes)	−0.452 [0.103]**	−0.172 [0.074]*	−0.815 [0.106]**	−0.383 [0.162]*	−0.098 [0.112]	−0.931 [0.161]**	−0.545 [0.132]**	−0.264 [0.097]**	−0.698 [0.141]**
Self-financing condition (1 = yes)	0.153 [0.103]	0.059 [0.075]	0.001 [0.105]	0.112 [0.150]	0.092 [0.101]	0.098 [0.145]	0.195 [0.141]	0.046 [0.111]	−0.095 [0.150]
Mixture condition (1 = yes)	−0.124 [0.103]	−0.175 [0.075]*	−0.372 [0.108]**	−0.102 [0.148]	−0.061 [0.106]	−0.447 [0.147]**	−0.166 [0.140]	−0.296 [0.106]**	−0.243 [0.159]
Extra information (1 = yes)	0.493 [0.066]**	0.352 [0.049]**	0.135 [0.069]						

Party treatment (Rep. = 0; Dem. = 1)	-0.038 [0.068]	-0.031 [0.051]	-0.020 [0.072]	-0.060 [0.098]	-0.149 [0.070]*	-0.015 [0.102]	-0.003 [0.094]	0.085 [0.072]	-0.062 [0.100]
Respondent's PID (−3 = Str. Rep.; 3 = Str. Dem.) × Party treatment (Rep. = 0; Dem. = 1)	0.646 [0.037]**	0.328 [0.027]**	0.071 [0.038]	0.721 [0.050]**	0.330 [0.036]**	0.017 [0.052]	0.563 [0.053]**	0.322 [0.040]**	0.141 [0.055]*
Respondent's PID (−3 = Str. Rep.; 0 = Ind./Not sure; 3 = Str. Dem.)	-0.356 [0.026]**	-0.166 [0.020]**	-0.090 [0.026]**	-0.370 [0.038]**	-0.138 [0.027]**	-0.074 [0.036]*	-0.342 [0.036]**	-0.194 [0.029]**	-0.106 [0.038]**
Constant	0.906 [0.275]**	0.302 [0.204]	-0.449 [0.298]	0.921 [0.410]*	0.154 [0.294]	-0.299 [0.408]	1.313 [0.350]**	0.755 [0.263]**	-0.409 [0.416]
Observations	1463	1463	1463	733	733	733	730	730	730
R-squared	0.256	0.145	0.082	0.267	0.138	0.116	0.223	0.138	0.069

Note: OLS regression coefficients with robust standard errors in brackets. Omitted funding source treatment condition is no mention of candidate funding. Controls included, but suppressed from table: female (1 = yes), age (years), age-squared/100, race (indicators for Black, Hispanic, and Other), and education (linear). *$p < 0.05$; **$p < 0.01$.

Source: 2012 MTurk Study (MTurk 1)

control condition, but it is also different from the contributions from individuals condition when it comes to *Vote Intent* and the perception that the candidate would not serve special interests.[27]

There is no identifiable difference between the interest group and individuals condition on the *Candidate Evaluation Index* when the extra information is presented to the respondents ($p = .406$), but such differences do exist in the absence of the extra information.[28] Thus, while there is some evidence that the effects of our interest group treatment is muted with additional information about the candidate, the effects are still apparent—they are distinguishable from both the absence of any funding information and from an identical candidate that received most of his money from individual contributions (and also a self-financed candidate and one that receives a mixture of contributions).

* * *

The second experiment we conducted using the Mechanical Turk service (MTurk 2) is described in Panel C of Appendix Table 4.1. Whereas the CCES and MTurk 1 experiments sought to assess how the source of donations to the candidate affected voters' perception of him, MTurk 2 attempted to gauge whether people evaluate a candidate differently when outside groups spend relatively large sums on his behalf. In MTurk 2 (described in greater detail in the appendix), we therefore presented participants with a vignette in which the amount of money that the candidate raised did not change—it was held constant at $600,000. Participants were also told that the candidate "spent $50,000 of his own money" during the campaign; this amount did not change. We did, however, randomize two crucial components of the candidate's biography. First, we either provided no information aside from the candidate's basic biography, or we told respondents either that "super PACs" or "interest groups" had spent money "to support his candidacy." We also varied the amount that the group (randomly assigned to be either super PACs or interest groups) spent: "no money," $350,000, or $1.2 million.[29] Finally, we hold constant $350,000 in spending by outside groups (either "super PACs" or "interest groups," matching the initial treatment) *against* the candidate.

As noted, the design of the MTurk 2 experiment features a control condition in which respondents received no information about outside money.[30] As with MTurk 1, the control condition supplies a natural comparison group for the randomized treatments regarding outside spending. The control reflects a lack of information that many voters might have about outside spending during an election, and allows us to observe whether providing such information has any effect on evaluations of the candidate.

For MTurk 2, we analyzed data from 1,565 participants who completed the study in the summer of 2013. The results from MTurk 2 are presented in Table 4.4, and we once again remind readers that the treatment indicators

Table 4.4   Effect of Super PAC v. Interest Group Funding Source Treatment on Candidate Evaluations

	(1) Vote Intent (−3 = very unlikely; +3 = very likely)	(2) Candidate Evaluation Index (M = 0, SD = 1; negative-positive)	(3) Candidate would NOT serve special interests (−3 = Disagree strongly; 3 = Agree strongly)
Interest group funding: $1.3m (1 = yes)	−0.354 [0.133]**	−0.047 [0.089]	−0.982 [0.115]**
Interest group funding: $350k (1 = yes)	−0.283 [0.127]*	−0.009 [0.083]	−0.336 [0.111]**
Interest group funding: none (1 = yes)	0.44 [0.112]**	0.318 [0.079]**	0.697 [0.134]**
Super PAC funding: $1.3m (1 = yes)	−0.415 [0.136]**	−0.111 [0.093]	−0.494 [0.119]**
Super PAC funding: $350k (1 = yes)	−0.095 [0.121]	0.038 [0.085]	−0.299 [0.109]**
Super PAC funding: none (1 = yes)	0.371 [0.123]**	0.108 [0.087]	0.428 [0.119]**
Respondent's PID (−3 = Str. Rep.; 0 = Ind./Not sure; 3 = Str. Dem.)	0.042 [0.034]	0.06 [0.024]*	−0.004 [0.032]
Constant	1.036 [0.359]**	0.024 [0.256]	0.111 [0.358]
Observations	1565	1565	1565
R-squared	0.060	0.054	0.132

Note: OLS regression coefficients with robust standard errors in brackets. The omitted funding source treatment condition is the control (no funding source information) group. Controls included, but suppressed from table: female (1 = yes), age (years), age-squared/100, race (indicators for Black, Hispanic, and Other), education (linear), income (linear), political interest (3-point scale), and political ideology (linear). *$p < 0.05$; **$p < 0.01$.
Source: 2013 MTurk Study (MTurk 2)

utilize the "no additional information" category for comparison, so they can be interpreted as the effect on an outcome measure of receiving an informational treatment compared to receiving no information about outside spending. With that in mind, the experiment yields interesting results with regard to the *Vote Intent* outcome. Specifically, respondents were significantly less likely to vote for the candidate when they learned that outside groups had spent on his behalf, regardless of whether the money came from "super PACs" or "interest groups." That is, there are no statistical differences between the effect on vote intent of hearing that a candidate was supported by super PACs as opposed to interest groups, nor does the magnitude of the support matter when the candidate is supported by "interest groups." Although both super PAC conditions result in lower vote intentions than the control condition, participants downgraded their vote intention significantly more for candidates who had benefited from "super PAC" expenditures of $1.3 million than they did for those who received $350,000 worth of support.[31] Participants also indicated that they were significantly *more* likely than the control condition to vote for a candidate who received no external support from either super PACs or interest groups when such groups spent $350,000 against him.

These results align well with respondents' judgments about the extent to which the candidate would "serve special interests." For all four conditions in which the candidate benefitted from outside spending—that is, super PACs or interest groups spent either $350,000 or $1.3 million to support him—he was judged to be more likely to serve special interests than a candidate in the control condition. Interestingly, the magnitude of the outside spending was a significant determinant of the extent to which participants judged a candidate as likely to serve special interests when they were told that an "interest group" had made independent expenditures, but not when told that super PACs had done so. Specifically, participants who were told that the candidate had benefitted from $1.3 million in spending by interest groups were significantly more likely to feel that the candidate would serve special interests than those told interest groups had spent $350,000, but no statistical difference exists between the two treatments denoting super PAC spending amounts.[32] We take this as evidence that the information about "interest group" support provided a stronger cue about the candidate's ties to "special interests" than information about "super PAC" spending. Indeed, the effect of $1.3 million spent by "interest groups" on perceptions of a candidate's likelihood to serve special interests is approximately twice that of $1.3 million spent by "super PACs," which is a statistically significant difference.[33] Finally, as with *Vote Intent*, the treatments reflecting a scenario in which groups spend nothing for the candidate but $350,000 to oppose him are oppositely signed relative to the other treatments: Regardless of whether they are referred to as "super PACs" or "interest groups," respondents are significantly more likely to say that the candidate would *not* serve special interests when outside groups spend against him.

There were few significant results in MTurk 2, however, when it came to the *Candidate Evaluation Index*. Respondents evaluated the candidate no differently when told that super PACs or interest groups spent on his behalf than when they received no additional information about outside spending in the race, nor did hearing that "super PACs" had spent no money for Smith but $350,000 against him affect participants' evaluations of him. However, when told that "interest groups" had spent $350,000 against the candidate (but nothing on his behalf), respondents evaluated him significantly more favorably. The relatively few significant findings on overall evaluations aside, the clear pattern in MTurk 2 is that knowledge of outside spending can affect both voter perception of the extent to which a candidate is beholden to special interests, and this judgment in turn appears to contribute to decisions about whether to vote for him. Specifically, candidates who benefit from outside spending—regardless of the size or source of that spending—are seen as more likely to "serve special interests" and are consequently less likely to be voted for. The converse is true of candidates who receive no help from outside groups, but who find themselves attacked by outside money.

SUMMARIZING THE EXPERIMENTS

Our experiments demonstrate that knowledge of the financial aspects of an election can shape voters' perceptions of a candidate. Specifically, four main findings emerge. First, in both experiments that examined contribution sources (CCES and MTurk 1), we find a negative association between participants being informed that a candidate had taken large amounts of interest group funding and all of our outcome measures. These findings suggest that, to the extent that voters are informed about candidates who are heavily reliant upon contributions from interest organizations, they are less likely to support a candidate who is heavily backed by special interests. This negative association between interest group funding and our outcome measures stands in contrast to the positive correlation between PAC funding and electoral success observed in previous observational work (e.g., Alexander 2005), a point we return to below.

Second, our findings with regard to the effect of self-funding with *earned* money agree with previous research that has treated all self-funding in the same fashion when examining the relationship between self-financing and electoral success, and that has found little such consistent correlation (e.g., Alexander 2005; Brown 2013; Steen 2006). However, our CCES experiment also isolated the effect of *inherited* money, with a different result: We find a negative association between self-financing a campaign primarily with inherited money and both candidate evaluations and vote intent. These findings suggest that voters may differentiate between different types of self-funded candidates, depending upon the source of the candidate's wealth as an informational shortcut. As such, the negative association apparent in some observational work (Alexander 2005)—or even the apparent attenuated (Steen 2006) or null (Brown 2013) effect of self funding relative to contributions in other observational research—may be driven by voter backlash against so-called "silver spoon" candidates.

Third, our findings regarding the effects of knowledge about contribution sources hold when participants are presented with a less overt treatment. MTurk 1 added a control condition in which participants were given no information about candidate funding, and to which we compare treated subjects. That experiment also randomized the provision of additional biographical information after the funding treatment, and forced participants to make their own judgments about the relative impact of dollar amounts. Faced with these conditions, the experiment produced the same broad results as the CCES experiment: Interest-backed candidates were judged more harshly on both the vote intent and general evaluation measures, while evaluations of self-funders were not significantly different.

Fourth, our MTurk2 experiment examines the effect of information about outside spending. The results suggest that when people are told that candidates benefit from either super PAC or interest group funding, they are more likely to feel that the candidate will serve special interests, and are less likely to vote for him. When told that a candidate had received no money from outside groups, but that he had also been attacked by them, the opposite was true: Participants in the MTurk 2 study judged him as less likely to be beholden to special interests, and were in turn more likely to vote for him.

CONCLUSION

Money matters. Our examination of the effect of both campaign and outside group spending suggests that both types of expenditures can affect election outcomes. However, not all funding influences voters in the same manner. Both the campaign spending of and outside spending for challengers are associated with a higher share of the general election vote for challengers. However, challengers also appear to perform better both when more outside money is spent for *incumbents* and when incumbents' campaigns spend more. Moreover, the results of our survey experiments suggest that candidate funding sources can play a role in shaping voter perceptions of candidates. Most notably, we find that when voters are informed of candidate funding sources there is a negative overall association between candidates who fund primarily with interest group contributions—or who benefit from independent expenditures of outside groups—and candidate evaluations, including vote intent.

At first glance, it may be difficult to reconcile our findings that congressional challengers performed better when they spent more money (or when it was spent for them) with the experimental results suggesting that raising large sums from (or having them spent by) interest groups costs a candidate votes. Indeed, the negative association between interest group funding and vote intent that we observe contrasts with Alexander (2005), who found a positive correlation between the percentage of PAC funding received by candidates for open U.S. House seats and their share of the general election vote, as well as with Brown (2013), who found a positive association between external (non-self) funding and electoral success. We believe, however, that our experiments merely underscore that the relationship between money and votes is quite complex and emerges from sometimes countervailing forces.

For instance, Alexander (2005) concluded that the voting public is apathetic to information about the funding sources of interest-backed candidates, noting that "the public is undoubtedly aware of the fact that most candidates accept PAC donations, and although the issue is raised frequently in dueling campaign press releases and ads, the flying allegations do not appear to be sticking" (357). Rather, Alexander suggests that a higher percentage of PAC funding can be viewed as a proxy for unobservable (to the researcher) factors that indicate candidate strength, such as "recommendations from party leaders, private polling data, or knowledge of factors unique to particular districts or candidates" (357).

Likewise, Brown (2013) finds that self-financing does not affect votes, while external contributions are a positive predictor of electoral success. Brown further argues that although money itself is apparently not driving outcomes, demonstrating an ability to raise large sums is part of what it takes to be a good candidate, since being well funded sends a signal to voters about the campaign's strength. Indeed, Brown suggests that "perhaps candidates fundraise to signal their viability to voters. Even if voters are not persuaded at all by slick campaign advertisements, they may nevertheless glean information from the fact that a candidate was able to raise enough money to produce slick ads in the first place" (2013, 38).

Our findings suggest, however, that candidates may want to narrowcast this signal if their funding is heavily dependent upon PAC sources or independent expenditures from outside groups, as the "interest-supported" brand carries a backlash risk with the mass electorate. Specifically, the "flying allegations" to which Alexander alludes might actually be sticking, but the negative effects are likely outweighed by much stronger ones derivative of candidate traits that are difficult to observe. In other words, we believe that the resolution to the issue of dissonance between our experimental findings and those of observational studies in the area of interest financing is that both are probably correct. There is some risk of a backlash from taking PAC money, but the very fact that a candidate attracts large PAC contributions can be viewed as a proxy for inherent strength that generally makes such a risk worth bearing. Challengers in particular can leverage contributions for more votes, and money has to come from somewhere. Assuming that voters do receive and process this information, we believe that our experimental findings depict a more complete picture of the electoral dynamics that candidates confront.

With regard to self-funded candidates, conclusions from previous observational studies have ranged from a negative relationship to a very weak positive one between a candidate's level of self-financing and her general election vote percentage; the only apparent consensus is that self-financing does not seem to be as beneficial as other funding sources (e.g., Alexander

2005; Brown 2013; Steen 2006). As noted above, these studies have been unable to determine whether this is because self-funded candidates face a backlash from voters, or whether high levels of self-financing mark a weak candidate unable to raise money from private donors due to unobservable (to the researcher) traits.

Although Brown's (2013) theoretical framework advances a persuasive argument in support of the latter claim, we find that the former is also likely accurate under certain conditions. Specifically, our CCES experiment shows that respondents distinguish between candidates who self-fund with money they inherited and money they earned; compared to candidates funding only with individual contributions, the former are judged more harshly, while the latter are not. In some cases respondents made significant distinctions between the two types of self financing.

It is important to note that like all research designs, our survey experiments have their limitations. Our study examines immediate responses to information about campaign money and, in so doing, informs debates about the effect of money on politics. Although these initial reactions are important in advancing our understanding of voters' preference formation, we cannot say how they are affected in the temporal context of a long political campaign. For instance, if voters immediately judge candidates who benefitted from independent expenditures more harshly upon receipt of that information, perhaps this judgment diminishes over time as other information about the candidate becomes known.

Nonetheless, by replicating our core findings across three experiments employing slightly different designs, we believe that they are valid with regard to assessing voter reaction to candidate funding sources and outside group support. In particular, by providing raw dollar amounts and additional biographical information, the MTurk experiments deliver treatment in a setting designed to closely simulate the conditions in which a voter would encounter information about a candidate's financial backers. Granted, the effects we observe in this lab setting could get "washed out" over the course of an actual campaign. However, they could also be larger, if candidates trumpet their funding sources or those of their opponents to a greater degree than our more subtle one-sentence treatments do. Regardless, the experiments reported above are informative with regard to how voters react to information about funding sources, and strongly suggest that previous observational analyses likely mask some complexity in the relationship between candidate funding sources and electoral success.

NOTES

1. Professor Gary C. Jacobson graciously shared data on congressional elections with us.
2. Examining incumbent-contested elections excludes 138 open-seat elections and 351 races with incomplete information, meaning that either the incumbent

did not meet major-party opposition or spending data were not available for one of the candidates in the election.

3. $p < .01$.
4. $p = .221$.
5. We plot challenger's share of the two-party general election vote, as it serves as the dependent variable in the models presented above. The challenger's share of the two-party vote is of course inversely related to incumbent vote share.
6. The Pearson correlation between incumbent spending and challenger vote share was .55, which is quite close to the .54 correlation coefficient between incumbent independent expenditures and challenger vote share (we describe this relationship below).
7. As just one example of the rise in campaign spending, the average campaign expenditure by a major party challenger to a U.S. House seat in 1974 was approximately $40,000; in 2010 the average was nearly $700,000 (Campaign Finance Institute, www.cfinst.org/pdf/vital/VitalStats_t2.pdf).
8. For a discussion of literature in this area, see Maestas and Rugeley (2008).
9. For a more thorough discussion of funding sources, see Brown (2013).
10. Lexis-Nexis searches show that the word "billionaire" appeared in about 20 percent of news stories about Meg Whitman during the 2010 campaign, and in nearly half of those about Greene.
11. Indeed, this is an argument many self-funders make (for example, see Cave and Luo 2010 on the 2010 midterm election).
12. Each study received approval from an Institutional Review Board.
13. The CCES is a collaborative effort among researchers at a number of universities to create a large, national survey. Pooling their resources, researchers contribute to "common content," or a set of questions that all respondents answer, followed by the "private content," another set of questions specific to each individual team. Our survey experiment appeared on Yale University's private content. We thank Yale's Center for the Study of American Politics for the financial support for this survey.
14. We chose to describe the fictitious candidate as one who was running for an open seat (i.e., one in which there was no incumbent running) because we wanted to mitigate the chances that participants would simply think about their own representative or senator when evaluating the fictitious candidate.
15. The full vignette also appeared at the top of this page.
16. See the appendix for more description of these outcome measures.
17. All reported p-values in this chapter are two-tailed. Here, $p < .01$ and $p = .024$, respectively.
18. $p = .353$. The three coefficients reported in column (1) of Table 4.2 are not statistically distinguishable from one another at conventional levels. The smallest p-value for a test of the equality of these coefficients (all three pairwise comparisons) is for the comparison of the coefficient of −7.270 on "contributions from individuals and interest groups" to the coefficient of −2.494 on "money made in the private sector" ($p = .055$).
19. The *Candidate Evaluation Index* is a standardized index with mean = 0 and standard deviation = 1.
20. $p < .01$ in both cases.
21. $p = .043$ and $p = .031$, respectively.
22. $1.3 million is a large sum of money, but is a fairly typical funding total for an open-seat candidate (Campaign Finance Institute 2013).
23. $p < .05$ in all cases.
24. $p = .226$, = .020, and < .01 for columns (1), (2), and (3) in Table 4.3, respectively.

25. The smallest *p*-value is .139, for self-financing in column (1).
26. The interest groups condition is also significantly different from both the self-financing and mixture conditions on *Vote Intent*, the *Candidate Evaluation Index* (only different from self-financing), and that the *Candidate would NOT serve special interests* ($p < .01$, except for comparison of interest groups to mixture for the *Candidate Evaluation Index* where $p = .977$).
27. $p < .01$ in all cases.
28. $p < .01$.
29. For instance, the "no money" condition would either read: "Super PACs spent no money in support of his candidacy" or, "Interest groups spent no money in support of his candidacy."
30. It also features a possible condition in which respondents were told that outside groups had been active in the race but in which the candidate received no supporting funds.
31. $p = .034$.
32. $p < .001$ and $p = .145$, respectively.
33. $p < .001$.

5 Super PAC Ads in the 2012 Presidential Election

In the summer of 2004, a few months before voters would head to the polls to decide between President George W. Bush and his challenger, John Kerry, an organization called Swift Boat Veterans for Truth (later named Swift Vets and POWs for Truth, SVPT) began airing ads questioning Kerry's suitability to be president. As we noted in Chapter 2, the ads focused on Kerry's military service record and portrayed him as an opportunist and "sellout." The ads were noteworthy not simply because of their claims—attack ads are commonplace in American politics (Geer 2006)—but also because they amounted to a possibly misleading campaign from a relatively unknown group (see: Lehigh 2004).

SVPT operated in a pre-*Citizens United* world. As such, it was registered as a 527 and could therefore only engage in issue advocacy, not express advocacy for the election or defeat of a candidate. Considering the larger amounts of money flowing to outside groups, coupled with their enhanced ability to sponsor express advocacy in the post–*Citizens United* era, it might be reasonable to expect more negative and misleading ads to permeate elections; this might be especially likely given that outside groups are less accountable to voters than candidates or parties. On the other hand, perhaps outside groups behave in a manner similar to campaigns with regard to their negativity, so although there may be more ads after *Citizens United*, the ratio of negative ads to positive ones may be largely the same as before. Alternatively, maybe group-funded ads are just as negative as they ever were before they could expressly advocate for the election or defeat of one candidate over another. As one prominent legal scholar described the Court's decision in *Citizens United*: "Prior to the *Citizens United* decision, corporations had the constitutional right to spend unlimited funds telling voters that 'Candidate Smith hates puppies.' *Citizens United* added only protection for these corporations to convey an incremental 'Vote Smith Out' exhortation" (Levitt 2010, 220). This statement implies that the content of the ads might not change all that much, except for the possible addition of a short sentence. We say "possible" because it is likely—to use Levitt's example—that if an ad tells people "candidate Smith hates puppies," it does not have to add, "don't vote for him." It is rather strongly implied, just like the accusations against Kerry in the SVPT ads rather strongly implied to not vote for him, even if the SVPT did not expressly say so.

The SVPT ads were notable, but are they the rule or the exception? Groups might choose to air more negative ads—that is, run an ad attacking one candidate rather than an ad supporting the other—but this does not necessarily mean the attack[1] ads they run are any different than the attack ads candidates run, on average. Put another way, a greater percentage of group ads may be negative, as indeed seems to have been the case during the 2012 election (see: Chapter 3; also Fowler and Ridout 2012)—whereas 85 percent of group ads were negative in that they only attacked a candidate but did not promote the other candidate, 54 and 51 percent of candidate and party ads were negative, respectively.[2] But that does not necessarily mean either that groups air more total negative ads, or that the negative ads they do air are significantly *more* "negative" (in a broad sense, but defined more specifically below) than those of candidates and parties. Are, for instance, group-funded ads more misleading and less informative than ads purchased by campaigns? In this chapter, we address both these points.

STUDY 1

We begin by examining whether super PACs air ads that differ significantly in their content from those aired by the candidates' campaigns. In particular, we focus on two presumably positive attributes of advertising—how "informative" and "fair" an ad is perceived to be—and two presumably negative attributes of advertising—how "misleading" and "negative" an ad is perceived to be. Much of the scholarly literature on and popular discussion of attack advertising focuses on the potential deleterious effects of its misleading and negative nature (see Geer 2006 for a summary). Ansolabehere and Iyengar (1995) contend, for example, that attack advertising demobilizes voters (also see Patterson 2002).[3] As Geer (2006) notes, however, all advertising—even positive ads that only promote a candidate—can be misleading. Further, Geer argues and provides evidence that attack ads can be informative, that there is often more documentation of the attacks volleyed in a negative ad than there is of the promoting done in a positive ad. With this in mind—that is, granting that there can be some beneficial aspects to attack advertising—our question is whether super PAC ads fare any better or worse on these measures than candidate ads.

To begin to address this question we conducted a study in which participants evaluated a series of negative ads devoid of their sponsors. We stripped the sponsors from the ads because we did not want knowledge or feelings about the sponsor (Mitt Romney, Barack Obama, or the relevant super PACs) to color perceptions of the ad content. We focused on negative ads–defined as ads that only mention an opponent, except for the sponsorship information (Fowler and Ridout 2012)—because they comprised a majority (nearly 64 percent) of the ads aired in the presidential race between June 1, 2012 and Election Day (Fowler and Ridout 2012, Table 8).

To select the ads for our study, we relied on the resource compiled by the Political Communication Lab (PCL) at Stanford University.[4] The PCL kept an inventory of all ads aired during the 2012 presidential election between Mitt Romney (the Republican challenger) and Barack Obama (the Democratic incumbent). In total, there were 204 ads that aired after the major parties made their candidates' nominations official at their late-summer conventions. We separated this set of ads by their sponsor: (1) a candidate (Obama or Romney), (2) a political party (Democratic National Committee or Republican National Committee), or (3) the super PACs most closely associated with each candidate (Priorities USA for Obama, or Restore Our Future for Romney).

Table 5.1 displays the breakdown of these 204 unique ads by their sponsor. One thing that is immediately clear is that most ads were sponsored by the candidates: The Romney and Obama campaigns combined to sponsor 63 percent of the 204 unique ads. Moreover, as the second column of Table 5.1 shows, the two candidates aired 81 percent (719,497 of 884,079) of the total spots that aired by the candidates, their parties, or the two super PACs from June 1, 2012 through Election Day. The two super PACs sponsored 27 percent of the unique ads and 14 percent (121,547 of 884,079) of the total spots. The parties sponsored the fewest number of unique ads—only 19—and aired only 5 percent (43,035 of 884,079) of the total spots between June 1, 2012 and Election Day. This distribution of ads likely reflects the stricter regulations placed on parties in terms of raising funds compared to

Table 5.1 Number of Unique Ads and Total Number of Ads Aired in the 2012 Presidential Election, by Sponsor

	Number of Unique Ads Sponsored, September 7, 2012 through Election Day[a]	Total Number of Ads Aired, June 1, 2012 through Election Day[b]
Barack Obama	63	511,513
Mitt Romney	66	207,984
Democratic National Committee	3	7,210
Republican National Committee	16	35,825
Priorities USA	10	58,990
Restore Our Future	46	62,557
Total	204	884,079

[a] *Source:* Stanford's Political Communication Lab, http://pcl.stanford.edu/campaigns/2012/
[b] *Source:* Fowler and Ridout (2012, Table 2)

super PACs and other outside groups, such as 501(c)4s, and the smaller role party committees play in the post–*Citizens United* system (La Raja 2012). For this reason, we focused our study on ads sponsored by the candidates and super PACs.

Before proceeding with the description of our study, we note that the second column of Table 5.1 helps address one point we wish to make in this chapter: who is responsible for the bulk of negative advertising. Although it may be the case that a greater proportion of group ads (85 percent) were negative in 2012 than candidate (54 percent) or party (51 percent) ads, this does not necessitate that groups were responsible for the bulk of negative advertising. To determine this, we simply multiply the total number of ads sponsored by candidates, parties, or super PACs (the last column of Table 5.1) by the proportion of ads they aired that were negative. Doing so suggests that Obama and Romney combined to air nearly 390,000 negative ads, whereas the two super PACs combined to air a little over 100,000.[5] (By the same calculus, the parties accounted for only about 22,000 negative ads.[6]) This comparison indicates it would be inaccurate to suggest the super PACs were solely, or even primarily, responsible for the negative ads voters encountered during the 2012 election.

Granted, this comparison does not include the ads aired by groups other than the two super PACs. For example, two of the top presidential race advertisers in 2012 were sister organizations American Crossroads (a super PAC) and Crossroads GPS (a 501(c)(4)), founded by Republican operatives Karl Rove (former Deputy Chief of Staff to President George W. Bush) and Ed Gillepsie (who served as Counselor to the President during the same administration). The two groups were the third and fifth highest presidential race advertisers in 2012, respectively, combining to air 143,163 spots between June 1, 2012 and Election Day. American Crossroads (81,553) aired more than the other two Super PACs more closely tied to the presidential candidates, Restore our Future (62,557) and Priorities USA (58,990), while Crossroads GPS (61,610) aired roughly the same amount as those two super PACs (Fowler and Ridout 2012, Table 2). It is possible that their ads were particularly negative or misleading, a possibility that warrants further study. In other words, the total number of negative ads aired by groups is obviously larger than 100,000.

To get a better sense of the total number of group ads that were negative, we rely on the Wesleyan Media Project estimate that a total of roughly 1.14 million ads aired during the 2012 presidential general election (Fowler and Ridout 2012, Figure 1). As Table 5.1 shows, 884,079 of these 1.14 million ads (or 78 percent) are accounted for by the six entities listed there. This leaves approximately 255,921 (1,140,000–884,079) ads that must also have been aired by some group (because there were no other candidates or parties than the ones listed in Table 5.1). Applying the same calculus as above (i.e., multiplying 255,921 by 85 percent), suggests an additional 217,533 negative ads were sponsored by groups. Combining the two super PACs with the rest of the groups then, results in an estimate of a little more than 320,000 negative ads sponsored by groups.[7] Although a large number, it is still less than the total number of negative ads aired by the two candidates (388,528). In short, groups aired a good deal of negative ads, but so did candidates. Did their ads differ in ways that are of concern to scholars and policymakers though?

* * *

Recall that because the parties aired so few ads in comparison to the candidates and super PACs (and related groups), we focus our study on candidate and super PAC ads. From the universe of 129 candidate-sponsored ads and 56 super PAC–sponsored ads, we randomly chose one negative ad from each of the four sponsors: Obama, Romney, Priorities USA, and Restore Our Future. By randomly selecting the ad, we hope to avoid bias in our conclusions that could result from selecting a particularly negative ad by any one sponsor. Next, we also selected the negative ad that was aired closest to Election Day (November 6) for each sponsor.[8] We chose these ads to see if ads aired closest to Election Day, when advertising should have the most important effects for a campaign given its quickly diminishing effects (Gerber et al. 2011; Hill et al. 2013), differ by their sponsorship, regardless of whether a randomly selected set of ads from earlier in the campaign does or does not.

The key characteristics of the ads that were selected—including complete voiceover text—are summarized in Table 5.2. The two ads sponsored by Obama were "Fair Share" (randomly selected) and "Cynical" (closest to Election Day). "Fair Share," which originally aired on September 25, 2012, attacked Romney over comments he made at a private, closed-door fundraiser in May of 2012. After a surreptitiously taped video of the meeting was leaked, the media and subsequently Romney's opponents homed in on one comment in particular, which came to be known as Romney's "47 percent comment." According to a transcript of the video obtained by *The New York Times*, an audience member asked Romney, "Over the past three years, all everybody's been told is, don't worry, we'll take care of it. How are you going to do it, with two months before the election, to convince everybody you've got to take care of yourself?" In response, Romney said,

Well, there are 47 percent of the people who will vote for the president no matter what. There are 47 percent who are with him, who are dependent upon government, who believe that they are victims, who believe that government has a responsibility to care for them, who believe that they are entitled to health care, to food, to housing, to you-name-it. That that's an entitlement and government should give it to them. And they will vote for this president no matter what. I mean, the president starts off with 48, 49 . . . I mean, he starts off with a huge number. These are people who pay no income tax; 47 percent of Americans pay no income tax. So our message of low taxes doesn't connect. He'll be out there talking about tax cuts for the rich. I mean, that's what they sell every four years. And so my job is not to worry about those people.

Table 5.2 Presidential Ads Used in Study 1

Ad (Original Air Date)	Sponsor	Selection Method	Text of Ad
Same Promises (10/23/12)	Priorities USA	Randomly selected	[Female Voice on Camera] We had a good group of people; good group of employees out there. [Male Voice on Camera] This was a booming place, and Mitt Romney and Bain Capital turned it into a junkyard. [Different Female Voice on Camera] I was suddenly 60 years old. I had no health care. [Different Male Voice on Camera] Mainly I was thinking about was my family. How am I gonna take care of my family? [Different Male Voice on Camera] He promised us the same thing he's promising the United States. He'll give you the same thing he gave us—nothin'.
Connect the Dots (10/31/12)	Priorities USA	Aired closest to Election Day	[Male Narrator] Mitt Romney and Rick Scott. Connect the dots. Scott ran a company that paid a record fine for committing Medicare fraud. Then as governor, Scott cut millions from health care. Romney was director of a company that stole millions from Medicare. Now, Romney's plan would end Medicare as we know it. We've seen this picture before. Just connect the dots. If Mitt Romney wins, the middle class loses.
Disappearing (9/19/12)	Restore Our Future	Randomly selected	[Female Narrator] Millions of Americans are disappearing from the workforce because they can't find jobs. The overall unemployment rate doesn't even count them anymore. Eight million Americans have dropped out of the workforce since Obama became president. Counting people who dropped out or can't find full-time jobs, the real unemployment rate is nearly 19 percent. [Male News Anchor] "This is the worst economic recovery America has ever had." [Female Narrator] Looking forward to a second Obama term?
Flatline (11/2/12)	Restore Our Future	Aired closest to Election Day	[Male Narrator] Beep, beep, beeeeeep. If you saw this line in the ER, you'd be panicked. Well, this flatline is Barack Obama's economy: 23 million looking for full-time work; middle-class incomes falling; spending and debt exploding. And Obama's second-term agenda is the same as the first. If you don't jumpstart America's economy now, your economy stays dead four more years. Demand better.

Fair Share (9/25/12)	Barack Obama	Randomly selected	[Male Narrator] When Mitt Romney dismissed 47 percent of Americans for not pulling their weight, he attacked millions of hard-working people making 25, 35, 45 thousand dollars a year. They pay Social Security taxes, state taxes, local taxes, gas, sales, and property taxes. Romney paid just 14 percent of taxes last year on over 13 million in income—almost all from investments. Instead of attacking folks who work for a living, shouldn't we stand up for them?
Cynical (11/1/12)	Barack Obama	Aired closest to Election Day	[Male Narrator] Wholly inaccurate. Clearly misleading. That's what news outlets are calling Mitt Romney's latest ads, suggesting auto jobs are being sent to China. GM calls Romney's ads, "politics at its cynical worst." And Chrysler's CEO said, "It's simply not true." We know the truth, Mitt. [Mitt Romney] "That's exactly what I said. My, my, the headline you read, which is let Detroit go bankrupt."
Dear Daughter (9/17/12)	Mitt Romney	Randomly selected	[Female Narrator] Dear daughter, welcome to America. Your share of Obama's debt is over 50 thousand dollars, and it grows every day. Obama's policies are making it harder on women. The poverty rate for women? The highest in 17 years. More women are unemployed under President Obama. More than 5.5 million women can't find work. That's what Obama's policies have done for women. Welcome, daughter.
Can't Afford Another Term (10/30/12)	Mitt Romney	Aired closest to Election Day	[Male Narrator] If you want to know President Obama's second-term agenda, look at his first: gutted the work requirement for welfare; doubled the number of able-bodied adults without children on food stamps; record unemployment; more women in poverty than ever before; borrowed from China and increased the debt to over 16 trillion, passing the burden on to the next generation. We may have made it through President Obama's first term; it's our children who can't afford a second.

Note: All ads can be viewed at http://pcl.stanford.edu/campaigns/2012/.

I'll never convince them they should take personal responsibility and care for their lives. What I have to do is convince the 5 to 10 percent in the center, that are independents, that are thoughtful, that look at voting one way or the other depending upon, in some cases, emotion, whether they like the guy or not, what he looks like.[9]

Obama's "Fair Share" ad, which aired only eight days after Romney's comments were made public, suggested that with his comments Romney "attacked millions of hard working people [who] pay Social Security taxes, state taxes, local taxes, gas, sales, and property taxes [whereas] Romney paid just 14 percent of taxes last year on over 13 million in income." The ad concluded by rhetorically asking, "Instead of attacking folks who work for a living, shouldn't we stand up for them?"

"Cynical," which aired on November 1, 2012, was also sponsored by Obama and focused on claims made in Romney ads attacking the Obama administration that auto jobs were being sent to China. "Cynical" referenced comments by auto companies saying that Romney's claims were "politics at its cynical worst" (General Motors) and "simply not true" (Chrysler). The ad concluded with a clip from a news interview, in which Romney stumbled over words and cut off his comments before he could explain them: "That's exactly what I said. My, my, the headline you read, which is let Detroit go bankrupt."

The two ads sponsored by Romney were "Dear Daughter" (randomly selected; originally aired on September 17, 2012) and "Can't Afford Another Term" (closest to Election Day; aired on October 30, 2012). "Dear Daughter" featured video of a mother holding an infant, and opened with the female narrator saying, "Dear daughter, welcome to America." The female narrator then proceeded to list various ways in which the Obama administration had made life and the future more difficult for women and children (leaving children in debt, "policies are making it harder on women," "the poverty rate for women—the highest in 17 years," and "more women are unemployed under President Obama") all while the infant and mother are pictured on screen. The ad concluded by saying, "That's what Obama's policies have done for women. Welcome, daughter."

"Can't Afford Another Term" attacked Obama on a number of policy dimensions. The ad claimed that in his first term Obama had "gutted the work requirement for welfare," "doubled the number of able-bodied adults without children on food stamps," created "record unemployment" that resulted in "more women in poverty than ever before," and "borrowed from China and increased the debt to over $16 trillion, passing the burden on to the next generation." While these statements were being made by the male narrator, the video showed sources for the different claims and, toward the end, focused on the concerned face of a young girl. The ad concluded with the line, "*We* may have made it through President Obama's first term; it's our children who can't afford a second."

The two ads sponsored by pro-Obama super PAC Priorities USA were "Same Promises" (randomly selected; originally aired on October 23, 2012) and "Connect the Dots" (closest to Election Day; aired on October 31, 2012). "Same Promises" featured five former employees of an unnamed company that Romney's firm Bain Capital took over and dismantled. While the individuals briefly told why they were upset about what happened to their workplace and unnamed town, the screen displayed images of a dilapidated town overlaid with the words, "Mitt Romney and Bain Capital laid off thousands of workers," followed by, "While driving companies into bankruptcy, Romney and Bain made hundreds of millions of dollars." The ad concluded with a former worker saying, "He [Romney] promised us the same thing he's promising the United States. He'll give you the same thing he gave us—nothin'."

"Connect the Dots" linked Romney and Florida governor Rick Scott, suggesting that both were hostile to Medicare. Although the ad was geared toward Florida residents, its potential appeal was broader as it focused on the issue of Medicare and health care more generally. The ad alleged that Scott "ran a company that paid a record fine for committing Medicare fraud" and then cut millions from health care as governor. Similarly, the ad claimed, "Romney was director of a company that stole millions from Medicare" and that he "would end Medicare as we know it." The ad showed images of Romney and Scott shaking hands, and concluded with the line, "If Mitt Romney wins, the middle class loses."

The two ads sponsored by pro-Romney super PAC Restore Our Future were "Disappearing" (randomly selected; originally aired on September 19, 2012) and "Flatline" (closest to Election Day; aired on November 2, 2012). Both attacked Obama over his handling of the economy. "Disappearing" featured still shots of workers in various white- and blue-collar jobs, while stating that nearly 8 million American workers had "disappeared" from the work force and that the "real unemployment rate" was at 19 percent. The ad also showed a clip of a male news anchor (Scott Pelley of CBS) saying, "This is the worst economic recovery America has ever had," and concluded by asking, "Looking forward to a second Obama term?"

"Flatline" opened with a picture of a heart monitor flatlining, with the beep, beep, beeeeeeep noise that accompanies such a flatline in the emergency room. It then attacked Obama on his handling of the economy, with the male narrator saying, "If you saw this line in the ER, you'd be panicked. Well, this flatline is Barack Obama's economy." After mentioning many of the perceived problems with the late-fall 2012 economy—unemployment, increasing debt, "middle-class incomes falling"—the ad concluded by saying, "If you don't jumpstart America's economy now, your economy stays dead four more years. Demand better."

* * *

We recruited participants for our study through Amazon.com's Mechanical Turk (MTurk) interface. In total, 725 individuals completed our study by watching all eight ads and answering the questions about them. Participants in our study answered the same set of questions following each ad. We asked them, "To what extent do you think the ad was . . ." "fair," "informative," "interesting," "misleading," "memorable," "negative," and "untruthful." The response options were: "not at all," "a little," "somewhat," and "very." We focus on responses to the questions measuring the extent to which the ad was perceived to be fair, informative, misleading, and negative here, as they are most relevant for our purposes.

Figure 5.1 displays participant responses to these four questions for each ad; again, their sponsorship was not included when people viewed them. Within each question, the ads are arranged in the order in which they were viewed by participants in the study. The darkest part of the bars represents the percentage of respondents who responded "not at all" to the question, with the bars lightening in color from there; the lightest sections correspond to those respondents who selected "very." For example, the top bar in the figure indicates that about 20 percent of people thought the "Same Promises" ad sponsored by pro-Obama super PAC Priorities USA was not at all fair, a little more than 36 percent thought it was a little fair, 32 percent thought it was somewhat fair, and the remaining 12 percent said the ad was very fair.

In terms of the perceived fairness of the ads—the first set of bars—the "Dear Daughter" ad sponsored by the Romney campaign was perceived as the least fair, with just over 50 percent of respondents saying the ad was not at all fair. The next highest ads in terms of perceived *unfairness* were the "Can't Afford" ad, also sponsored by the Romney campaign, and the "Flatline" ad, sponsored by the pro-Romney super PAC Restore Our Future. The Obama-sponsored ads appear to have been perceived as the most fair, but readers should bear in mind that our sample has more Democrats than Republicans in it—a concern we address below. The larger point in looking at views about the fairness of the eight ads is that it does not appear to be the case that super PAC–sponsored ads were viewed as particularly more or less fair than their candidate-sponsored counterparts.

The second set of bars in Figure 5.1 plots how informative people thought the ads were. Four ads were viewed as somewhat or very informative by a majority of respondents: "Same Promises" and "Connect the Dots," both of which were sponsored by pro-Obama super PAC Priorities USA, "Disappearing," sponsored by pro-Romney super PAC Restore Our Future, and "Fair Share," sponsored by the Obama campaign. That three of these four ads were sponsored by super PACs suggests that super PAC ads do convey information to voters, perhaps more so than candidate-sponsored ads. Or, at the very least, it seems unlikely given these results that super PAC attack ads are *less* informative than candidate-sponsored attack ads.

Somewhat surprising perhaps, only two of the eight ads were viewed as somewhat or very misleading by a majority of respondents; both of these ads were sponsored by the Romney campaign. Almost 59 percent of respondents thought the "Dear Daughter" ad was somewhat or very misleading, and just over 50 percent thought the "Can't Afford Another Term" ad was misleading. To be clear, this is not to say that *all* Romney ads were particularly misleading in 2012. Rather, the evidence presented in Figure 5.1 suggests

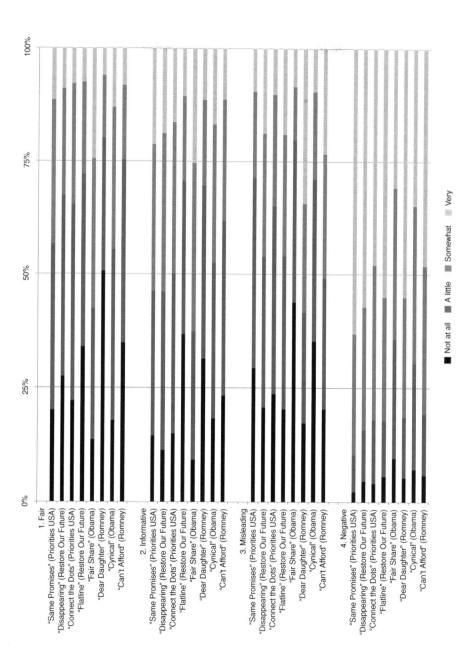

Figure 5.1 Evaluations of Eight Presidential Ads Used in Study 1
Source: MTurk Study 1

that the randomly selected Romney ad we chose ("Dear Daughter") and the one that Romney's campaign chose to air closest to Election Day ("Can't Afford Another Term") were viewed as somewhat more misleading than super PAC–sponsored ads that met the same criteria. This is true even in comparison to only those sponsored by the pro-Romney super PAC Restore Our Future, both of which had around 46 percent of respondents saying they were somewhat or very misleading. At the very least, it does not appear to be the case that Super PAC–sponsored ads were *more* misleading when compared to ads sponsored by the candidates.

Finally, Figure 5.1 plots responses to how "negative" respondents felt the eight ads were. Although all the ads are considered to be "negative" for the most part—across the eight ads, between 64 percent and nearly 90 percent of responses indicate that the ads are somewhat or very negative—there is some variation. For instance, the Obama campaign's ads were perceived to be the least negative, with over 30 percent of respondents indicating they were either "not at all" or only "a little" negative. Super PAC–sponsored ads were considered to be the most negative, with only 10 to 18 percent of respondents selecting "not at all" or "a little" across those four ads. The Romney campaign's ads fall somewhere between Obama's and the super PACs' ads.

In short, an initial look at evaluations of the ads suggests that although the super PAC–sponsored ads are perceived to be a bit more "negative" on average than candidate-sponsored ads, they are not necessarily viewed as more misleading, less fair, or any less informative. Indeed, in some cases, super PAC–sponsored ads are perceived to be less misleading and more informative, but these differences vary by ad.

* * *

Figure 5.1 combines all respondents together, giving us a picture of how the average person responded to the ads. It seems reasonable to expect, however, that different types of people may have varying reactions to the ads. The most obvious factor that would drive responses is partisan affiliation; likely, Democrats will look more favorably upon ads that support Democrats, and vice versa. Most notably given our focus on attack ads, research on the effects of negative advertising has found that partisans tend to polarize in response to negative ads (Ansolabehere and Iyengar 1995; Iyengar, Jackman, and Hahn 2008). For instance, an ad attacking Obama would result in Republicans disliking Obama (a little) more, whereas Democrats may actually *like* Obama (a little) more as a result of the ad that attacks their party's preferred candidate.

Figures 5.2 and 5.3 display responses separated by respondent partisan identification.[10] To better visualize similarities and differences between super PAC ads and candidate-sponsored ads, the figures display the average difference between the two groups. We do so by first assigning each response option a score. For each item, if a respondent selected "not at all," that response is assigned a score of 0; if they chose "a little" the corresponding score is 1;

"somewhat" is 2; and "very" is 3. We then add the two same-sponsored ads together (for example, both super PAC ads sponsored by Priorities USA), resulting in a combined score that ranges from 0 to 6 (where 0 would be a respondent who selected "not at all" for both ads and 6 would be a respondent who selected "very" for both ads). Next, we divide the combined score by two to get the average score of the two ads. This process gives us an average score for the ads aired by a given sponsor (i.e., separately for Obama, Romney, and the two super PACs). To obtain the difference in average evaluations between super PAC ads and candidate ads, we subtract the average super PAC ads score from the average candidate ads score. Because we think there might be differences by partisan affiliation, we do this separately for self-identified Democrats, Republicans, and independents.[11] Thus, for each item (fair, informative, misleading, and negative) we have an average difference in evaluations (super PAC ads – candidate ads) among Democrats, Republicans, and independents. These differences in evaluations are plotted for ads attacking Romney (i.e., the average difference between Priorities USA ads and Obama ads) in Figure 5.2 and for ads attacking Obama (i.e., the average difference between Restore Our Future ads and Romney ads) in Figure 5.3.

The "whiskers" around the average difference represent the confidence we have in that estimate, based on the 95 percent confidence interval surrounding the difference. When we have more respondents, our confidence increases, which is why the confidence intervals for Democrats are smaller than those for Republicans and independents. These confidence intervals are important for two reasons. First, they allow us to easily visualize whether any difference is statistically significantly different from zero. Basically, if the confidence interval overlaps with the vertical line at zero (0.0) in Figures 5.2 or 5.3, then we cannot say this difference is statistically different from zero; but if the confidence interval does *not* overlap with the vertical line at zero then we can be reasonably certain (again, with 95 percent statistical confidence) that the difference is statistically significant.[12]

Second, the confidence intervals help us visualize whether partisans differ in their evaluations of the ads. The statistical significance of these differences—for example, the difference between Republicans evaluations of an ad subtracted from the difference between Democrats evaluations of the ad, typically referred to as a "difference-in-differences"—are not as easily visualized as the simple differences from zero. But generally speaking, the more two confidence intervals overlap, the less certain we are that the difference between any two partisan groupings is statistically meaningful. Where we discuss any such differences below, we formally test the difference-in-differences and report them as "statistically significant" if those tests reveal a minimum of 95 percent statistical confidence that the difference-in-differences is statistically significant.[13]

To more clearly illustrate what the bars indicate, readers might consider one example. Among Democrats the Obama-sponsored ads attacking

Romney received an average fairness score of 1.73 (indicating the average score was just below "somewhat" fair); among the same set of Democrats, Priorities USA-sponsored ads attacking Romney received an average fairness score of 1.46, about halfway between "a little" and "somewhat" fair. This difference of about 0.27 points is displayed in Figure 5.2 as the darkest gray bar of the three at the top of the figure. Because the confidence interval of this approximately 0.27-point difference does not overlap (or, contain) zero, we consider this to be a statistically significant difference from zero. In other words, we can say with 95 percent confidence that Democrats viewed Priorities USA-sponsored ads as somewhat less fair than Obama-sponsored ads. This greater perceived fairness of the Obama-sponsored ads among Democrats is similar to the difference of about 0.34 points we observe among independents (i.e., the difference between Democrats and independents is not statistically significant because the confidence intervals quite

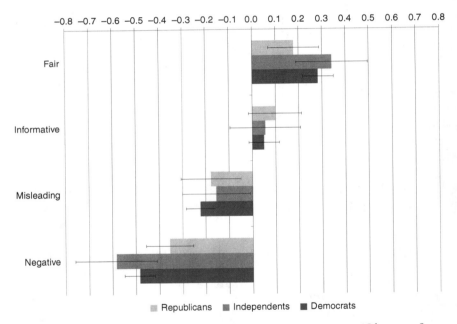

Figure 5.2 Difference in Evaluations of Ads Attacking Romney (Obama – Super PAC), by Respondent Party Identification

Note: The bars represent the difference between the average score of the two super PAC ads subtracted from the average score of the two Obama-sponsored ads. Whiskers represent 95 percent confidence intervals around that difference. Positive numbers indicate that Obama-sponsored ads were considered "more" of that characteristic than the pro-Obama super PAC Priorities USA-sponsored ads. Negative numbers indicate that Priorities USA-sponsored ads were considered "more" of that characteristic than Obama-sponsored ads. For example, Obama's ads were considered more "fair" and Priorities USA's ads were considered more "misleading."

Source: MTurk Study 1

clearly overlap one another—the confidence interval for independents contains the entirety of the confidence interval for Democrats). It also is the case however that Republicans perceive the Obama-sponsored ads as more fair—a difference in that direction of about 0.18 points that is statistically distinguishable from zero. Moreover, the differences between Democrats and Republicans are not significantly different from one another. In other words, both Democrats and Republicans perceived the Obama-sponsored ads as more fair, and although Democrats perceived them as somewhat fairer than Republicans did, this difference-in-differences of about 0.10 points is not statistically significant.[14] Nor is this difference substantively meaningful—on a scale that ranges from 0 to 3, there is only a 0.10 difference in terms of how Democrats and Republicans differed in their evaluations of the Obama and Priorities USA ads.

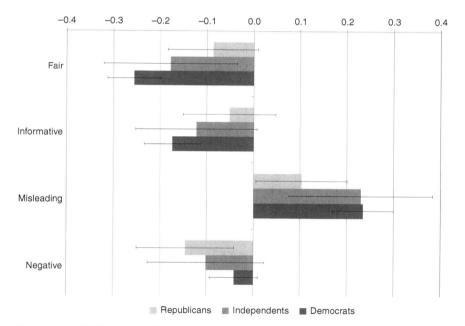

Figure 5.3   Difference in Evaluations of Ads Attacking Obama (Romney – Super PAC), by Respondent Party Identification

Note: The bars represent the difference between the average score of the two super PAC ads subtracted from the average score of the two Romney-sponsored ads. Whiskers represent 95 percent confidence intervals around that difference. Positive numbers indicate that Romney-sponsored ads were considered "more" of that characteristic than the pro-Romney super PAC Restore Our Future-sponsored ads. Negative numbers indicate that Restore Our Future-sponsored ads were considered "more" of that characteristic than Romney-sponsored ads. For example, Romney's ads were considered more "misleading" and Restore Our Future's ads were considered more "fair."

Source: MTurk Study 1

At least three points are worth highlighting from Figures 5.2 and 5.3. First, the Obama-sponsored ads were considered fairer and more informative than the pro-Obama super PAC Priorities USA-sponsored ads. As noted above, this difference in fairness is statistically significant for all partisans (Democrats, Republicans, and independents), whereas the difference in perceived levels of information contained in the ads is smaller (less than 0.1 points) for all partisans, and not statistically significant (the confidence intervals for Democrats, Republicans, and independents all contain zero). Still, the data presented in Figure 5.2 suggest that the Obama-sponsored ads had what might be considered more "positive" attributes than the Priorities USA-sponsored ads. Conversely, the data presented in Figure 5.3 suggest that Romney-sponsored ads were less fair and less informative than the pro-Romney super PAC Restore Our Future-sponsored ads. Further, Democrats, Republicans, and independents alike considered the Romney-sponsored ads to be less informative and less fair than the Restore Our Future-sponsored ads; however, the difference on whether the ad was informative is statistically significant for neither Republicans nor independents, and the difference on fairness also failed to achieve statistical significance for Republicans. In short, when it comes to "positive" characteristics of the ads, Figure 5.2 suggests that *Democratic* attack ads sponsored by pro-Obama super PACs were *less* "positive" than Obama-sponsored ads, whereas Figure 5.3 suggests *Republican* attack ads sponsored by pro-Romney super PACs were *more* "positive" than Romney-sponsored ads.

Second, in terms of potentially "negative" characteristics of the ads, we again observe a difference between the Democratic and Republican attack ads. Ads sponsored by Obama were perceived to be less misleading and particularly less negative than ads sponsored by the pro-Obama super PAC Priorities USA for all partisans (see Figure 5.2), whereas ads sponsored by Romney were perceived to be less negative (the differences are not statistically significant for independents or Democrats, however) *but* more misleading (for all partisans) than ads sponsored by the pro-Romney super PAC Restore Our Future (see Figure 5.3). Again, as was the case with the "positive" characteristics of the ads, the data do not suggest a clear pattern in differences between super PAC ads and candidate ads. Rather, they perhaps suggest a potential difference in tactics between the candidates and how they chose to "use" their super PACs. The data suggest that as the challenger Romney may have felt the need to attack Obama with more misleading ads (compared to the super PAC that also attacked Obama, Restore Our Future), whereas as the incumbent Obama did not feel the same urgency (and his ads were, as a result, perceived to be *less* misleading and negative compared to the super PAC that also attacked Romney, Priorities USA).

Third, there are some differences in how partisans evaluated the ads. Most notably, there tend to be smaller differences in evaluations between candidate ads and super PAC ads among Republicans than Democrats and independents. Of the eight items plotted in Figures 5.2 and 5.3, the only differences that are larger for Republicans than Democrats or independents are the difference in informativeness of the ads attacking Romney (Figure 5.2) and the difference in negativity of the ads attacking Obama (Figure 5.3), although those differences are not statistically significant.[15] In every other case, either Democrats or independents exhibit the largest differences. And in some cases, these differences are statistically significant. For example, compared to Republicans, Democrats considered the Obama-sponsored ads to be much less negative than Priorities USA-sponsored ads. The 0.13 difference-in-differences (0.36 difference for Republicans / 0.49 difference for Democrats) is statistically significant.[16] In terms of the ads attacking Obama, compared to Republicans, Democrats thought the Romney-sponsored ads were less fair, less informative, and more misleading than the Restore Our Future-sponsored ads.[17]

In short, the data presented in Figures 5.2 and 5.3 provide a bit more nuance to the picture than we gleaned from Figure 5.1. Pooling all the ads together, as in Figure 5.1, suggests that super PAC–sponsored ads are perceived to be a bit more "negative" on average than candidate-sponsored ads, but are not necessarily viewed as more misleading, less fair, or any less informative. Figures 5.2 and 5.3 suggest that there are partisan differences in terms of how individuals respond to the *content* of the ads, but that these differences tend to be relatively small. More important, the data presented in Figures 5.2 and 5.3 suggest that there are differences in evaluations of whether candidate or super PAC ads were more or less negative, etc. For instance, the greater negativity observed in Figure 5.1 appears to be driven by the fact that Obama-sponsored ads were considered to be much less negative than pro-Obama super PAC Priorities USA-sponsored ads, while Romney-sponsored ads were considered to be a little less negative than the pro-Romney super PAC Restore Our Future's ads.[18] Further, this more nuanced picture indicates that the ads Romney ran were viewed as more misleading, less fair, and less informative than the ones his most closely associated super PAC, Restore Our Future, did. Obama, on the other hand ran ads that were viewed as less misleading, fairer, and more informative than his most closely associated super PAC, Priorities USA. The explanation for these differences, if any, is unclear. It could have been a difference in tactics—maybe Obama chose to take the "high ground" as the incumbent, whereas Romney wanted to be seen as attacking his opponent—or perhaps the ad that we randomly selected and that aired closest to Election Day for each entity are not representative of the entire set. Whatever the case, our study can rule out sponsorship information as an explanatory factor, as the "paid for by" details were removed from the ads before we showed them to participants. In other words, any differences reported above stem from something about the ads themselves, and not from a reaction to their sponsor.

* * *

Because the effect of most advertisements does not last very long, typically only a few days at most (Gerber et al. 2011; Hill et al. 2013), we might be particularly interested in how people evaluated the set of ads that aired closest to Election Day.[19] Figures 5.4 and 5.5 display the same type of information as Figures 5.2 and 5.3, but only contain information about the difference in scores from the ads that were aired closest to Election Day.[20] Figure 5.4 displays this information for ads attacking Romney: evaluations of Priorities USA's "Connect the Dots" ad subtracted from evaluations of Obama's "Cynical" ad. Figure 5.5 displays this information for ads attacking Obama: evaluations of Restore Our Future's "Flatline" ad subtracted from evaluations of Romney's "Can't Afford Another Term" ad. For instance, the top set of bars in Figure 5.4 indicates that Priorities USA's "Connect the Dots" ad was thought to be less fair than Obama's "Cynical" ad by all partisans, which is consistent with the pattern we observed in Figure 5.2 when we averaged across the two ads by each sponsor.

Although the picture for fairness of the ads attacking Romney looks the same, the differences between Election Day ads are not all consistent with

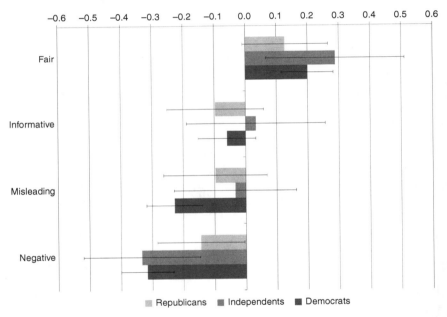

Figure 5.4   Difference in Evaluations of Ads Attacking Romney (Obama – Super PAC), by Respondent Party Identification: "Election Day" Ads

Note: This analysis was restricted to the ads that were aired closest to Election Day. The bars represent the difference between the score of the super PAC ad subtracted from the score of the Obama-sponsored ad. Whiskers represent 95 percent confidence intervals around that difference. Positive numbers indicate that the Obama-sponsored ad was considered "more" of that characteristic than the pro-Obama super PAC Priorities USA-sponsored ad. Negative numbers indicate that the Priorities USA-sponsored ad was considered "more" of that characteristic than the Obama-sponsored ad. For example, Obama's ad was considered more "fair" and Priorities USA's ad was considered more "negative."

Source: MTurk Study 1

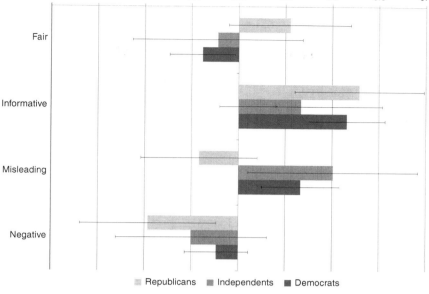

Figure 5.5 Difference in Evaluations of Ads Attacking Obama (Romney – Super PAC), by Respondent Party Identification: "Election Day" Ads

Note: This analysis was restricted to the ads that were aired closest to Election Day. The bars represent the difference between the score of the super PAC ad subtracted from the score of the Romney-sponsored ad. Whiskers represent 95 percent confidence intervals around that difference. Positive numbers indicate that the Romney-sponsored ad was considered "more" of that characteristic than the pro-Romney super PAC Restore Our Future-sponsored ad. Negative numbers indicate that the Restore Our Future-sponsored ad was considered "more" of that characteristic than the Romney-sponsored ad. For example, Romney's ad was considered more "informative" and Restore Our Future's ads were considered more "negative."

Source: MTurk Study 1

the average pattern observed in Figures 5.2 and 5.3. Both Republicans and Democrats, for instance, perceived Obama's "Cynical" ad to be less informative than Priorities USA's "Connect the Dots" ad, whereas the average pattern in Figure 5.2 was one in which the average of Obama's ads was more informative than the average of Priorities USA's ads.[21] This switch is driven by the fact that the ad Obama chose to air closest to Election Day was considered to be less informative—by more than 0.30 points (from 1.79 to 1.46)—than the ad we randomly selected from all his earlier attack ads. While there was also a decline in the perceived informativeness of Priorities USA ads as Election Day grew closer, it was not as stark—a little less than 0.10 points (from 1.61 to 1.52).[22]

Consistent with the average pattern, however, Obama's "Cynical" ad was considered less misleading and less negative by Democrats and Republicans, but these differences tend to be smaller when we only compare the ads aired closest to Election Day in Figure 5.4. When we look at the data more closely, this smaller difference in evaluations of the ads aired closest to Election Day appears to be driven by an uptick in the perceived negativity and misleading nature of Obama's "Cynical" ad compared to his ad aired earlier in the campaign season, "Fair Share." "Cynical's" average negativity score was 1.97 and its average misleading score was 1.04, whereas "Fair Share's" negativity score was 1.86 (a difference of about 0.10 points) and its misleading score was 0.85 (a difference of almost 0.20 points). In other words, the ad Obama chose to air closest to Election Day was perceived to be more negative and more misleading than the ad he aired earlier. Priorities USA's ad that was aired closer to Election Day was also perceived to be more misleading than the one it aired earlier, but not by as much as Obama's (a jump of only about 0.10 points instead of 0.20 for Obama). Contra Obama's pattern of increased negativity closer to Election Day, however, Priorities USA's ad that was aired closer to Election Day was perceived to be less negative than the one it aired earlier.

As was the case with ads attacking Romney, Figure 5.5 suggests the ads attacking Obama closest to Election Day do not follow the average pattern either (compare Figure 5.5 to Figure 5.3). For instance, whereas on average Romney-sponsored ads were seen as less informative than Restore Our Future-sponsored ads by all partisans (see Figure 5.3), when we compare the two ads aired closest to Election Day, the Romney-sponsored ad ("Can't Afford Another Term") is considered more informative than the Restore Our Future-sponsored ad ("Flatline") by all partisans. This shift is largely driven by the fact that the Restore Our Future ad "Flatline" was considered much less informative than its earlier ad ("Disappearing); there was a difference of about 0.60 points (1.62 to 1.04) between the two. Romney's ad that was aired closest to Election Day was seen as more informative than his earlier ad, but only by about 0.15 points (1.26 versus 1.11).

The ads attacking Obama that were aired closest to Election Day also produced some interesting partisan differences. Most notably perhaps, compared to the Restore Our Future ad, Republicans considered the Romney ad fairer and less misleading, whereas Democrats considered it less fair and more misleading. Both of these difference-in-differences are statistically significant ($p < .05$, two-tailed). These differences are apparent despite the fact that both Democrats and Republicans considered the Romney ad to be less negative, consistent with the average pattern observed in Figure 5.3. However, Republicans did consider it to be much less negative than Democrats—a difference of almost 0.20 points among Republicans compared to a difference of only 0.05 points among Democrats ($p < .05$, two-tailed for test of difference-in-differences).

* * *

What does this study tell us about super PAC ads compared to other ads directly overseen by the campaign? The main conclusions we draw are that people respond differently to different ads, and that sometimes different people (different partisans, for example) respond differently to the same ads. And, at least based on this study, it appears that *both* super PACs and candidates make ads that vary in how misleading and negative they are perceived, and also how fair and informative they are thought to be.

Of course, we were not able to examine all ads. It is possible that ads sponsored by other super PACs or other groups not as closely associated with a candidate are particularly negative or misleading, a possibility that warrants further study. Still, although candidates may shy away from sponsoring negative ads for fear of a backlash (Dowling and Wichowsky forthcoming; Fowler and Ridout 2012), they do air negative ads. Indeed, 54 percent of campaign-sponsored advertising was negative in 2012 according to Wesleyan Media Project data (Fowler and Ridout 2012, Table 8), and as we describe above, because of the sheer volume of candidate advertising, the candidates (Obama and Romney) accounted for a majority of the negative ads aired in 2012. Further, our initial study suggests these candidate-sponsored ads do not necessarily differ from those sponsored by super PACs in a consistent manner in terms of how they are evaluated by citizens.

STUDY 2

Of course, it is possible that citizens responded more negatively to an ad when they knew the sponsor was a super PAC. That is, the content of super PAC ads might not have been consistently less informative or more misleading and negative than candidate ads, but having a non-candidate sponsor (typically revealed by the "paid for" information at the end of an ad) results in advertising being *perceived* as less informative, more misleading, and/or more negative. In other words, our first study indicates that, on average, people do not perceive the *content* of super PAC and candidate ads to be all that different. Now, we entertain the additional question of whether knowing who sponsors presidential advertising changes people's perceptions of the ad.

In order to see what effect, if any, knowledge of sponsorship has on perceptions of presidential ads, an ideal study would hold constant the content of the ad and simply vary (i.e., randomize) the sponsor. We did just this in our second study via a survey experiment (see Chapter 4 for details on survey experiments).[23] Specifically, for our experimental study, we selected the two ads that the candidates chose to sponsor closest to Election Day—Obama's "Cynical" and Romney's "Can't Afford Another Term"—and made three versions of each. First, we kept the originals with the candidate sponsorship information. Second, we used the same versions of the ads used in the study described above—with the sponsorship information removed. Last, we replaced the candidate sponsorship information with the corresponding super PAC sponsorship information. In other words, we created a version of "Cynical" in which the pro-Obama super PAC Priorities USA was the sponsor instead of Obama and a version of "Can't Afford Another Term" in which the pro-Romney super PAC Restore Our Future was the sponsor. In both cases, we used the actual sponsorship information (audio and visual) from ads sponsored by the super PACs.

We then randomly assigned participants who agreed to take part in a study ($N = 1,187$) to watch one of these six ads with equal probability. Table 5.3 displays the number of participants who were assigned to each experimental condition (i.e., each ad), along with more information about the ad such as sponsorship text. After watching the randomly assigned ad, participants then answered the same questions as those in the study reported above did—"To what extent do you think the ad was . . ." "fair," "informative," "interesting," "misleading," "memorable," "negative," and "untruthful." We once again focus on responses to the questions measuring the extent to which the ad was perceived to be fair, informative, misleading, and negative, as they are most relevant for our purposes. The response options were the same as before: "not at all," "a little," "somewhat," and "very." If people responded differently to these presidential ads depending on who the sponsor is, then we should observe differences across experimental conditions on these measures.

Figure 5.6 displays the average response for these four measures—on a scale from 0 to 3, where 0 equals "not at all," 1 equals "a little," 2 equals "somewhat," and 3 equals "very"—by the six experimental conditions. (For the interested reader, Appendix Figure 5.1 presents the raw response data, akin to Figure 5.1 for Study 1.) As with our previous figures in this chapter, the whiskers represent 95 percent confidence intervals; in this case, the 95 percent confidence interval around each mean. So, for example, the very top bar of Figure 5.6 indicates participants randomly assigned to watch the "Cynical" ad sponsored by Obama had an average score of 1.35 on fairness (in between "a little" and "somewhat"). The whiskers indicate that the 95 percent confidence interval is between 1.21 and 1.49. What the whiskers also tell us, when we compare them to the two other bars representing participants assigned to the other two conditions in which the "Cynical" ad was watched but with either no sponsor or Priorities USA as the sponsor, is that this mean of 1.35 is not statistically distinguishable from the other two conditions.[24] As with the previous study, the more two confidence intervals overlap, the less likely the two numbers (in this case, means) are statistically distinguishable from one another, but we also test this formally. The main comparisons we want to make are across sponsorship conditions, holding the ad constant. That is, we want to compare the three versions of the "Cynical" ad to one another (represented by the set of bars without vertical lines), and separately the three versions of the "Can't Afford Another Term" ad to one another (represented by the set of bars with dark vertical lines).

For the "Cynical" ad, which attacked Romney over claims he made about auto jobs being sent to China, the three groups are not statistically distinguishable from one another on any of the four measures. There are a few differences that approach conventional levels of statistical significance

Table 5.3 Presidential Ads Used in Study 2

Ad (Original Air Date)	Sponsor (Randomly Assigned)	N	Text of Ad	Sponsorship Voiceover
Cynical (11/1/12)	Barack Obama	176	[Male Narrator] Wholly inaccurate. Clearly misleading. That's what news outlets are calling Mitt Romney's latest ads, suggesting auto jobs are being sent to China. GM calls Romney's ads, "politics at its cynical worst." And Chrysler's CEO said, "It's simply not true." We know the truth, Mitt. [Mitt Romney] "That's exactly what I said. My, my, the headline you read, which is let Detroit go bankrupt."	[Barack Obama] I'm Barack Obama and I approve this message.
Cynical (11/1/12)	Priorities USA	242		[Male Narrator] Priorities USA Action is responsible for the content of this advertising.
Cynical (11/1/12)	No Sponsor	187		[None]
Can't Afford Another Term (10/30/12)	Mitt Romney	183	[Male Narrator] If you want to know President Obama's second-term agenda, look at his first: gutted the work requirement for welfare; doubled the number of able-bodied adults without children on food stamps; record unemployment; more women in poverty than ever before; borrowed from China and increased the debt to over 16 trillion, passing the burden onto the next generation. We may have made it through President Obama's first term; it's our children who can't afford a second.	[Mitt Romney] I'm Mitt Romney and I approve this message.
Can't Afford Another Term (10/30/12)	Restore Our Future	170		[Male Narrator] Restore Our Future is responsible for the content of this message.
Can't Afford Another Term (10/30/12)	No Sponsor	229		[None]

Note: All of the original ads can be viewed at http://pcl.stanford.edu/campaigns/2012/.

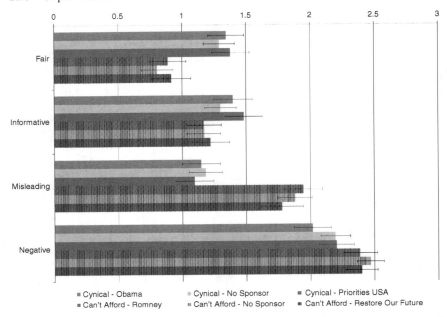

Figure 5.6 Evaluations of Presidential Ads from Study 2, Randomly Assigned Sponsor

Note: Participants were randomly assigned to watch one of the six ads. The bars represent the mean score; whiskers represent 95 percent confidence intervals around that mean.

Source: MTurk Study 2

though. For example, the Priorities USA condition scores approximately 0.18 units higher on informativeness than the no sponsor condition[25] and the Obama condition scores approximately 0.18 units lower in terms of its perceived negativity than both the no sponsor condition and Priorities USA condition.[26] On the whole, however, we find relatively small and statistically insignificant differences across treatment conditions for the ad attacking Romney. Similarly, for the "Can't Afford Another Term" ad, which attacked Obama on a number of policy dimensions but mainly focused on the economy, the three groups are not statistically distinguishable from one another on any of the four measures.

So, although the ad attacking Romney was considered more fair and informative and less misleading and negative than the ad attacking Obama, this is likely a function of our sample having more Democrats than Republicans in it.[27] What this study tells us is simply changing the sponsor of a presidential ad to be a super PAC—instead of a candidate—does little to alter people's perceptions of the ad. No matter who the sponsor was—or if the ad had no sponsor (as in Study 1), people's perceptions of the ad were roughly the same. The results of this study suggest that simply watching ads sponsored by super PACs, as opposed to candidates, during the campaign did not result in greater perceptions of negativity or less information being gleaned. Rather, the *content* of the ad likely matters more and, as we found in Study 1, candidates and super PACs did not systematically differ in consistent ways in terms of whose content was more or less fair, informative, misleading, and negative.

CONCLUSION

Combining the results of Studies 1 and 2, we reach the following conclusions. First, super PAC–sponsored ads are not necessarily more negative or misleading than candidate-sponsored ads. In fact, some super PAC ads are considered *less* negative and misleading than those aired by the candidates. In addition, super PAC ads can be considered just as informative and fair as candidate ads. Again, the content of the ad appears to be more important for people's perceptions of the ads—and the content of super PAC ads is not necessarily all that different than those of candidate ads. Further evidence that it is the content of the ad that matters most is seen in Study 2. The fact that we observe little difference between an ad sponsored by a candidate (Obama or Romney) and the same ad sponsored by a super PAC (Priorities USA or Restore Our Future) suggests that people do not necessarily perceive presidential ads differently depending on their sponsor.[28] And so, as evidenced by data on advertising from the 2012 election (Fowler and Ridout 2012), although super PACs (and related groups) appear to be much more likely to sponsor negative ads than positive ads compared to candidates (and parties), this does not mean the negative ads super PACs run are any more or less negative than those that candidates choose to run. Coupled with the fact that the candidates aired more total ads (see Table 5.1) and even a greater number of negative ads than super PACs (and related groups), we are left with the impression that the ads super PACs (and related groups) run are not solely or even necessarily primarily responsible for any perceived increase in negativity in campaigns at the presidential level.

NOTES

1. We use "attack" and "negative" interchangeably to describe an ad that attacks one candidate but does not mention the other.
2. This difference contrasts with elections in the late 1980s and early 1990s when a smaller percentage of group ads were negative (Brooks and Murov 2012; see Ansolabehere and Iyengar 1995 for data on the 1980s and 1990s).
3. In their meta-analysis of the negative advertising literature, Lau, Sigelman, and Rovner (2007) find no "reliable evidence that negative campaigning depresses turnout, though it does slightly lower feelings of political efficacy, trust in government, and possibly overall public mood" (1176). The most recent study we are aware of suggests negativity only demobilizes after

a person has selected a preferred candidate and the negativity is primarily focused on that candidate (Krupnikov 2011).

4. See: http://pcl.stanford.edu/campaigns/2012/.
5. For Obama and Romney: $(511,513+207,984)*0.54 = 388,528$; for Priorities USA and Restore Our Future: $(58,990+62,557)*0.85 = 103,315$.
6. $(7,210+35,825)*0.51 = 21,948$
7. $255,921*0.85 = 217,533$
8. The PCL included an air date with the list of ads.
9. See: www.nytimes.com/2012/09/19/us/politics/mitt-romneys-speech-from-mother-jones-video.html?pagewanted=all&_r=0.
10. Self-reported partisan identification was ascertained earlier in the survey, prior to evaluating the eight campaign advertisements. The question was, "Generally speaking, do you usually think of yourself as a Democrat, a Republican, an Independent, or what?" independents were then asked, "Do you think of yourself as closer to the Democratic Party, closer to the Republican Party, or equally close to both parties?" while Democrats and Republicans were asked, "Would you call yourself a strong [Democrat / Republican] or not a very strong [Democrat / Republican]?" We classify independents who say they lean toward one party or the other as self-reported partisans (that is, either Democrats or Republicans). Our sample consisted of 156 Republicans, 90 independents, and 479 Democrats.
11. In other words, separately for Democrats, Republicans, and independents, and for each question (fair, informative, misleading, and negative), we calculate: difference in evaluation of ads attacking Romney = [(Obama1 + Obama2)/2] – [(Priorities USA1 + Priorities USA2)/2]; and Difference in evaluation of ads attacking Obama = [(Romney1 + Romney2)/2] – [(Restore Our Future1 + Restore Our Future 2)/2].
12. i.e., $p < .05$, two-tailed.
13. i.e., $p < .05$, two-tailed.
14. $p = .12$, two-tailed.
15. $p > .05$, two-tailed.
16. $p < .05$, two-tailed.
17. $p < .05$, two-tailed for all three difference-in-differences.
18. The average difference (across the three partisan groupings) in negativity between Obama- and Priority USA-sponsored ads was about 0.47 points; for Romney- and Restore Our Future-sponsored ads the average difference is only 0.07 points.
19. We note that Hill et al. (2013) do find evidence that some presidential advertising can have an effect that lasts up to six weeks. But, for the most part, the evidence presented in Hill et al. (2013) and Gerber et al. (2011) suggests that the effect of advertising decays quickly.
20. In other words, separately for Democrats, Republicans, and independents, and for each question (fair, informative, misleading, and negative), we calculate: Difference in evaluation of ads attacking Romney = Obama Closest to ED – Priorities USA Closest to ED; and Difference in evaluation of ads attacking Obama = Romney Closest to ED – Restore Our Future Closest to ED.
21. In Figure 5.2 the informative bars all go to the right of the vertical line at 0, whereas in Figure 5.4 the Republicans and Democrats are to the left of that line, although the confidence intervals do overlap zero, suggesting we cannot rule out the possibility that these differences are different from zero.
22. In Appendix Table 5.1, we present the average score for each question, separately for each ad.

23. For examples of other recent work that does so, see Brooks and Murov (2012), Dowling and Wichowsky (forthcoming), and Weber, Dunaway, and Johnson (2012).
24. $p > .05$, two-tailed for all three pairwise comparisons—Obama v. no sponsor, Obama v. Priorities USA, and Priorities USA v. no sponsor.
25. $p = .059$, two-tailed.
26. $p = .053$ and $.056$, respectively.
27. Recall that the MTurk population is a convenience sample that appears more representative than student samples, but is not completely representative of the U.S. population. An MTurk sample is typically younger, less likely to own a home, more likely to self-identify as liberal and with the Democratic Party, and more likely to report no religious affiliation; see Berinsky, Huber, and Lenz (2012).
28. We note that recent work focusing on congressional elections suggests the sponsor of an ad may matter for evaluations of the candidates involved (see, for example Brooks and Murov 2012; Dowling and Wichowsky forthcoming; Weber et al. 2012). Because our studies were conducted after the 2012 presidential election, using real ads, we did not ask people to evaluate the candidates, as it is likely their opinions of Obama and Romney were already solidified. More generally, as we discuss in Chapter 7, who sponsors an ad may be more relevant for elections in which the candidates are not as well known as they are in presidential elections.

6 Public Opinion of Campaign Finance after *Citizens United*

On June 17, 1972, there was a break-in at the Democratic National Committee's offices located in the Watergate Hotel in Washington, D.C. The intruders were caught attempting to steal secret documents and wiretap phones. They turned out to be connected to President Richard Nixon's reelection campaign; one was a former CIA operative serving as security director for the committee to reelect the President (Lewis 1972). The investigation that followed revealed that President Nixon's reelection committee "accepted illegal contributions, gave ambassadorships and other political appointments to large donors, granted favors to businesses that made large campaign contributions, and used a slush fund to finance the break-in itself and other illegal activities" (Herrnson 2005, 108). Not only did the Watergate scandal eventually result in the resignation of President Nixon in August 1974, but it also spurred public calls for reform of the campaign system, culminating in the passage of the Federal Election Campaign Act (FECA) in 1974. According to a March 1974 public opinion poll, only 18 percent of the public reported opposition to a reform bill that was very similar to what was ultimately passed in the FECA.[1]

The Supreme Court has long recognized the relationship between campaign finance laws and public opinion. In upholding a challenge to the FECA's contribution limits in *Buckley v. Valeo* (424 U.S. 1 (1976)), the Supreme Court held that although political contributions did contain an element of speech—a contributor is expressing support for a particular candidate—they could be permissibly limited. It based this decision on a belief that, particularly in the wake of Watergate, it was in the government's interest to ensure the public's faith in government, as the FECA was widely seen as a prudent measure to tamp down corruption. Importantly, the Court held in *Buckley* that this interest was so crucial that no evidence of untoward behavior was actually required. The Court asserted,

> It is unnecessary to look beyond the Act's primary purpose—to limit the actuality and appearance of corruption resulting from large individual financial contributions—in order to find a constitutionally sufficient justification for the $1,000 contribution limitation. . . . To the extent

that large contributions are given to secure a political *quid pro quo* from current and potential office holders, the integrity of our system of representative democracy is undermined. Although the scope of such pernicious practices can never be reliably ascertained, the deeply disturbing examples surfacing after the 1972 election demonstrate that the problem is not an illusory one. (424 U.S. 1 (1976) at 423–424)

The Bipartisan Campaign Reform Act (BCRA), passed in 2002, was also highly popular. Unlimited soft money contributions, which could be raised by parties outside of FECA spending limits, had come to play a central role in federal campaign finance. The national Democratic and Republican parties had combined to raise more than $517 million in soft money contributions in the 2000 election, and the Democrats had raised more in soft money than in "hard" contributions subject to statutory limitations during that campaign.[2] Public opinion surveys prior to passage of the BCRA "revealed that substantial majorities considered large political contributions and political fund raising a major source of corruption [and that the] public was particularly troubled by large, soft money donations and believed that restrictions should be placed on the amounts that corporations and unions may contribute to political campaigns" (Herrnson 2005, 113). Moreover, a national poll conducted as part of the American National Election Studies indicated that support for "major campaign finance reform" was not a partisan phenomenon, with 59 percent of "strong Republicans" and 71 percent of "strong Democrats" supporting such legislation in 2002 (La Raja 2008, 109). There were certainly several major political obstacles to the passage of the BCRA (see: Corrado 2003; La Raja 2008, Ch. 4). Nonetheless, public support was helpful in terms of securing its ultimate passage (Herrnson 2005, 113).

It is perhaps no surprise that the two most sweeping campaign finance laws that have been passed in the last 40 years enjoyed strong public support. In virtually all policy areas, public opinion is important for understanding whether change is enacted, and also whether any such change is politically sustainable (Patashnik 2008). This is likely especially true in the case of campaign finance, as it is in other areas directly related to elections, because elected officeholders have little incentive to change the rules by which they were elected in the first place. Some have called for another set of reforms in the wake of the federal court decisions in *Citizens United*, *SpeechNow*, and *Carey* (see: Franz 2012; La Raja 2012). For instance, we noted the (to this point) failed efforts to pass the DISCLOSE Act in Chapter 3. Given the apparent importance of public support to securing such reforms, it seems prudent to consider the state of public opinion concerning both campaign finance laws and the conduct of campaigns and elections more generally.

As we noted in Chapters 1 and 2, there was considerable media attention devoted to the changes in campaign finance laws brought about by the federal court decisions in early 2010. However, that media attention does not itself necessitate an equally attentive public (Zaller 1992). Moreover, given the level of nuance often required in complex campaign finance regulations, it is unclear whether any amount of media coverage can effectively educate the public about the state of federal campaign finance law. So, what does the public think about the *Citizens United* decision? More generally, what knowledge does the public have about current campaign finance laws? The answers to these questions will go a long way toward informing us about the likely success of new reform proposals following the federal court decisions in *Citizens United*, *SpeechNow*, and *Carey*.

PUBLIC ATTITUDES TOWARD CAMPAIGN FINANCE

The Supreme Court (*Buckley v. Valeo*) and scholars (Blass et al. 2012; La Raja 2008; Persily and Lammie 2004) alike have recognized that campaign finance regulations have potential implications for the public's confidence in the democratic process. Yet, prior studies concerning public opinion about campaign finance law have found that although the public reports dissatisfaction with existing campaign finance law (La Raja 2008; Mayer 2001; Persily and Lammie 2004; Shaw and Ragland 2000), it has also generally lacked information about campaign finance regulations and has placed campaign finance relatively low on its policy priorities (e.g., Mayer 2001).

Although debates over campaign finance regulations often pit individual speech rights against a collective interest in governmental transparency, historically the Supreme Court has been tolerant of restrictions on political money. Ever since *Buckley*, the Court has consistently held that the government has an interest in preventing not only any actual corruption resulting from political contributions, but also the mere *appearance* of corruption. As noted above, this logic rests on the assumption that even if no corruption exists, a widespread perception of corrupt behavior alone is able to undermine public confidence in the government. The Court's willingness to accept restrictions on the speech rights of donors absent any evidence of a deleterious impact of money marks campaign finance as a unique policy space, and implicitly recognizes the importance of public opinion in crafting regulations in this area (see Persily and Lammie 2004). The *Citizens United* decision did not allow corporate and labor organizations to contribute directly to candidates, but coupled with the *SpeechNow* decision, a wider range of groups are now permitted to infuse unlimited sums into the political system. Indeed, in Chapter 3 we found that super PACs made approximately $600 million in independent expenditures during the 2012 federal elections alone; this figure is quite similar to the more than $500 million in unlimited soft money raised in 2000 (see above). Considering the Court's emphasis on preventing the appearance of corruption, it therefore seems worthwhile to examine both mass knowledge of campaign finance regulation during the 2012 election and public opinion concerning the Court's decision in *Citizens United*.

This is particularly relevant given that, as was the case following the Watergate scandal, the public has not held the federal government in high esteem recently. Since 2011, Gallup has typically found public approval of Congress to be less than 20 percent, hitting an all-time low of 10 percent in two separate months of 2012 (Newport 2012). It is not clear whether perceived corruption drives such low approval, but a majority of Americans do seem to believe that money influences government action (Blass et al. 2012; Mayer 2001; Persily and Lammie 2004). It is therefore not surprising that the federal campaign finance system has proven unpopular as well, with majorities of the public consistently reporting dissatisfaction with campaign finance laws (La Raja 2008; Mayer 2001; Persily and Lammie 2004; Shaw and Ragland 2000).

Yet, there is reason to harbor some skepticism regarding not only the mass public's knowledge of the actual rules that it wants to change, but also the strength of its will to change them. Mayer (2001) demonstrated that on most factual questions regarding federal campaign finance laws, a majority of respondents either did not know the correct answer or chose an incorrect response, and campaign finance reform consistently ranked at or near the bottom of the list of issues on which respondents desired political action (see also: La Raja 2008, 108). Moreover, the stringency of campaign finance regulation does not appear to be linked with public concern about corruption (Persily and Lammie 2004; Rosenson 2009), a desire for additional regulation (Blass et al. 2012), or mass political efficacy (Miller and Panagopoulos 2011; Primo and Milyo 2006). In addition, the presence of more money in an election does little on its own to shape individuals' confidence in government (Sances 2013). Trust in government is instead more closely associated with personal characteristics such as the respondent's approval of the president or her willingness to trust others (Persily and Lammie 2004).

Compared to previous changes in the campaign finance regulatory environment, *Citizens United* was unique in that it explicitly allowed corporate spending in American politics. As noted above and previously in this book, this shift was widely reported in the media and was referenced by the president during a nationally televised address. It is possible that the intensity of elites' discussion of *Citizens United* raised mass awareness of the correspondent campaign finance issues with a visibility that previous changes had failed to achieve (see: Zaller 1992). The *Citizens United* case may therefore have spurred greater mass knowledge of federal campaign finance law, and consequently—depending on the public's feelings about the ruling—may stimulate reform. On the other hand, it is possible either that the average person did not pay much attention to the decision, or agreed with the ruling, suggesting that there is unlikely to be widespread impetus for reform.

ARE CORPORATIONS PEOPLE? PUBLIC OPINION ABOUT THE *CITIZENS UNITED* DECISION

The first question we address is whether the public was supportive of the Supreme Court's ruling in *Citizens United*. To be sure, there was no shortage of public opinion surveys following the Court's decision in January 2010. The surveys conducted at that time suggest that support for the Court's decision rested, at least in part, on how the question was asked. For example, a *Washington Post*–ABC News telephone survey conducted February 4–8, 2010 ($N = 1,000$) found that 80 percent of the public (strongly or somewhat) opposed the Court's decision, while only 18 percent (strongly or somewhat) supported it (Eggen 2010). Similarly, in a survey conducted online by Hart Research Associates nearly a year later (from December 27, 2010 to January 3, 2011, $N = 500$), roughly 65 percent of respondents "disapproved" of the decision (if they had heard about it) or (if they had not heard about it, but read a brief description about it) had an "unfavorable" reaction to it (Nance 2011). One issue with these questions, however, is that they were somewhat leading. For example, the *Washington Post*–ABC News telephone survey asked, "[D]o you support or oppose the recent ruling by the Supreme Court that says corporations and unions can spend as much money as they want to help political candidates win elections?"[3] This question is fairly broad, makes no mention of the Court's rationale, and also does not specify that corporations and unions cannot donate directly to candidates, but can only "help" them win elections by spending their own money on express advocacy our donating to outside groups.

In contrast, when the public was asked about specific aspects of the case or the general principles discussed therein, support for the Court's decision was much higher. For example, a telephone survey conducted by Victory Enterprises from March 1–2, 2010 ($N = 600$ "likely" voters) found that a majority of people did not "believe that the government should have been able to prevent Citizens United . . . from airing ads promoting its movie" and that the government should not "have the power to limit how much some people speak about politics in order to enhance the voices of others." The first question is in some ways *too* specific to the *Citizens United* case; that is, rather than focusing on general principles, it focuses on what Citizens United itself wanted to do—make a movie. The second question is somewhat leading, or perhaps disingenuous in its use of the word "people," as the rights of *individual* people were not technically at issue in *Citizens United*; rather, the rights of corporations and unions were discussed in that case.

We measure public opinion regarding the rights of corporations in elections by improving on previous public opinion questions in this area in two ways. First, we ask a "richer" question that contains more information about what the Court's actual decision was in order to gauge current public opinion concerning the *Citizens United* decision. Second, we take a step back and ask a more basic/abstract question: Are corporations people?

Study 1: Public Opinion about the *Citizens United* Decision

To measure public opinion regarding the Court's decision in *Citizens United*, we asked approximately 1,200 respondents on the 2011 Cooperative Congressional Election Study (CCES) the following question:

> In January 2010, the United States Supreme Court ruled on a case that challenged existing state laws that restricted the money corporations and unions could spend directly on political advertising. The Supreme Court overturned these laws on the basis that they violated free speech, and ruled the First Amendment allows corporations and unions to use their general treasury funds to support or oppose specific candidates.
>
> Do you agree or disagree with this Supreme Court decision that allowed corporations and unions to use their general treasury funds to support or oppose specific candidates?[4]

The response options were: "strongly agree," "somewhat agree," "somewhat disagree," and "strongly disagree." The order in which the responses appeared was rotated so that half of the participants were randomly assigned to receive "strongly agree" listed first and the other half were randomly assigned to receive "strongly disagree" listed first.

This question provides content about the First Amendment rationale behind the Court's decision and, more importantly, attempts to provide balanced information—both how the system was prior to the Court's ruling (some states had laws restricting the amount of money corporations and unions could spend in elections) and how it is after (these laws are no longer in effect). Also, readers will note that the question does not specifically name the actual case, *Citizens United* v. *FEC*. Leaving the name of the case out of the question allows respondents to focus on whether they agree with the decision, rather than any thoughts/feelings conjured up by the mention of "Citizens United." Readers may also note that the question asserts that the Court "ruled on a case that challenged existing *state* laws" (emphasis added). This is because although *Citizens United* pertained to federal law, it also pertained to states in which bans on corporate and union independent expenditures, or any other type of independent expenditure for that matter, were in place. In all, twenty states had some type of independent expenditure ban prior to the *Citizens United* decision; the remaining thirty states did not. The twenty states that did have some ban saw their ban overturned by the Court's ruling. See Spencer and Wood (2014) for further discussion.

Responses to this question are summarized in Figure 6.1.[5] The figure depicts the percentage of respondents who answered "somewhat agree" (light gray part of the bars) and "strongly agree" (dark gray part of the bars) for the full sample at the top of the figure. That area of the figure indicates that, overall, approximately 30 percent of the public agrees with the Court's decision to allow corporations and unions to use their general treasury funds to support or oppose specific candidates for office. In the fall

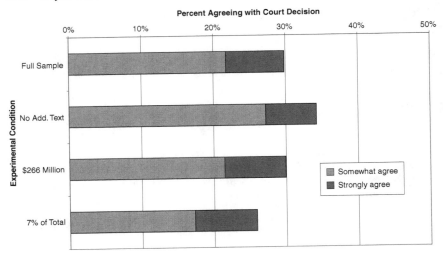

Figure 6.1   Support for the *Citizens United* Decision (in November 2011 Survey)
Note: Weighted analysis. N = 1,196 (Full Sample); 407 (No Add. Text), 395 ($266 Million), 394 (7% of Total).
Source: 2011 CCES

of 2011 at least, it appears that a solid majority (approximately 70 percent) disagreed with the *Citizens United* decision.

Moreover, the percentage of respondents who stated that they agreed with the Court's decision did not vary much when we changed the wording of the question. Specifically, we employed a standard question wording experiment (Druckman et al. 2006; Schuman and Presser 1981). In question wording experiments, some respondents are given one version of the question, while another set of respondents are given a different version. Researchers then compare the distribution of responses from the two versions to see if the difference in question wording mattered for public opinion on the question at hand. In theory, researchers could have as many different versions of the question as they think important. In our case, we employed three versions.

Prior to asking respondents whether they agreed or disagreed with the Court's ruling, we told one-third of the respondents the total amount of money spent by groups (i.e., entities other than candidates and political parties) in 2010 (see Dwyer 2010). We provided this information as a cue to respondents because many likely lack information about how much money was spent by groups, thus helping them to determine the extent to which outside money might have been a factor (italics added for emphasis, but not in original):

In January 2010, the United States Supreme Court ruled on a case that challenged existing state laws that restricted the money corporations and unions could spend directly on political advertising. The Supreme Court overturned these laws on the basis that they violated free speech, and ruled the First Amendment allows corporations and unions to use their general treasury funds to support or oppose specific candidates. *Corporations, unions, and other special interest groups spent $266 million to influence the 2010 congressional elections.*

A separate one-third of the respondents were told the total amount of money groups spent as a percentage of the total amount of money spent in 2010. We provided this information to discern whether information about relative spending levels would matter in the same manner as raw spending totals (italics added for emphasis, but not in original):

In January 2010, the United States Supreme Court ruled on a case that challenged existing state laws that restricted the money corporations and unions could spend directly on political advertising. The Supreme Court overturned these laws on the basis that they violated free speech, and ruled the First Amendment allows corporations and unions to use their general treasury funds to support or oppose specific candidates. *Corporations, unions, and other special interest groups spent $266 million of the nearly $4 billion total (7% of the total) that was spent to influence the 2010 congressional elections.*

The remaining one-third of respondents received no additional information (the question text they saw is the same as the first iteration of the question described above). By varying the question across respondents, we can see whether providing people with information about how much money is spent by outside groups might influence public opinion.

Somewhat interestingly, we find little movement in responses across the different question wordings in Figure 6.1. In the absence of any information about the amount of money spent by groups, 34 percent of respondents agreed with the Court's decision. Thirty percent of respondents who were given information about the total amount of money spent by groups in 2010 agreed with the Court's decision, while 26 percent who were given the total amount of money spent by groups as a percentage of the grand total did so. The similarity in the proportion of respondents who agreed with the decision—regardless of the amount of information they received—suggests that a relatively low percentage of the public agrees with the Court's decision, and that opinion is fairly stable in the face of factual information about spending by groups. If anything, information about money spent reduces agreement with the Court's opinion.

In addition, agreement with *Citizens United* is fairly stable across partisan lines. Figure 6.2 displays responses to the question by respondent party identification. The top group of bars indicates that 27 percent of

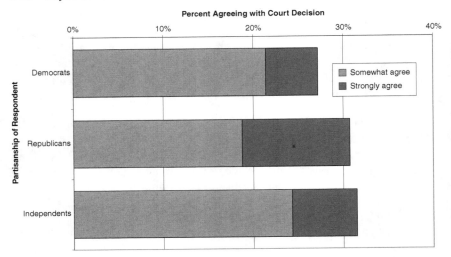

Figure 6.2 Support for the *Citizens United* Decision (in November 2011 Survey), by Respondent Party Identification
Note: Weighted analysis. N = 1,196.
Source: 2011 CCES

Democrats agreed with the decision compared to 31 percent of Republicans and 32 percent of independents. That there is such little movement across partisan groups suggests that, on average, partisans evaluated the *Citizen United* decision (at least as it was presented in the question we asked) similarly.

In sum, public agreement with the Supreme Court's decision in *Citizens United* was approximately 30 percent in November 2011. Moreover, this level of agreement was fairly consistent across partisan lines. Importantly, the question we used to measure agreement with the Court's decision did not mention the decision, *Citizens United*, by name, which likely would have influenced responses. Rather, the question we asked focused on the First Amendment justification for the Supreme Court's ruling and the state laws that were struck down ("First Amendment allows corporations and unions to use their general treasury funds to support or oppose specific candidates"). When presented in this fashion, agreement with the Court's decision was relatively low. This may suggest that there would be broad support for overturning the Court's *Citizens United* decision if its impact were communicated in this manner. Alternatively, 30 percent represents a nontrivial number of people in agreement, suggesting efforts to reform the campaign finance system post–*Citizens United* might be met with pushback. Before jumping to any conclusions though, we wanted to ask the public a more basic question, engaging the premise of the Court's ruling: "Are corporations people?"

Study 2: Should Corporations Have the Same First Amendment Rights as People?

Responses to the public opinion question asked in Study 1 suggest that more than a few people (approximately 30 percent) agreed with the Court's decision in *Citizens United*. Moreover, Republicans were slightly more likely to agree with the outcome of that case than were Democrats. Whether these views reflect more general views about the rights of corporations in elections, however, is unclear. Granted, the question used in Study 1 does not specifically mention *Citizens United*, but it does mention aspects of the case and (for some respondents) information about the 2010 congressional elections. This information may influence responses. As a first attempt at assessing whether, in the abstract, individuals think corporations should be afforded the same First Amendment rights as individual citizens, in Study 2 we asked a separate set of respondents the following question:

> In thinking about the U.S. Constitution's First Amendment protections of freedom of speech and assembly, do you think corporations should have the same rights as individuals?

The response options were: "Yes, corporations should have the same rights as individuals," "No, corporations should not have the same rights as individuals," and "don't know." The order of the "Yes" and "No" response options was randomized. "Don't know" was fixed as the third response option.[6]

As with Study 1, we again employed a simple question wording experiment. In particular, we asked two other versions of the question in addition to the one stated above, which we refer to as our no additional text condition. In our other two conditions, participants were either presented with information that prompted them to think more specifically about elections (elections prompt) or lobbying (lobbying prompt). Participants were randomly assigned to one of these three conditions with equal probability so that one-third of the respondents received no additional text, one-third received the elections prompt, and the remaining one-third received the lobbying prompt. Participants assigned to the elections condition saw the following question (italics added for emphasis, but not in original):

> In thinking about the U.S. Constitution's First Amendment protections of freedom of speech and assembly, do you think corporations should have the same rights as individuals? *That is, should both individuals and corporations have the same constitutional rights to spend money to influence elections?*

Participants assigned to the lobbying condition saw the following question (italics added for emphasis, but not in original):

> In thinking about the U.S. Constitution's First Amendment protections of freedom of speech and assembly, do you think corporations should

have the same rights as individuals? *That is, should both individuals and corporations have the same constitutional rights to lobby the government?*

This question directly asks people about their views regarding the rights of corporations vis-à-vis individuals. The elections and lobbying prompts address the question of whether there are specific arenas for which respondents are more or less willing to think corporations should have the same First Amendment protections as people. If individuals are less willing for corporations to be afforded the same rights as individuals in one arena (elections or lobbying) over another, it might suggest that they are more concerned about the appearance of corruption in that arena.

Responses to this question are presented in Figure 6.3.[7] The figure depicts the percentage of respondents who answered "yes" (light gray bars), "no" (dark gray bars), and "don't know" (white bars) for the full sample, and then for each experimental condition. The far left of the figure indicates that 59 percent of respondents think that corporations should *not* have the same rights as individuals, 23 percent think they should, and 18 percent are unsure. In other words, a solid majority of the population believes that corporations are not entitled to the same First Amendment rights as individuals, and, it seems, would disagree with the Court's stated rationale in its *Citizens United* ruling.

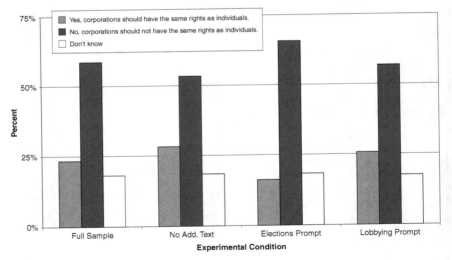

Figure 6.3   Beliefs about the First Amendment Rights of Corporations Compared to Individuals

Note: Weighted analysis. N = 980 (Full Sample); 318 (No Add. Text), 325 (Elections Prompt), 337 (Lobbying Prompt).

Source: February 7–10, 2012 YouGov/Polimetrix survey

Interestingly, when we examine the data by experimental condition, we find that the percentage of respondents who think corporations are not entitled to the same rights as individuals varies by experimental condition. We note that the percentage of respondents who respond "don't know" is roughly the same, around 18 percent, for all three conditions, so we focus on differences in "yes" and "no" answers. Among respondents who were provided with no additional text—depicted in the second set of bars from the left—53 percent think corporations should not have the same rights as individuals and 28 percent think they should. Among respondents who were provided with the elections prompt—depicted in the second set of bars from the right—66 percent think corporations should not have the same rights as individuals and 16 percent think they should. Finally, among respondents who were provided with the lobbying prompt—depicted in the set of bars on the far right—57 percent think corporations should not have the same rights as individuals, while 26 percent think they should. Thus, when encouraged to think about elections, a greater percentage of the public appears concerned about granting equal rights to corporations, compared to both lobbying and a condition in which no additional information was given.[8] Moreover, the percentage (66 percent) that thinks corporations should not have the same rights as individuals is very similar to the proportion of respondents (70 percent) who disagreed with the Court's *Citizens United* decision in the more specific question presented in the previous section.

Do partisans have different opinions on this matter? Readers will recall that the results of Study 1 (see Figure 6.2) suggest that Republicans may be more likely to think corporations should have the same rights as individuals, as they were somewhat more supportive of the principles of the *Citizens United* decision than Democrats. Figure 6.4 presents an initial test of this possibility by breaking down the responses to the "Do corporations have the same rights as individuals?" question by respondent party identification. The figure does not display the "don't know" responses, but they represent the empty space between the end of a bar and 100 percent. Although independents responded "don't know" at higher rates (22 percent in the full sample) than Democrats (14 percent) and Republicans (17 percent), the percentage of respondents answering "don't know" was relatively constant across experimental conditions within party identification.

The top group of bars indicates that 15 percent of Democrats think corporations should have the same rights as individuals (over 70 percent do not) compared to 42 percent of Republicans (only 41 percent of Republicans do not). The opinion of independents is closer to that of Democrats than Republicans—19 percent of independents think corporations should have the same rights as individuals, while 59 percent do not. Thus, it appears there are sizable partisan differences concerning the rights of corporations vis-à-vis individuals, with Democrats (and independents) much less supportive of the idea that corporations should be afforded the same First Amendment rights as individuals.[9]

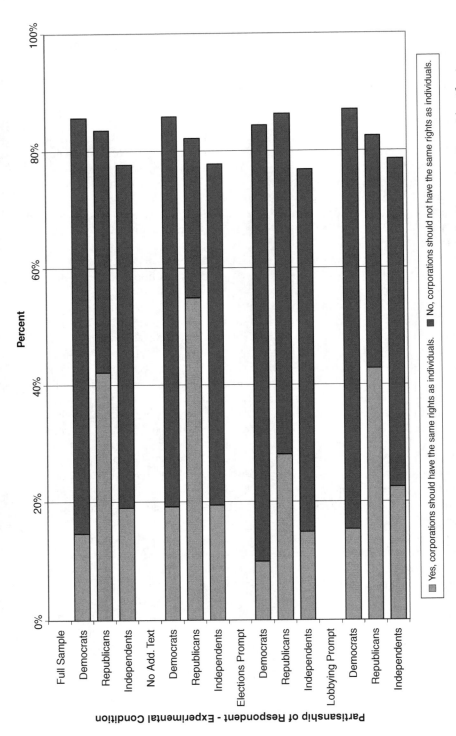

Figure 6.4 Beliefs about the First Amendment Rights of Corporations Compared to Individuals, by Respondent Party Identification

Note: Weighted analysis. N = 980 (Full Sample); 318 (No Add. Text), 325 (Elections Prompt), 337 (Lobbying Prompt).

Source: February 7–10, 2012 YouGov/Polimetrix survey

The next three groups of bars display these results by experimental condition, and reveal that the gap between Democrats and Republicans is most pronounced when no additional text is given (19 and 55 percent, respectively) and in the lobbying condition (15 and 43 percent, respectively). The partisan gap in opinion is less pronounced, however, when participants were encouraged to think about elections: 10 percent of Democrats, 15 percent of independents, and 28 percent of Republicans think corporations should have the same rights as individuals. Thus, there appears to be more bipartisan support for the idea that corporations should *not* have equivalent First Amendment rights when it comes to electioneering as opposed to lobbying. In particular, this bipartisan support appears to be driven by the fact that Republicans are more willing to grant equivalent First Amendment rights to corporations when it comes to lobbying (or when no policy arena is named).[10]

These findings suggest that there may be public support for reinstating some restrictions on corporate spending in elections that *Citizens United* ruled unconstitutional. However, one potential obstacle to doing so is that many people do think corporations should have equal First Amendment rights to those of individuals when it comes to elections, and even more so when it comes to other policy arenas, such as lobbying. Another potential hurdle is whether there is much knowledge of the current campaign finance system in the first place.

PUBLIC KNOWLEDGE OF CAMPAIGN FINANCE LAW IN THE 2012 ELECTION

In the months following its release, the *Citizens United* decision garnered significant media attention. For instance, a Lexis-Nexis search returns more than 3,000 mentions of "Citizens United" in English print media between January 1, 2010 (shortly before the case was decided) and November 6, 2012 (Election Day 2012). The joint terms "Citizens United" and "Supreme Court" return nearly 1,000 mentions. A Google News search of the latter combination returned nearly 2,000 articles, while a general Google Internet search finds more than 9 million pages. Yet for all that attention, it remains to be seen whether the mass public understands the state of campaign finance regulation. They may have held an opinion on the *Citizens United* decision (see above), but whether they understand how the system operates is a separate question. So, how much did people know about the state of federal (presidential) campaign finance rules during the 2012 election?

To find out, we fielded two nationally representative surveys conducted in the weeks immediately before the general election on November 6, 2012. We asked the same set of questions on both surveys—the 2012 Cooperative Congressional Election Study (CCES) and the 2012 Cooperative Campaign Analysis Project (CCAP)—both of which were fielded by YouGov/

Polimetrix.[11] On both the CCES and CCAP, we asked respondents a series of questions designed to assess their knowledge of the legality of various activities during presidential elections.[12] These questions are listed in Table 6.1. Respondents were randomly assigned to answer six questions about rules pertaining either to corporations *or* individuals. For example, a respondent would have been asked either "to the best of your knowledge is it legal today for corporations to donate money to candidates in presidential elections" or "to the best of your knowledge is it legal today for citizens to donate money to candidates in presidential elections," but not both.[13] Approximately 500 respondents answered each battery in each survey, for a total of roughly 1,000 responses to the questions about corporations and 1,000 to the questions about citizens. For all questions, participants could respond that the activity was "illegal," "legal," or that they "don't know." Table 6.1 displays responses to questions about permissible contributory behavior of corporations and citizens. In addition to displaying the percentage of respondents who selected each answer, the table also specifies whether the activity was in fact illegal or legal according to federal law governing presidential elections in 2012.

For all six questions regarding corporations, a majority of respondents either did not know the correct answer or answered incorrectly. For instance, a majority (58.4 percent) said that it was legal for "corporations to donate money to candidates in presidential elections." Only 13.7 percent of respondents correctly answered that such activity is illegal. (*Citizens United* left unchanged the fact it has been illegal for corporations to contribute any amount of money to federal candidates since 1907.) Similarly, a minority of respondents correctly answered that it is legal for corporations to purchase electioneering advertising (45.1 percent) or to contribute to some groups who buy political advertising without disclosing the corporation's identity (37.5 percent). (Corporations may contribute to nonprofit 501(c)(4) "social welfare" organizations, which need not disclose their donors to the Federal Election Commission.) Likewise, only a minority of respondents correctly answered that corporations cannot donate unlimited sums to presidential candidates or parties (43.3 percent), or that they cannot donate to presidential candidates without disclosing the corporation's identity (41.8 percent).

Table 6.1 displays a similar pattern of knowledge—or lack thereof—of allowable behavior for individual citizens. Only minorities of participants correctly responded that individuals could not make unlimited contributions to presidential candidates in 2012 (47.8 percent), or that individuals were barred from contributing to presidential candidates anonymously (38.0 percent). Likewise, a minority of respondents knew that individuals may donate to groups (such as 501(c)(4) organizations) without disclosing their identity (40.0 percent), or that they may donate unlimited funds to groups (such as super PACs) that buy political advertising (42.7 percent). Later in the survey, we asked a slightly different question designed to tap knowledge about rules regarding super PACs, without referring to them by name: "To the

Table 6.1 Knowledge of Campaign Finance Rules Pertaining to Corporations and Citizens

To the best of your knowledge, is it legal today for . . .	Corporations				Citizens			
	Illegal	Don't Know	Legal	Law	Illegal	Don't Know	Legal	Law
corporations/citizens to spend money to purchase advertising supporting or opposing candidates in presidential elections?	19.1	35.8	45.1	LEGAL	10.3	28.4	61.2	LEGAL
corporations/citizens to donate money to candidates in presidential elections?	13.7	28.0	58.4	ILLEGAL	3.5	15.2	81.4	LEGAL
corporations/citizens to contribute unlimited sums of money to groups who buy political advertising in presidential elections?	25.0	34.7	40.3	LEGAL	25.2	32.2	42.7	LEGAL
corporations/citizens to contribute unlimited sums of money to candidates and/or political parties during presidential elections?	43.3	31.4	25.3	ILLEGAL	47.8	25.0	27.3	ILLEGAL
corporations/citizens to contribute to candidates for president without disclosing their (the corporations'/citizens') identity?	41.8	37.0	21.3	ILLEGAL	38.0	33.8	28.1	ILLEGAL
corporations/citizens to contribute to some groups who buy political advertising without disclosing their (the corporations'/citizens') identity?	21.6	40.9	37.5	LEGAL	22.3	37.7	40.0	LEGAL

Note: Cell entries are percentage of respondents selecting each response category. *N* ranges from 1,002 to 1,014. Complete question wording included in the appendix.

Source: 2012 CCES and 2012 CCAP surveys. Combined responses. Weighted analysis.

best of your knowledge, is it legal today for some groups to accept unlimited donations from citizens if the money is only spent on political advertising or similar communications?"[14] Forty-three percent of respondents answered correctly that this activity was legal—almost exactly the same number for the similar question in Table 6.1. In other words, roughly the same percentage of people (43 percent) knew that citizens could "contribute unlimited sums of money to groups who buy political advertising" as knew that groups could "accept" those unlimited donations, so long as it was only spent on political advertising.

Table 6.1 does reveal two areas in which a majority of respondents displayed knowledge of campaign finance regulations: A majority correctly answered that individuals may legally purchase electioneering advertising themselves (61.2 percent) and that they may donate to presidential candidates in presidential elections (81.4 percent). Still, a majority of respondents was able to correctly answer only two of the twelve questions; Table 6.1 is hardly suggestive of a public with high knowledge of campaign finance regulations, even after *Citizens United*.

In an effort to determine whether respondents' knowledge of campaign finance law differs according to the amount of attention they pay to politics, Table 6.2 contains the percentage of participants who chose each answer (legal, illegal, or don't know), tabulated by their level of political interest. We classify individuals as having a high level of political interest if they reported that they "follow what's going on in government and public affairs" *most of the time*.[15] About 41 percent of respondents meet this definition of high political interest. We classify the remainder of respondents as having low political interest compared to this group.

Two trends are apparent in Table 6.2. First, high-interest respondents were quite knowledgeable about 2012 campaign finance law, and were more knowledgeable on average than low-interest respondents. A majority of high-interest respondents were able to answer 11 of the 12 questions correctly, ranging from a high of 92 percent of high-interest respondents knowing that it was legal for citizens to donate to candidates in presidential elections to a bare majority knowing that it was legal for corporations (53.5 percent) and citizens (50.9 percent) to contribute to some groups who buy political advertising without disclosing their identity. The lone instance in which a majority of high-interest respondents did not know a specific legal provision was the question asking whether corporations were legally able to donate money to presidential candidates (displayed in the second row of Table 6.2). On this question, only 14.6 percent of high-interest participants correctly responded that corporations could *not* legally make direct contributions; this is practically indistinguishable from low-interest respondents, of which 13.1 percent answered correctly.

Notably, on this question a greater percentage of high-interest respondents actually selected the *incorrect* answer "legal" (74.4 percent) as opposed to "don't know" (only 11 percent). Conversely, although low-interest respondents

Table 6.2 Knowledge of Campaign Finance Rules Pertaining to Corporations and Citizens, by Respondent's Level of Political Interest

	Corporations						Citizens					
	Illegal		Don't Know		Legal		Illegal		Don't Know		Legal	
To the best of your knowledge is it legal today for . . .	High	Low	High	Low	High	Low	High	Low	High	Low	High	Low
corporations/citizens to spend money to purchase advertising supporting or opposing candidates in presidential elections?	22.4	16.8	20.0	46.1	57.5	37.0	9.1	11.3	15.6	38.3	75.3	50.4
corporations/citizens to donate money to candidates in presidential elections?	14.6	13.1	11.0	39.1	74.4	47.8	1.7	4.8	6.3	22.0	92.0	73.2
corporations/citizens to contribute unlimited sums of money to groups who buy political advertising in presidential elections?	24.6	25.3	16.0	47.1	59.4	27.7	21.9	27.7	17.8	43.2	60.3	29.2
corporations/citizens to contribute unlimited sums of money to candidates and/or political parties during presidential elections?	50.9	38.4	16.9	40.9	32.2	20.7	62.0	36.8	12.7	34.5	25.4	28.8
corporations/citizens to contribute to candidates for president without disclosing their (the corporations'/citizens') identity?	51.8	35.1	21.6	47.1	26.6	17.8	54.3	25.6	21.1	43.6	24.7	30.8
corporations/citizens to contribute to some groups who buy political advertising without disclosing their (the corporations'/citizens') identity?	22.6	20.9	23.9	52.1	53.5	27.0	24.3	20.8	24.8	47.6	50.9	31.7

Note: Cell entries are percentage of respondents selecting each response category. *N* ranges from 1,002 to 1,014 for each question. Complete question wording included in the appendix.

Source: 2012 CCES and 2012 CCAP surveys. Combined responses. Weighted analysis.

also selected the incorrect answer "legal" at a high rate (47.8 percent), low-interest respondents were more apt to respond "don't know" (39.1 percent) than high-interest respondents. This suggests that high-interest respondents may have felt more certain in their incorrect belief of this law or, alternatively, that they were more willing to give a nonequivocal response. However, though it is certainly the case that low-interest respondents appear more willing to select "don't know"—a higher percentage of low-interest respondents compared to high-interest respondents select "don't know" for all twelve questions—there are other questions in which high-interest respondents select "don't know" at a higher rate, suggesting that many incorrectly believed corporations could donate to a candidate during the presidential election. We return to this point below.

Second, knowledge among low-interest respondents effectively mimicked that of the sample as a whole. A majority of low-interest respondents demonstrated understanding of only two facts: that individuals may purchase advertising themselves (50.4 percent), and that individuals may donate to a presidential candidate (73.2 percent). Even on these two questions though, the gap in knowledge between high- and low-interest respondents is about 20 percentage points. In fact, the only question to reveal little difference between high- and low-interest respondents was the one concerning whether corporations could donate to candidates or parties (mentioned above).

In short, for eleven of the twelve questions, we find large differences in the ability of high- and low-interest respondents to identify activities permissible under federal law.[16] This suggests it is likely that elite discourse about the *Citizens United* decision, and campaign finance in the 2012 election more generally, was absorbed by those who pay more attention to politics (see Zaller 1992). This is the case even when there was relatively widespread elite misperception of exactly what *Citizens United* did and did not do (on this issue, see, for example, Kaminer 2012), which perhaps helps to explain why nearly 75 percent of high-interest respondents (incorrectly) reported that corporations can "donate money to candidates in presidential elections."

CONCLUSION

Through a series of Supreme Court and regulatory decisions, the rights of corporations have been greatly expanded when it comes to spending their money to influence elections. For many scholars and pundits, the "final straw" (Levitt 2010) in the increasing rights of corporations to partake in electioneering was the Court's decision in *Citizens United* to grant corporations (and unions) the right to spend their general treasury funds on express political advocacy. Many prominent individuals—including the president—and groups criticized the Court's decision in *Citizens United*. Further, many public interest groups decried the decision, disagreeing with the Court's reasoning and also marshaling evidence that the public opposed the Court's decision (e.g., Public Citizen 2011). Other public interest groups, however, supported the Court's decision, suggesting that the public favored the "principles" of the Court's ruling (e.g., Center for Competitive Politics 2010). Thus, while there was competing elite discourse regarding *Citizens United*, the public also appeared at odds over the Court's decision.

For all of the public discussion surrounding the constitutionality of corporate and union electioneering, however, the survey evidence presented in Study 2 suggests that public knowledge of campaign finance law was lacking in many respects during the 2012 election. The responses of high-interest respondents indicate that those who pay close attention to politics are more likely to demonstrate knowledge of campaign finance rules. However, on the whole there is little evidence that elite discourse about campaign finance in the wake of *Citizens United* fueled an increase in mass knowledge of related policy. Indeed, given the very low percentage of correct responses among high-interest respondents regarding the legality of corporate donations to candidates, it is possible that elites themselves have not grasped the most immediate effect of *Citizens United*: Corporations may spend money to support or oppose, but may not donate to, candidates and parties.

The generally low level of knowledge about campaign finance rules among respondents suggests that it may prove difficult to reform the regulatory system resulting from *Citizens United*. Specifically, reformers are likely to confront not only the typical policymaking hurdles, but also a public lacking sufficient information to form an opinion about the existing campaign finance environment—much less the political will to change it. In other words, the results presented in the second part of this chapter suggest that reform efforts may find little success because many citizens are not entirely sure what a given law is, never mind if it should be changed. Still, it could be the case that the public agrees on a set of basic principles for campaign finance laws. That is to say, a citizen may not *know* what a given law is, but she might have a good idea of what she thinks the law *should* be.

On this matter, we find mixed evidence in the first part of this chapter. There certainly is a majority of individuals who indicate they do not support the idea that corporations should be granted the same rights as individuals when it comes to elections. However, a nontrivial number of individuals are in agreement with the Court's reasoning that corporations should be treated as people, at least when it comes to participating in elections. This suggests another reason why reform may prove difficult: In addition to a lack of public knowledge regarding the state of campaign finance regulations, several individuals agree with the principles of the Court's rulings. For example, approximately 30 percent of the public agreed with the Court's decision to allow "corporations and unions to use their general treasury funds to support or oppose specific candidates"[17] and 23 percent of the public thought that "corporations should have the same rights as individuals." Further, the more basic question revealed partisan differences. For example, 15 percent of Democrats (and 19 percent of independents) think corporations should have the same rights as individuals compared to 42 percent of Republicans. However, Democrats and Republicans do exhibit greater agreement regarding the rights of corporations vis-à-vis individuals when it comes to elections (10 percent of Democrats and 28 percent of Republicans think corporations should have the same rights as individuals), than they do lobbying (15 percent of Democrats and 43 percent of Republicans think corporations should have the same rights as individuals).

Coupled with the already failed attempts at instituting certain reforms like the DISCLOSE Act, the evidence presented in this chapter suggests that efforts to reform the campaign finance system may be met with pushback, and not just from corporations and unions (or other groups), but from citizens who indicate agreement with the Court's ruling in *Citizens United*.

NOTES

1. Harris Survey, March, 1974. Accessed September 30, 2013 from the iPOLL Databank, The Roper Center for Public Opinion Research, University of Connecticut: http://0-www.ropercenter.uconn.edu.umiss.lib.olemiss.edu/data_access/ipoll/ipoll.html.
2. Campaign Finance Institute. "Hard and Soft Money Raised by National Party Committees, 1992–2012." Accessed December 18, 2013 from: www.cfinst.org/pdf/vital/VitalStats_t13.pdf.
3. Exact question wording is not available for the Hart Research Associates poll.
4. The 2011 CCES was fielded by YouGov/Polimetrix over the Internet. YouGov/Polimetrix uses a combination of sampling and matching techniques to approximate a nationally representative random digit dialing (RDD) sample. All of the analysis using these data employs the analytical weights provided with the dataset in an effort to represent a national sample. Our survey experiment appeared on Yale University's private content. We thank Yale's Center for the Study of American Politics for the financial support for this survey.
5. The sample is restricted to the 1,196 respondents who answered this question and other (demographic and political characteristic) questions used in other analysis reported in this chapter.
6. The survey was conducted from February 7–10, 2012. All of the analysis using these data employs the analytical weights provided with the dataset in an effort to represent a national sample.
7. The sample is restricted to the 980 respondents who answered this question and other (demographic and political characteristic) questions used in other analysis reported in this chapter.
8. This conclusion is supported if we regress respondents' beliefs about whether corporations are entitled to the same First Amendment rights as individuals (scored −1 = No, 0 = DK, 1 = Yes) on indicators for the experimental conditions (with no additional text serving as the excluded category) and demographic and political controls. This analysis, reported in column 1 of Appendix Table 6.1, indicates that the belief that corporations should have the same rights as individuals is negatively associated with assignment to the elections prompt condition. Further, although there is a (small) negative association

between the lobbying prompt condition and the outcome measure, the difference between the –.213 elections prompt coefficient and –.071 lobbying prompt coefficient is statistically significant (*p* = .024).

9. This conclusion is supported if we regress respondents' beliefs about whether corporations are entitled to the same First Amendment rights as individuals (scored –1 = No, 0 = DK, 1 = Yes) on indicators for the experimental conditions (with no additional text serving as the excluded category) and demographic and political controls, including indicators for respondent partisanship (Democrat and Republican as separate indicators, with independent serving as the reference category). This analysis, reported in column 1 of Appendix Table 6.1, indicates that Republicans believe that corporations should have the same rights as individuals at higher rates than both independents (*p* < .01) and Democrats (*p* < .01).

10. This conclusion is supported if we regress respondents' beliefs about whether corporations are entitled to the same First Amendment rights as individuals (scored –1 = No, 0 = DK, 1 = Yes) on indicators for the experimental conditions (with no additional text serving as the excluded category) and demographic and political controls, separately for Democrats, Republicans, and independents. This analysis, reported in columns 2–4 of Appendix Table 6.1, indicates that the belief that corporations should have the same rights as individuals is negatively associated with assignment to the elections prompt condition for all three groups. However, it is only statistically significant for Republicans (column 3), for whom the elections prompt coefficient is significantly different from both the no additional text coefficient (*p* < .01) and the lobbying prompt coefficient (*p* < .05).

11. Both the CCES and CCAP are cooperative projects that include a "common content" section (which includes an array of basic demographic and political questions) and modules designed by individual research teams, each of which take approximately 10 minutes to complete. Our questions were included on a team module with a target sample of 1,000 respondents in each survey. The CCES was fielded from October 1 to November 3, 2012; the CCAP was fielded from October 27 to November 3, 2012. Our questions appeared on Yale University's private content. We thank Yale's Center for the Study of American Politics for the financial support for this survey.

12. There are a variety of concerns about using opt-in surveys, especially those fielded on the Internet (AAPOR Executive Council Task Force 2010). A common concern is that opt-in participants are likely to be more politically interested or informed than the average citizen. To the extent this is the case, however, it should bias our survey results toward finding greater knowledge of campaign finance rules and regulations among the mass public. In other words, the results we present, if anything, likely overstate public knowledge of campaign finances rules. This is important given that we find public knowledge is not particularly high, even using this sample *and* during an election in which campaign finance was particularly salient. The final sample (*N* = 1,000 for each survey) is weighted to be representative of the U.S. adult population (age 18 and over). All of the data presented below use sampling weights provided by YouGov/Polimetrix. Appendix Table 6.2 presents selected demographic and political characteristics of this combined (CCES and CCAP) sample.

13. Underline in original question text.

14. Appendix Table 6.3 presents the full set of responses to this additional question.

15. Full question wording: "Some people seem to follow what's going on in government and public affairs most of the time, whether there's an election going on or not. Others aren't that interested. Would you say you follow

what's going on in government and public affairs . . .?" (Most of the time; Some of the time; Only now and then; Hardly at all; Don't know).

16. The differences range between 12 and 32 percentage points. We note that for the most part these differences are the result of greater percentages of low-interest respondents answering "don't know" compared to high-interest respondents. That is, the gap in factually *incorrect* responses between high- and low-interest respondents is not as large as the difference between them in terms of factually *correct* responses.

17. A 2010 Gallup poll found that the majority of the public agrees with the Court that "campaign money is 'free speech'" (Saad 2010). Specifically, 57 percent responded that they "consider money given to political candidates to be a form of free speech," with 37 percent indicating that they do not. Differences between the Gallup responses and our responses could be a result of Gallup's question priming people to think about whether political donations are "free speech," sampling variability, or the different times in which the surveys were fielded.

7 Prospects for Campaign Finance Reform

On Tuesday January 31, 2012, Americans for a Better Tomorrow, Tomorrow (ABTT) filed paperwork with the FEC indicating that the super PAC had raised more than $1 million. The day before, Stephen Colbert had regained the presidency of ABTT after having briefly ceded control to John Stewart while Colbert formed an exploratory presidential campaign committee. As president of ABTT once again, Colbert requested that the group's treasurer, Shauna Polk, submit a supplemental memo to the FEC with ABTT's disclosure report. In that memo, Colbert is quoted as saying, " 'Yeah! How you like me now, F.E.C? I'm rolling seven digits deep! I got 99 problems but a non-connected independent-expenditure only committee ain't one!' "[1]

Colbert's riff on popular recording artist Jay-Z's hit song, "99 Problems," highlighted the ease with which "non-connected independent-expenditure only committees" (i.e., super PACs) could be formed and raise money. Even President Obama, who stated his opposition to super PACs and corporate spending several times immediately after the *Citizens United* and *Speech-Now* rulings, eventually endorsed a super PAC in early 2012. These were just two of the over 1,000 super PACs that were created in the 2012 election cycle, 255 of which spent money totaling approximately $600 million.[2] Clearly, creating a super PAC to operate in the 2012 election was not a problem, but do super PACs (and similar groups) pose a problem for democracy moving forward?

The preceding chapters can be seen as both confirming the fears of reformers in some areas and allaying their immediate concerns in others, and thus do not provide an unambiguous answer to this question. Advocates of campaign finance reform argue that the changes brought about by federal court decisions in 2010 necessitate changes to the campaign finance system, and they have offered a variety of proposals to change that system. As such, it is worth considering options for reform that have been proposed since the passage of *Citizens United*, *SpeechNow*, and *Carey*, in light of the evidence presented both in the previous chapters of this book and in other current campaign finance scholarship.

THE DISCLOSE ACT

We briefly discussed the DISCLOSE Act in Chapter 3, but it merits further discussion here as well. The DISCLOSE Act was proposed twice in Congress. It failed to garner enough votes on the first attempt (in the 111th Congress), and was not even put to a vote in the 112th Congress.[3] Nevertheless, the notion that all donors to election-related committees should be disclosed publicly has traditionally received strong support from the public (Thee-Brenan 2010) and the Supreme Court alike (Briffault 2010; Garrett 2004; Hasen 2012; Levitt 2010; Magleby 2002). Even in *Citizens United*, the Court upheld congressionally imposed disclosure requirements, and did so again in a subsequent decision in that same year: *Doe v Reed* (130 S. Ct. 2811 (2010)). In *Doe*, the Court ruled that a group that had placed a referendum on same-sex marriage on the ballot in the state of Washington must disclose the identity of its donors since signing such a petition was tantamount to the very public act of legislating. Given both the popularity of disclosure among the public and its traditional support at the Supreme Court, disclosure is likely to remain an important regulatory tool for the foreseeable future.

The main problem with the current disclosure regime in the eyes of reformers is that "social welfare" 501(c)(4) organizations do not have to publicly disclose their donors. Since they can still spend up to 50 percent of their funds on independent expenditures for political ads, many 501(c)(4)s can spend a great deal of money on political advertising. Alternatively, social welfare groups can make a large lump sum donation to super PACs, which would disclose the social welfare organization—and not original 501(c)(4) donors—as the contributor (Ronayne 2011; Torres-Spelliscy 2011). The social welfare organizations often have names that suggest widespread support, such as "Citizens for Strength and Security" (funded by labor unions) or "Citizens for Better Medicare" (funded by the pharmaceutical industry), so in the end such a disclosure does not necessarily give the public much information about the interests funding a political organization such as a super PAC.

Full disclosure of such information seems to be in the spirit of both *Citizens United* and *Doe*. As Justice Kennedy argued in the *Citizens United* majority opinion, disclosure "permits citizens and shareholders to react to the speech of corporate entities in a proper way. This transparency enables the electorate to make informed decisions and give proper weight to different speakers and messages" (*Citizens United v FEC*, 130 S.Ct. 876, at 914 (2010)). Thus, while the DISLCOSE Act has yet to gain much steam in Congress, we believe that the preponderance of evidence suggests that a well-considered challenge to the nondisclosure of independent expenditures by social welfare organizations might find success before the Supreme Court.

Our findings suggest that full financial disclosure can serve an important function in voters' preference formation. The most direct piece of evidence we presented that speaks to the question of whether strengthened disclosure requirements might change the conduct of elections comes out of the experiments in Chapter 4. We found that voters evaluate candidates less favorably when told they are heavily supported by super PACs (or a generic interest group), compared to candidates who have a more diversified funding portfolio. This finding suggests that funding sources weigh on voters' minds, and it seems reasonable to expect that knowledge of super PAC funders might also be an important element of preference formation. Group-sponsored ads tend to be effective because they give cover to allied candidates, as that candidate does not receive as much "backlash" for going on the attack when he or she is not the one sponsoring the ad (see: Brooks and Murov 2012; Weber et al. 2012). Recent experimental work, however, finds that if the donors behind a group-sponsored attack ad are divulged after the ad, the group-sponsored ad is not as effective (Dowling and Wichowsky 2013). This suggests that group-sponsored ads might not be as influential if a measure such as the DISCLOSE Act was passed.

On the other hand, full disclosure may not impact all aspects of federal elections. In Chapter 5 we found no significant differences in terms of how misleading and negative or fair and informative people perceived an ad to be when participants watched the same ad attacking a presidential candidate, but with different sponsors (candidate or super PAC). This is likely due to the fact that people know how they feel about a presidential candidate, and process information in line with their feelings about him/her (see: Lenz 2012). If most people have fairly well-formed opinions of presidential candidates, information in an ad (including the sponsor) is likely to change neither the way they think of the presidential candidates nor their evaluation of the ad itself.

It might be the case, however, that in elections for the U.S. Senate and, especially, the U.S. House—where candidates are not as well known—greater disclosure of donors may make more of a difference. Or, perhaps even simply making aggregate funding information more readily available to voters (as we did in our experiments in Chapter 4)—in the ads, for instance, instead of in news stories/articles that would require effort to look up[4]—would make a difference. For instance, Levitt (2010) recommends that "Democracy Facts"—stylized like a nutrition label and including information about the percentage of a group's financial support coming from its top five contributors, the names of those top five donors, and the total number of the group's financial supporters—accompany all political advertising, instead of the more simplistic and less informative current disclaimer of who paid for the ad. Whether any such proposals concerning donor disclosure would secure enough votes to pass, however, remains to be seen. Nonetheless, our findings indicate that regardless of the normative qualities of disclosure, information about the sources of political money can be an important factor in and of itself when it comes to forming voter preferences.

PUBLIC ELECTION FUNDING

Other proposals attempt to shift where political money comes from by offering candidates large subsidies from the government treasury designed to either replace or supplement private donations. Most "public funding" plans originate from a perspective that views private funding—and particularly large contributions from individuals or interest groups via PACs—with suspicion. Indeed, public funding is often packaged as an effort to prevent such contributors from "buying elections," to bolster the financial position of challengers vis-à-vis incumbents, and to free candidates from the onerous burdens on their time necessitated by fundraising (see: Miller 2011). At the state level, "Clean Elections" laws have been enacted for elections to at least some offices in about half a dozen states. These laws effectively provide candidates with full funding: In exchange for large subsidies sufficient to fund a credible campaign, candidates forego raising money from private donors (see: Miller 2013). In legislative elections in Arizona, Connecticut, and Maine, Clean Elections laws have been shown to vault inexperienced candidates who might otherwise be deemed as "low quality" to viability (Miller 2013), and to decrease the vote margins of incumbents when their challengers accept subsidies (Malhotra 2008; Mayer et al. 2006; Werner and Mayer 2007). Moreover, candidates who accept Clean Elections subsidies spend less time fundraising (Francia and Herrnson 2003) and more time interacting with the voting public, resulting in more people voting in those elections (Miller 2013).

Other public funding systems preserve a role for private donations, but incentivize the solicitation of small contributions from individuals. For instance, candidates for municipal office in New York City are eligible to receive grants from the city that match small donations (up to $175 in the 2013 election) on a six-to-one basis. That is, for every New York City resident that a candidate can persuade to donate $175, the city's public funding program will kick in an additional $1,050. The clear goal of the New York City system is to encourage participating candidates to seek small contributions from New Yorkers over large ones from interest groups and/or outsiders, diminishing their potential to affect the outcome of the election. There is evidence that the New York City system has enhanced the role of small donors, and has led to a donor pool that is more in line with the demographic composition of the city (Malbin et al. 2012). Kraus (2006; 2011) also found that public funding broadened the donors that participated in New York City elections, and slowed the growth of spending over time in those elections. In short, both Clean Elections laws and matching funds programs like the one in New York City appear to alter the core dynamics of elections, diminishing the role of large donors (in the case of New York City's program) or eliminating that role altogether (as in Clean Elections systems).

At the federal level, the proposed "Fair Elections Now Act" (FENA) would combine elements of each type of public funding system, allowing congressional candidates to accept large initial subsidies—the proposed grant for House candidates is more than $1 million—and to receive matches for subsequent small donations from individuals. In other words, after receiving the initial lump sum from the treasury, FENA candidates would be able to continue raising funds with no limit on the amount that could be raised, so long as all subsequent contributions were from individuals and were smaller than $100.[5] Any additional funds would then be matched on a 4-to-1 basis ($4 for every $1 raised in small donations) by public funds. The matching contributions would (in theory) help to ensure that candidates who opt into the FENA system could compete against well-financed candidates who did not, while avoiding entanglements with large donors.

Like the DISCLOSE Act, the FENA has been put before Congress on more than one occasion, but to no avail. Although passage seems unlikely, the act has repeatedly been introduced in every session of Congress since *Citizens United* (Miller 2013), and its effects on the broader campaign finance environment are therefore worth considering. Most obviously, the FENA would significantly alter the dynamics of contributions, and would certainly diminish the capability of would-be donors to contribute large sums to candidates. However, so long as *Citizens United*, *SpeechNow*, and *Carey* set the rules for spending by outside groups, it seems naïve to expect that the FENA would eliminate "big money" in American politics. The so-called hydraulic theory of campaign finance holds that money will always find its way into the system, seeping like water into the smallest of openings. As such, it seems reasonable to expect that if donors were cut off from making large contributions, they could easily either establish or contribute to a super PAC that would purchase ads on a candidate's behalf. Importantly, the results from the experiments we report in Chapter 5 suggest that super PAC advertising is not all that consistently different from candidate advertising, at least in the realm of the presidential ads we studied. Moreover, in Chapter 4 we found some evidence that such spending by outside groups may have made a difference in the outcome of a U.S. House election. Specifically, the more outside groups spent on behalf of challengers, the better they did on Election Day.

Whether such spending amounts to "buying" elections—perhaps the worst fear of reformers—remains to be seen. As we note in Chapter 4, the relationship between outside spending and challenger success likely exists (at least in part) in the opposite direction, with strong challengers more likely to attract spending by outside groups. Moreover, another finding from Chapter 4—that group spending is *negatively* correlated with the electoral success of House incumbents—could be seen as a sign that outside groups attempt to protect incumbents by aiding them when they are met by a strong challenge. There is, in short, much that remains to be discovered regarding the net effect of outside spending in incumbent-contested elections. We therefore believe that untangling the effect of outside spending in political campaigns is an important topic for future research.

For now, it is important to note that outside money does appear to matter. While public funding has proven to be an effective tool when it comes to reducing direct ties between donors and candidates, there is little reason to believe that even fully funding all federal candidates would diminish the role of outside money after *Citizens United*. So long as independent expenditures can be made in a relatively unencumbered fashion, there is nothing in any current or proposed public funding program that would prohibit them from being made, nor is there any obvious reason to expect that either the tone of group-funded ads or their effect on election outcomes would be much different in publicly funded federal elections.

CONSTITUTIONAL AMENDMENTS

If passed, proposals like the DISCLOSE ACT and the FENA would almost certainly result in constitutional challenges, and the federal courts would ultimately decide their fate. As noted above, if the goal of "reform" is to limit the capacity of corporations, unions, super PACs, hybrid PACs, 527s, and/or social welfare 501(c)(4) groups to make independent expenditures advocating the election or defeat of federal candidates, then we view neither enhanced disclosure requirements nor public funding as viable reform attempts. As such, amending the constitution has emerged as another proposed mechanism for implementing changes to the campaign finance system—as we note in Chapter 3. Importantly, any amendment would require a two-thirds majority vote in both the House and the Senate, followed by subsequent approval by three-fourths of the states. Passing such an amendment would be a tall order; there have been only 27 successful amendments in U.S. history, and ten of those were part of the Bill of Rights. However, the clear advantage of such a path is that, if successful, a constitutional amendment barring corporate (or any other) expenditure during elections would become the supreme law of the land, which could not be overturned by the courts.

What might such an amendment look like? Two amendments proposed in January 2013 by Rep. Jim McGovern (D-MA) serve as possible examples. One of them, the "People's Rights Amendment," would end corporate personhood rights (HJ Res 21). The argument behind McGovern's proposal is straightforward: Corporations are not people. McGovern's proposed amendment would therefore go well beyond merely ending the ability of corporations to spend in elections, clarifying that corporations are not legally the same as people, and are therefore not afforded the same Constitutional rights. As the proposed amendment states,

> We the people who ordain and establish this Constitution intend the rights protected by this Constitution to be the rights of natural persons. The words people, person, or citizen as used in this Constitution do not include corporations, limited liability companies or other corporate

entities established by the laws of any State, the United States, or any foreign state, and such corporate entities are subject to such regulation as the people, through their elected State and Federal representatives, deem reasonable and are otherwise consistent with the powers of Congress and the States under this Constitution. (HJ Res 21, Sections 1 and 2)

A similar amendment was proposed in the Senate in June 2013 by Jon Tester (D-MT); however as of fall 2013, neither McGovern's "People's Rights Amendment" nor Tester's proposal appears to be gaining much momentum in Congress.

The other amendment proposed by Rep. McGovern (HJ Res 20) would empower both Congress and the states to regulate political spending by giving Congress the "clear authority in the Constitution to regulate the campaign finance system."[6] Senator Tom Udall (D-NM) proposed a similar amendment in the Senate in June 2013. These amendments would effectively eliminate the Supreme Court's ability to evaluate campaign finance regulations implemented by Congress or the states, stating:

> To advance the fundamental principle of political equality for all, Congress shall have power to regulate the raising and spending of money and in-kind equivalents with respect to Federal elections, including through setting limits on—(1) the amount of contributions to candidates for nomination for election to, or for election to, Federal office; and (2) the amount of expenditures that may be made by, in support of, or in opposition to such candidates. (HJ Res 20, Section 1)[7]

The rationale for these proposals is essentially that the Supreme Court is wrong when it equates political expenditures with speech. As Senator Udall put it when he introduced his version of the amendment,

> Money and free speech are not the same thing, and it is a tortured logic to say so. . . . We can't fix this broken system until we undo the false premise—that spending money on elections is the same thing as the constitutional right of free speech. There are only two ways to change this: The Supreme Court could reverse itself, which is not likely, or we can amend the Constitution, which would overturn bad decisions and prevent future ones. I believe the growing momentum demonstrates that this is the right time for us to act.[8]

Amendments such as these would certainly have ramifications for the conduct of elections. Most obviously, removing corporate personhood rights would allow the statutory elimination of any spending by corporations in elections. It would also likely enable the government to restrict donations to super PACs, effectively relegating them to "standard PAC status" as they would no longer be able to accept unlimited donations from either corporations or individuals. Although these developments would likely eliminate a good deal of outside spending (which, again, totaled more than $1 billion combined in 2012), we find it unlikely that outside spending would cease to exist.

An initial analysis of the top donors to super PACs in the 2012 election, for example, suggests that "the single largest donors are not organizations seeking to take advantage of their newfound rights pursuant to the *Citizens United* and *SpeechNow.org* cases. Instead, the largest donations come from wealthy individuals who since *Buckley* have had the First Amendment right to make unlimited independent expenditures" (Farrar-Myers et al. 2012, 107). For example, Farrar-Myers et al. (2012, Table 1B) report that six individuals or married couples each contributed nearly as much to super PACs as did the two highest organizations, the United Auto Workers (UAW) and National Education Association (NEA). These six individuals/couples alone account for over $183 million (more than one-quarter) of total contributions to super PACs in the 2012 election cycle. Returning to the notion of hydraulic theory, in which money is thought to find its way into the political system regardless of regulations, super PACs likely provided an opening to individual donors who may have opted to make "soft money" contributions prior to the passage of the BCRA (as noted in Chapter 6). Removing their ability to contribute to super PACs would not impede them from simply purchasing ads directly with their own money, and the experience of having done so in 2010 and 2012 would likely encourage such individuals to continue making expenditures, even as sole funders of advertising. In short, we believe that a constitutional amendment eliminating corporate personhood would certainly change things, but perhaps not as much as one might think.

An amendment granting Congress the power to regulate the campaign finance system as it deems fit, however, could have more far-ranging effects. Although the amendments do not specify any policies or regulations, they do discuss the possibility of limiting both the raising and spending of money for federal campaigns (see above).[9] Any proposals that would place caps on spending would likely be struck down by the courts absent the passage of a constitutional amendment. If an amendment were to be passed and ratified by the states, we would likely observe less spending by outside groups, as one aim is to be able "to regulate and limit independent expenditures, like those from super PACs."[10] One effect would be to greatly reduce the number of group-sponsored political advertisements citizens see; as we noted in Chapter 3, most independent expenditures are spent on advertising.

Along with fewer ads, people almost certainly would be subjected to less total negative advertising.[11] In Chapter 3 we found that the vast majority of independent expenditures are made in opposition to (rather than in support of) a candidate. We also show that the bulk of this money is spent on advertising; as corroborating evidence, the Wesleyan Media Project found that 85 percent of group ads in the 2012 presidential election were negative attack ads (Fowler and Ridout 2012). Many argue that the political system is too negative, and there is some evidence that negative ads demobilize or "turn off" the electorate (Ansolabehere and Iyengar 1995). However, it is also important to keep in mind, as Geer (2006) argues, that negative ads can provide useful information to voters; that in many cases the positive ads promoting candidates amount to nothing more than "puff" pieces in which voters learn little to nothing of substance about the candidates. On this front, we report in Chapter 5 that some super PAC ads were perceived to have more information content than candidate-sponsored ads. Moreover, the negative attack ads sponsored by super PACs are not necessarily perceived as more misleading or negative than candidate-sponsored ads. Whether super PAC ads will continue to be no different, on average, than candidate ads (at least in terms of how they are perceived by voters), is unclear. It is possible that, over time, the role of campaigns and groups could become more distinct, with groups on the attack and campaigns remaining positive. As Farrar-Myers et al. put it,

> If Super PACs become efficient and effective complements to candidate campaign strategies, the electoral system could easily become one grounded in functional coordination. Candidates, campaigns, and the parties could focus their fundraising activities on small donors who more readily translate into votes and on positive messages in their campaigns. The Super PACs and outside groups could then focus on the large donors and on undertaking attack ads and other negative-oriented campaign activities. As a result, candidates, parties, and campaigns could easily become beholden to the large contributors who finance the Super PACs that support them, if the more nuanced lessons of the 2012 campaign cycle can be further refined. Such a system then starts to look like a version of the campaign finance system that gave rise to the need for FECA and its 1974 amendment in the first place. (2012, 116)

A constitutional amendment granting Congress the power to limit the activities of super PACs, however, would likely limit the chances that such "functional coordination" fears become a reality.

PUBLIC OPINION AND PROSPECTS FOR REFORM

As the passage of the Federal Election Campaign Act (FECA) and the Bipartisan Campaign Reform Act (BCRA) imply, public opinion often plays an important role in the passage of significant federal campaign finance legislation. Accordingly, it is important to consider not only the potential effects of campaign finance reform proposals, as we do above, but also, to the extent possible, their level of public support.

In Chapter 6 we presented some public opinion data on support for the Court's *Citizens United* ruling. A cursory glance at the data suggests proposals to end corporate personhood rights, such as the constitutional amendments discussed above, might have widespread public support. When considering this question, it is important to keep in mind that *Citizens United* did not grant corporate personhood rights—that decision goes back to the late 1800s (*Santa Clara County v. Southern Pacific Railroad* 118 U.S. 394 (1886); see Stephens 2013; Tucker 2011). *Citizens United* merely extended the reach of corporations to elections. As such, the most relevant public opinion question for ascertaining public support for such an amendment to the Constitution is not (dis)agreement with *Citizens United*, but rather whether the public is supportive of the general notion that corporations should have the same First Amendment rights as individuals.

In our survey, approximately 60 percent of the public thought that corporations "should not have the same First Amendment rights as corporations." On its face, our survey might indicate that there may be enough support for a constitutional amendment like those described above. A closer look, however, suggests two reasons for caution. First, outlawing "corporate personhood" extends well beyond elections. When we gave respondents a particular frame of reference, they were more supportive of the idea of corporations having First Amendment rights equivalent to those of individuals when it comes to lobbying as opposed to elections: 26 percent versus 16 percent, respectively. One possible implication is that proposals or amendments that focus on the role of corporations in elections will likely receive more public support than those that attempt to eliminate corporate personhood altogether.

Second, there is a sizable partisan divide in the public's beliefs about the First Amendment rights of corporations vis-à-vis individuals. Specifically, Republicans were significantly more supportive of the idea that corporations should have the same rights as individuals compared to Democrats and independents; Republicans were roughly evenly divided, whereas sizable majorities of Democrats and independents thought corporations should not have the same First Amendment rights as individuals. It is also the case, however, that the difference between Republicans and Democrats/independents is not as stark when it comes to corporate rights *in elections*. When prompted to think about the First Amendment rights of corporations as they pertained specifically to elections, less than one-third of Democrats, Republicans, and independents alike thought corporations should be afforded the same rights as individuals. In contrast, when no prompt was given or respondents were prompted to think about lobbying activities, Republicans were much more favorable toward the idea that corporations should have the same First Amendment rights as individuals.

As of fall 2013, 16 states have passed either a resolution or a ballot initiative requesting Congress pass some constitutional amendment clarifying the personhood of corporations vis-à-vis individuals and/or granting Congress and the states power to implement and oversee campaign finance rules and regulations.[12] In the end, the public opinion data we present in Chapter 6 suggests any such attempts should be made with care. From the public's point of view, it is one thing to attempt to rid (or at least limit) corporate spending in elections; it is another to attempt to rid corporate personhood altogether. This is but one question that reformers, legislators, and the federal courts will have to engage as federal elections continue to move beyond the *Citizens United* decision.

NOTES

1. The Daily Beast. Accessed December 18, 2013 from: www.thedailybeast.com/cheats/2012/01/31/colbert-super-pac-raises-1m.html.
2. Center for Responsive Politics. Accessed December 18, 2013 from: www.opensecrets.org/outsidespending/fes_summ.php?cycle=2012.
3. In the 111th Congress the bill passed in the House, but fell one vote shy of the sixty needed to bring the bill to a vote in the Senate.
4. Citizens could also look up this information in the FEC database, which would likely be even more time consuming.
5. The lack of a spending limit on participating candidates has been mentioned as one potential shortcoming of the proposal. See: Miller (2013).
6. Quote from the June 18, 2013 press release for Senator Tom Udall (D-NM). Accessed September 20, 2013 from: www.tomudall.senate.gov/?p=press_release&id=1329.
7. Section 2 stipulates the same language, but for states.
8. Ibid.
9. Ibid.
10. Ibid.
11. Any argument that reforms to eliminate or reduce independent expenditures because they contribute to negative campaigns rests on the assumption that candidates or parties would not pick up the pace, so to speak, in terms of negativity. As far as we can tell, this is an untested assumption.
12. United for the People. Accessed September 30, 2013 from: www.united4thepeople.org/local.html.

References

AAPOR Executive Council Task Force. 2010. "Research Synthesis: AAPOR Report on Online Panels." *Public Opinion Quarterly* 74:711–81.

Abramowitz, Alan I. 1991. "Incumbency, Campaign Spending, and the Decline of Competition in U.S. House Elections." *Journal of Politics* 53:34–56.

Alexander, Brad. 2005. "Good Money and Bad Money: Do Funding Sources Affect Electoral Outcomes?" *Political Research Quarterly* 58:353–58.

Americans for Campaign Reform. "Money in Politics: Who Gives." Accessed September 26, 2013. www.acrreform.org/research/money-in-politics-who-gives/.

Ansolabehere, Stephen, and Alan Gerber. 1994. "The Mismeasure of Campaign Spending: Evidence from the 1990 U.S. House Elections." *Journal of Politics* 56:1106–18.

Ansolabehere, Stephen, and Shanto Iyengar. 1995. *Going Negative: How Political Ads Shrink and Polarize the Electorate*. New York: Free Press.

Aprill, Ellen P. 2011. "Regulating the Political Speech of Noncharitable Exempt Organizations after *Citizens United*." *Election Law Journal* 10:363–405.

Askin, Frank. 2002. "Of Bright Lines and Fuzzy Arguments: McCain-Feingold Tries to Rein in Sham Issue Advocacy." *Election Law Journal: Rules, Politics, and Policy* 1:373–85.

Barnes, Robert. 2010. "In the Court of Public Opinion, No Clear Ruling." *The Washington Post*, January 29. Accessed September 28, 2013. http://articles.washingtonpost. com/2010–01–29/news/36777908_1_alito-president-obama-supreme-court.

Berinsky, Adam J., Gregory A. Huber, and Gabriel S. Lenz. 2012. "Evaluating Online Labor Markets for Experimental Research: Amazon.com's Mechanical Turk." *Political Analysis* 20:351–68.

Blass, Abby, Brian Roberts, and Daron Shaw. 2012. "Corruption, Political Participation, and Appetite for Reform: Americans' Assessment of the Role of Money in Politics." *Election Law Journal: Rules, Politics, and Policy* 11:380–98.

Bond, Jon R., Cary Covington, and Richard Fleisher. 1985. "Explaining Challenger Quality in Congressional Elections." *Journal of Politics* 41:510–29.

Bowler, Shaun, and Jeffrey Karp. 2004. "Politicians, Scandals, and Trust in Government." *Political Behavior* 26(3): 271–87.

Briffault, Richard. 2010. "Campaign Finance Disclosure 2.0." *Election Law Journal: Rules, Politics, and Policy* 9:273–303.

Brooks, Deborah Jordan, and Michael Murov. 2012. "Assessing Accountability in a Post-*Citizens United* Era: The Effects of Attack Ad Sponsorship by Unknown Independent Groups." *American Politics Research* 40:383–418.

Brown, Adam R. 2013. "Does Money Buy Votes? The Case of Self-Financed Gubernatorial Candidates, 1998–2008." *Political Behavior* 35:21–41.

Buhrmester, Michael D., Tracy Kwang, and Samuel D. Gosling. 2011. "Amazon's Mechanical Turk: A New Source of Inexpensive, yet High-Quality, Data?" *Perspectives on Psychological Science* 6:3–5.

Cain, Bruce, John Ferejohn, and Morris Fiorina. 1987. *The Personal Vote: Constituency Service and Electoral Independence*. Cambridge, MA: Harvard University Press.

Campaign Finance Institute. 2013. "Expenditures of House Incumbents and Challengers, by Election Outcome, 1974–2010." Accessed September 28, www.cfinst.org/data/pdf/VitalStats_t3.pdf.

Carey, John M., Richard G. Niemi, and Lynda W. Powell. 2000. "Incumbency and Probability of Reelection in State Legislative Elections." *Journal of Politics* 62:671–700.

Cassie, William E., and Joel A. Thompson. 1998. "Patterns of PAC Contributions to State Legislative Candidates." In *Campaign Finance in State Legislative Elections*, edited by Joel A. Thompson and Gary F. Moncrief, 158–84. Washington, D.C.: Congressional Quarterly.

Cave, Damien, and Michael Luo. 2010. "More of the Rich Run as Populist Outsiders." *New York Times*, July 22. Accessed September 28, 2013. www.nytimes.com/2010/07/23/us/politics/23self.html?_r=0.

Center for Competitive Politics. 2010. "*Citizens United* Poll Shows Broad Support for Free Political Speech," March 4. Accessed September 28, 2013. www.campaignfreedom.org/doclib/20100304_CCPpoll03042010.pdf.

Christopher, Andrew N., Ryan D. Morgan, Pam Marek, Jordan D. Troisi, Jason R. Jones, and David F. Reinhar. 2005. "Affluence Cues and First impressions: Does It Matter How the Affluence Was Acquired?" *Journal of Economic Psychology* 26:187–200.

Christopher, Andrew N., and Barry R. Schlenker. 2000. "The Impact of Perceived Material Wealth and Perceiver Personality on First Impressions." *Journal of Economic Psychology* 21:1–19.

Christopher, Andrew N., Daniel L. Westerhof, and Pam Marek. 2005. "Affluence Cues and Perceptions of Helping." *North American Journal of Psychology* 7:229–238.

Citizens United. 2013. "Citizens United—Who We Are." Accessed September 28, 2013. www.citizensunited.org/who-we-are.aspx.

Confessore, Nicholas, and Michael Luo. 2012. "G.O.P. Donors Showing Thirst to Oust Obama in November." *New York Times*, January 31. Accessed September 28, 2013. www.nytimes.com/2012/02/01/us/politics/campaign-finance-reports-show-super-pac-donors.html?pagewanted=all&_r=0.

Confessore, Nicholas, and Michael Luo. 2013. "Groups Targeted by I.R.S. Tested Rules on Politics." *New York Times*, May 26. Accessed September 28, 2013. www.nytimes.com/2013/05/27/us/politics/nonprofit-applicants-chafing-at-irs-tested-political-limits.html?ref=michaelluo.

Corrado, Anthony. 2003. "The Legislative Odyssey of BCRA." In *Life After Reform*, edited by Michael J. Malbin, 21–39. Washington, D.C.: Rowman and Littlefield.

Cox, Gary, and Jonathan N. Katz. 1996. "Why Did the Incumbency Advantage in U.S. House Elections Grow?" *American Journal of Political Science* 40:478–97.

Dinan, Stephan. 2013. "Capitol Hill Least Productive Congress Ever: 112th Fought 'About Everything.'" *Washington Times*, January 9. Accessed September 28, 2013. www.washingtontimes.com/news/2013/jan/9/capitol-hill-least-productive-congress-ever-112th-/?page=all.

Dolan, Eric W. 2012. "Kucinich: Corporations Can Legally Buy Elections." *The Raw Story*, January 24. Accessed September 28, 2013. www.rawstory.com/rs/2012/01/24/kucinich-corporations-can-legally-buy-elections/.

Dowling, Conor, and Amber Wichowsky. Forthcoming. "Attacks without Consequence? Candidates, Parties, Groups and the Changing Face of Negative Advertising." *American Journal of Political Science*.

Dowling, Conor, and Amber Wichowsky. 2013. "Does It Matter Who's Behind the Curtain? The Rise of Anonymity in Political Advertising." *American Politics Research* 41:965–96.

Druckman, James N., Donald P. Green, James H. Kuklinski, and Arthur Lupia. 2006. "The Growth and Development of Experimental Research Political Science." *American Political Science Review* 100:627–35.

Dwyer, Devin. 2010. "Campaign Spending Scorecard: Record Cash, Little Impact." *ABC News*, November 10. Accessed September 30, 2013. http://abcnews.go.com/Politics/2010-election-campaign-spending-nonparty-groups-doubles-impact/story?id=12106892&singlePage=true.

Eggen, Dan. 2010. "Poll: Large Majority Opposes Supreme Court's Decision on Campaign Financing." *Washington Post*, February 16. Accessed September 28, 2013. http://articles.washingtonpost.com/2010–02–16/politics/36773318_1_corporations-unions-new-limits.

Eggen, Dan, and Chris Cillizza. 2011. "Romney Backers Launch 'Super PAC' to Raise and Spend Unlimited Amounts." *Washington Post*, June 23. Accessed September 28, 2013. www.washingtonpost.com/politics/romney-backers-launch-super-pac/2011/06/22/AGTkGchH_story.html.

Epstein, Jennifer. 2012. "Obama 'Worries' Over Super PACs." *Politico*, February 6. Accessed September 28, 2013. www.politico.com/news/stories/0212/72493.html.

Erikson, Robert S. 1971. "The Advantage of Incumbency in Congressional Elections." *Polity* 3:395–405.

Farrar-Meyers, Victoria Skinner, and Richard Skinner. 2012. "Super PACs and the 2012 Elections." *The Forum* 10:105–18.

Feigenbaum, James J., and Cameron A. Shelton. 2013 "The Vicious Cycle: Fundraising and Perceived Viability in US Presidential Primaries." *Quarterly Journal of Political Science* 8:1–40.

Ferejohn, John A. 1977. "On the Decline of Competition in Congressional Elections." *American Political Science Review* 71:166–76.

Fowler, Erika, and Travis Ridout. 2012. "Negative, Angry and Ubiquitous: Political Advertising in 2012." *The Forum* 10:51–6.

Francia, Peter L., John C. Green, Paul S. Herrnson, Lynda W. Powell, and Clyde Wilcox. 2003. *The Financiers of Congressional Elections*. New York: Columbia University Press.

Francia, Peter L., and Paul S. Herrnson. 2003. "The Impact of Public Finance Laws on Fundraising in State Legislative Elections." *American Politics Research* 31:520–39.

Franz, Michael. 2012. "Interest Groups in Electoral Politics: 2012 in Context." *The Forum* 10:62–79.

Franz, Michael, Joel Rivlin, and Kenneth Goldstein. 2006. "Much More of the Same: Television Advertising Pre- and Post-BCRA." In *The Election after Reform*, edited by Michael J. Malbin, 141–60. Washington, D.C.: Rowman and Littlefield.

Garrett, Elizabeth. 2004. "*McConnell v. FEC* and Disclosure." *Election Law Journal: Rules, Politics, and Policy* 3:237–44.

Garrett, Sam. 2013. "Super PACs In Federal Elections: Overview and Issues for Congress." *Congressional Research Service*, April 4. Accessed September 28, 2013.

Geer, John. 2006. *In Defense of Negativity: Attack Advertising in Presidential Campaigns*. Chicago: University of Chicago Press.

Gerber, Alan. 1998. "Estimating the Effect of Campaign Spending on Senate Election Outcomes Using Instrumental Variables." *American Political Science Review* 92:401–11.

Gerber, Alan. 2004. "Does Campaign Spending Work? Field Experiments Provide Evidence and Suggest New Theory." *American Behavioral Scientist* 47:541–74.

Gerber, Alan, James Gimpel, Donald Green, and Daron Shaw. 2011. "How Large and Long-Lasting Are the Persuasive Effects of Televised Campaign Aids?" *American Political Science Review* 105:135–50.

Gill, David, and Christine Lipsmeyer. 2005. "Soft Money and Hard Choices: Why Political Parties Might Legislate Against Soft Money Donations." *Public Choice* 123:411–38.

Glass, Russell. 2012. "One CEO's Case against Corporate Financing of Elections." *Forbes*, November 6. Accessed September 28, 2013. www.forbes.com/sites/ericsavitz/2012/11/06/one-ceos-case-against-corporate-financing-of-elections/.

Goodliffe, Jay. 2005. "When Do War Chests Deter?" *Journal of Theoretical Politics* 17:249–77.

Gora, Joel. 2011. "The First Amendment . . . United." *Georgia State University Law Review* 27: 935–88.

Green, Donald P., and Jonathan S. Krasno. 1988. "Salvation for the Spendthrift Incumbent: Reestimating the Effects of Campaign Spending in House Elections." *American Journal of Political Science* 32:884–907.

Gross, Donald A., and Robert K. Goidel. 2003. *The States of Campaign Finance Reform*. Columbus, OH: The Ohio State University Press.

Hasen, Richard L. 2012. "Chill Out: A Qualified Defense of Campaign Finance Disclosure Laws in the Internet Age." *Journal of Law & Politics* 27:557–683.

Herrnson, Paul S. 1992. "Campaign Professionalism and Fundraising in Congressional Elections." *Journal of Politics* 54:859–70.

Herrnson, Paul S. 2005. "The Bipartisan Campaign Reform Act and Congressional Elections." In *Congress Reconsidered*, edited by Lawrence C. Dodd and Bruce I. Oppenheimer, 8th ed., 107–135. Washington, D.C.: CQ Press.

Herrnson, Paul S., and Stephanie Perry Curtis. 2011. "Financing the 2008 Congressional Elections." In *Financing the 2008 Election*, edited by David B. Magleby and Anthony Corrado, 166–209. Washington, D.C.: Brookings Institution Press.

Hill, Seth, James Lo, Lynn Vavreck and John Zaller. 2013. "How Quickly We Forget: The Duration of Persuasion Effects from Mass Communication." *Political Communication*. Forthcoming.

Iyengar, Shanto, Simon Jackman, and Kyu Hahn. 2008. "Polarization in Less than 30 Seconds: Continuous Monitoring of Voter Response to Campaign Advertising." Paper presented at the annual meeting of the Midwestern Political Science Association.

Jacobson, Gary C. 1978. "The Effects of Campaign Spending in Congressional Elections." *American Political Science Review* 72:469–91.

Jacobson, Gary C. 1980. "Campaign Finance Regulation: Politics and Policy in the 1970s." In *Paths to Political Reform*, edited by William J. Crotty, 239–81. Lexington, MA: Lexington Books.

Jacobson, Gary C. 1990. "The Effects of Campaign Spending in House Elections: New Evidence for Old Arguments." *American Journal of Political Science* 34:334–62

Jacobson, Gary C. 2006. "Campaign Spending Effects in U.S. Senate Elections: Evidence from the National Annenberg Election Survey." *Electoral Studies* 25:195–226.

Jacobson, Gary C. 2009. *The Politics of Congressional Elections*, 7th ed. New York: Pearson/Longman.

Jacobson, Gary C., and Samuel Kernell. 1983. *Strategy and Choice in Congressional Elections*, 2nd ed. New Haven: Yale University Press.

Kaminer, Wendy. 2012. "*The New York Times*' Disingenuous Campaign Against *Citizens United*." *The Atlantic*, February 24. Accessed September 28, 2013. www.theatlantic.com/politics/archive/2012/02/the-new-york-times-disingenuous-campaign-against-citizens-united/253560/.

Kasindorf, Martin, and Judy Keen. 2004. "'Fahrenheit 9/11': Will It Change Any Voter's Mind?" *USA Today*, June 24. Accessed September 28, 2013. http://

usatoday30.usatoday.com/news/politicselections/nation/president/2004-06-24-fahrenheit-cover_x.htm.

Kirby, Brenda J. 1999. "Income Source and Race Effects on New-Neighbor Evaluations." *Journal of Applied Social Psychology* 29:1497–511.

Krasno, Jonathan S., and Donald P. Green. 1988. "Preempting Quality Challengers in House Elections." *Journal of Politics* 50:920–36.

Krasno, Jonathan S., Donald P. Green, and Jonathan Cowden. 1994. "The Dynamics of Campaign Fundraising in House Elections." *Journal of Politics* 56:459–74.

Kraus, Jeffrey. 2006. "Campaign Finance Reform Reconsidered: New York City's Public Finance Program after Fifteen Years." *The Forum* 3:1–27.

Kraus, Jeffrey. 2011. "Campaign Finance Reform Reconsidered: New York City's Public Finance Program after Fifteen Years." In *Public Financing in American Elections*, edited by Costas Panagopolous, 147–75. Philadelphia: Temple University Press.

Krupnikov, Yanna. 2011. "When Does Negativity Demobilize? Tracing the Conditional Effect of Negative Campaigning on Voter Turnout." *American Journal of Political Science* 55:797–813.

La Raja, Raymond. 2008. *Small Change: Money, Political Parties, and Campaign Finance Reform*. Ann Arbor: University of Michigan Press.

La Raja, Raymond. 2012. "Why Super PACs: How the American Party System Outgrew the Campaign Finance System." *The Forum* 10:91–104.

Lau, Richard R., Lee Sigelman, and Ivy Brown Rovner. 2007. "The Effects of Negative Political Campaigns: A Meta-analytic Reassessment." *Journal of Politics* 69:1176–1209.

Lehigh, Scot. 2004. "Kerry Comrades Have Credibility on Their Side." *The Boston Globe*, August 20. Accessed September 28, 2013. www.boston.com/news/politics/president/kerry/articles/2004/08/20/kerry_comrades_have_credibility_on_their_side/.

Lenz, Gabriel S. 2012. *Follow the Leader? How Voters Respond to Politicians' Policies and Performance*. Chicago: The University of Chicago Press.

Levinthal, Dave. 2012. "Hybrid PACs Pick Up Pace." *Politico*, February 14. Accessed September 28, 2013. www.politico.com/news/stories/0212/72849.html.

Levitt, Justin. 2010. "Confronting the Impact of Citizens United." *Yale Law and Policy Review* 29:217–34.

Levitt, Steven. 1994. "Using Repeat Challengers to Estimate the Effects of Campaign on Election Outcomes in the U.S. House." *Journal of Political Economy* 102:777–98.

Lewis, Alfred E. 1972. "5 Held in Plot Bug Democrats' Office Here." *Washington Post*, June 18, Page A01. Accessed September 30, 2013. www.washingtonpost.com/wp-srv/national/longterm/watergate/articles/061872-1.htm.

Lott, John R. Jr. 2000. "A Simple Explanation for Why Campaign Expenditures Are Increasing: The Government Is Getting Bigger." *Journal of Law and Economics* 43:359–93

Lowenstein, Daniel, Richard Hasen, and Daniel Tokaji. 2008. *Election Law: Cases and Materials*, 4th ed. Durham, NC: Carolina Academic Press.

Lowi, Theodore J. 2009. *Arenas of Power*. Boulder, CO: Paradigm Publishers.

Luo, Michael. 2010. "Groups Push Legal Limits in Advertising." *New York Times*, October 17. Accessed September 28, 2013. www.nytimes.com/2010/10/18/us/politics/18express.html?pagewanted=all.

MacNeal, Caitlin. 2013. "*Citizens United* Constitutional Amendments Introduced in the Senate." *Huffington Post*, June 19. Accessed September 28, 2013. www.huffingtonpost.com/2013/06/19/citizens-united-constitutional-amendment_n_3465636.html.

Maestas, Cherie D., and Cynthia R. Rugeley 2008. "Assessing the 'Experience Bonus' through Examining Strategic Entry, Candidate Quality, and Campaign Receipts in US House Elections." *American Journal of Political Science* 52:520–35.

Magleby, David B. 2002. *Financing the 2000 Election.* Washington, D.C.: Brookings Institution Press.

Magleby, David B. 2010. "Political Parties and Consultants." In *The Oxford Handbook of American Political Parties and Interest Groups,* edited by L. Sandy Maisel, Jeffrey M. Berry, and George C. Edwards. Oxford: Oxford University Press.

Malbin, Michael J. 2003. "Thinking about Reform." In *Life after Reform,* edited by Michael J. Malbin, 1–20. Washington, D.C.: Rowman and Littlefield.

Malbin, Michael J., Peter W. Brusoe, and Brendan Glavin. 2012. "Small Donors, Big Democracy: New York City's Matching Funds as a Model for the Nation and States." *Election Law Journal: Rules, Politics, and Policy* 11:3–20.

Malhotra, Neil. 2008. "The Impact of Public Financing on Electoral Competition: Evidence from Arizona and Maine." *State Politics and Policy Quarterly* 8:263–81.

Maurer, Bill. 2010. "Corporate Free Speech Is Not Un-American." *Seattle Times,* February 1. Accessed September 28, 2013. seattletimes.com/html/opinion/2010953796 _guest02maurer.html.

Mayer, Kenneth. 2001. "Hey, Wait a Minute: The Assumptions behind the Case for Campaign Finance Reform." In *A User's Guide to Campaign Finance Reform,* edited by Gerald C. Lubenow, 71–82. Lanham, MD: Rowman and Littlefield.

Mayer, Kenneth R., Timothy Werner, and Amanda Williams. 2006. "Do Public Funding Programs Enhance Electoral Competition?" In *The Marketplace of Democracy: Electoral Competition and American Politics,* edited by Michael P. McDonald and John Samples, 245–67. Washington, D.C.: Brookings Institution Press.

Mayhew, David R. 1974. *Congress: The Electoral Connection.* New Haven, CT: Yale University Press.

McCarty, Nolan, Keith T. Poole, and Howard Rosenthal. 2006. *Polarized America: The Dance of Ideology and Unequal Riches.* Cambridge, MA: MIT Press.

Miller, Michael G. 2011. "After the GAO Report: What Do We Know about Public Election Funding?" *Election Law Journal: Rules, Politics, and Policy* 10:273–90.

Miller, Michael G. 2013. *Subsidizing Democracy: How Public Funding Changes Elections, and How it Can Work in the Future.* Ithaca, NY: Cornell University Press.

Miller, Michael, and Costas Panagopoulos. 2011. "Public Financing, Attitudes toward Government and Politics, and Efficacy." In *Public Financing in American Elections,* edited by Costas Panagopolous, 238–48. Philadelphia: Temple University Press.

Mutz, Diana C. 2011. *Population-Based Survey Experiments.* Princeton: Princeton University Press.

Nance, Scott. 2011. "Survey: Four in Five American Support Amendment to Overturn Citizens United." *The Democratic Daily.* January 22. Accessed April 10, 2012. http://thedemocraticdaily.com/2011/01/22/survey-four-in-five-americans-support-amendment-to-overturn-citizens-united/.

Newport, Frank. 2012. "Congress Approval Ties All-Time Low at 10%." Gallup Politics. August 14. Accessed September 3, 2012. www.gallup.com/poll/156662/ congress-approval-ties-time-low.aspx.

Parsneau, Kevin. 2013. "Text of State of the Union Addresses, 1961–2012." Database.

Patashnik, Eric P. 2008. *Reforms at Risk: What Happens after Major Policy Changes Are Enacted.* Princeton: Princeton University Press.

Patterson, Thomas E. 2002. *The Vanishing Voter: Public Involvement in an Age of Uncertainty.* New York: Knopf.

Persily, Nathaniel, and Kelli Lammie. 2004. "Perceptions of Corruption and Campaign Finance: When Public Opinion Determines Constitutional Law." *University of Pennsylvania Law Review* 153:119–80.

Primo, David. 2002. "Public Opinion and Campaign Finance." *Independent Review* 7:207–19.

Primo, David, and Jeffrey Milyo. 2006. "Campaign Finance Laws and Political Efficacy: Evidence from the States." *Election Law Journal: Rules, Politics, and Policy* 5:23–39.

Prior, Markus. 2006. "The Incumbent in the Living Room: The Rise of Television and the Incumbency Advantage in U.S. House Elections." *Journal of Politics* 68:657–73.

Public Citizen. 2011. "12 Months After: The Effects of *Citizens United* on Elections and the Integrity of the Legislative Process." *Congress Watch* division of *Public Citizen*, January 18. Accessed September 28, 2013. www.citizen.org/12-months-after.

Ronayne, Kathleen. 2011. "Some Super PACs Reveal Barest of Details about Funders." *Center for Responsive Politics*, June 17. Accessed September 30, 2013. www.opensecrets.org/news/2011/06/some-super-pacs-reveal-barest.html.

Rosenson, Beth Ann. 2009. "The Effect of Political Reform Measures on Perceptions of Corruption." *Election Law Journal: Rules, Politics, and Policy* 8:31–46.

Rucker, Philip. 2011. "Mitt Romney Says 'Corporations Are People' at Iowa State Fair." *Washington Post*, August 11. Accessed September 28, 2013. http://articles.washingtonpost.com/2011-08-11/politics/35270239_1_romney-supporters-mitt-romney-private-sector-experience.

Saad, Lydia. 2010. "Public Aggress with Court: Campaign Money Is 'Free Speech'." *Gallup Politics*, January 22. Accessed September 28, 2013. www.gallup.com/poll/125333/public-agrees-court-campaign-money-free-speech.aspx.

Sances, Michael. 2013. "Is Money in Politics Harming Trust in Government? Evidence from Two Survey Experiments." *Election Law Journal: Rules, Politics, and Policy* 12:53–73.

Schuman, Howard, and Stanley Presser. 1981. *Questions and Answers in Attitude Surveys: Experiments on Question Form, Wording, and Context*. San Diego: Sage Publications.

Shaw, Greg, and Amy Ragland. 2000. "Trends: Political Reform." *Public Opinion Quarterly* 64:206–26.

Sniderman, Paul M. 2011. "The Logic and Design of the Survey Experiment: An Autobiography of a Methodological Innovation." In *Cambridge Handbook of Experimental Political Science*, edited by James Druckman, Donald P. Green, James Kuklinski, and Arthur Lupia, 102–14. Cambridge: Cambridge University Press.

Snyder, James M. 1990. "Campaign Contributions as Investments: The U.S. House of Representatives, 1980–1986." *Journal of Political Economy* 98:1195–227.

Spencer, Douglas M., and Abby K. Wood. 2014. "*Citizens United*, States Divided: Evidence of Elasticity in Independent Expenditures." *Indiana Law Journal*. Forthcoming.

Sorauf, Frank. 1988. *Money in American Elections*. Glenview, IL: Scott Foresman.

Steen, Jennifer A. 2006. *Self-Financed Candidates in Congressional Elections*. Ann Arbor: University of Michigan Press.

Stephens, Beth. 2013. "Are Corporations People? Corporate Personhood under the Constitution and International Law." *Rutgers Law Journal*. Forthcoming.

Stratmann, Thomas. 1992. "Are Contributors Rational? Untangling Strategies of Political Action Committees." *Journal of Political Economy* 100:647–64.

Thee-Brenan, Megan. 2010. Americans Want Disclosure and Limits on Campaign Spending. *New York Times*, October 28. Accessed September 30, 2013. http://thecaucus.blogs.nytimes.com/2010/10/28/americans-want-disclosure-and-limits-on-campaign-spending/.

Theriault, Sean M. 2008. *Party Polarization in Congress*. Cambridge: Cambridge University Press.

Thielemann, Gregory S., and Donald R. Dixon. 1994. "Explaining Contributions: Rational Contributors and the Elections for the 71st Texas House." *Legislative Studies Quarterly* 19:495–506.

Thompson, Joel A., William Cassie, and Malcolm E. Jewell. 1994. "A Sacred Cow or Just a Lot of Bull? Party and PAC Money in State Legislative Elections." *Political Research Quarterly* 47:223–37.

Thrush, Glenn. 2012. "Obama Super PAC Decision: President Blesses Fundraising for Priorities USA Action." *Politico*, February 6. Accessed September 28, 2013. www.politico.com/news/stories/0212/72531.html.

Toobin, Jeffrey. 2010. "Bad Judgment." *The New Yorker*, January 22. www.newyorker.com/online/blogs/newsdesk/2010/01/campaign-finance.html.

Torres-Spelliscy, Ciara. 2011. "Hiding behind the Tax Code: The Dark Election of 2010 and Why Tax-Exempt Entities Should Be Subject to Robust Federal Campaign Finance Disclosure Laws." *Nexus: Chapman's Journal of Law and Policy* 16:57–95.

Tucker, Anne. 2011. "Flawed Assumptions: A Corporate Law Analysis of Free Speech and Corporate Personhood in *Citizens United*." *Case Western Law Review* 61:495–548.

Vavreck, Lynn, and Douglas Rivers. 2008. "The 2006 Cooperative Congressional Election Study." *Journal of Elections, Public Opinion and Parties* 18:355–66.

Weber, Christopher, Johanna Dunaway, and Tyler Johnson. 2012. "It's All in the Name: Source Cue Ambiguity and the Persuasive Appeal of Campaign Ads." *Political Behavior* 34:561–84.

Weissman, Stephen R., and Ruth Hassan. 2006. "BCRA and the 527 Groups." In *The Election After Reform: Money, Politics, and the Bipartisan Campaign Reform Act*. Michael J. Malbin, ed. Lanham, MD: Rowman and Littlefield.

Werner, Timothy, and Kenneth R. Mayer. 2007. "Public Election Funding, Competition, and Candidate Gender." *PS: Political Science and Politics* 40:661–67.

Wertheimer, Fred. 2010. "Supreme Court Decision in *Citizens United* Case Is Disaster for American People and Dark Day for the Court." *Democracy 21* Press Release, January 21. Accessed September 28, 2013. www.democracy21.org/archives/whats-new/supreme-court-decision-in-citizens-united-case-is-disaster-for-american-people-and-dark-day-for-the-court/.

Will, George F. 2010. "As a Progressive, Obama Hews to the Wilsonian Tradition." *Washington Post*, March 11. Accessed September 28, 2013. www.washingtonpost.com/wp-dyn/content/article/2010/03/10/AR2010031002638.html.

Zaller, John. 1992. *The Nature and Origins of Mass Opinion*. Cambridge: Cambridge University Press.

Zeleny, Jeff. 2010. "*Obama's Themes: 'Rescue, Rebuild, Restore'*." *The Caucus: The Politics and Government Blog of the Times*, January 27. Accessed September 28, 2013. http://thecaucus.blogs.nytimes.com/2010/01/27/obamas-themes-rescue-rebuild-restore/?_r=0.

Appendixes

APPENDIX TO CHAPTER 4

To assess whether voters respond to information about candidates' funding sources when evaluating candidates, we conducted three survey experiments. All three experiments were administered online. The first experiment was included on the 2010 Cooperative Congressional Election Study (CCES). The two other experiments were administered on Amazon.com's Mechanical Turk (MTurk) interface in spring 2012 (MTurk 1) and summer 2013 (MTurk 2). Each study received human subjects approval from the human subjects committee at Yale University (2010 CCES and MTurk 1) or the University of Mississippi (MTurk 2). We describe each study in more detail in this appendix.

CCES Experiment

The 2010 CCES was administered by YouGov/Polimetrix over the Internet. YouGov/Polimetrix uses a combination of sampling and matching techniques to account for the fact that (opt-in) respondents may differ from the general population. This process is designed to approximate a random digit dialing (RDD) sample.[1] For more detailed information on this type of survey and sampling technique see Vavreck and Rivers (2008). More broadly, see AAPOR Executive Council Task Force (2010) for a report on the strengths and limitations of online panels.

An overview of the CCES experiment is provided in the text of Chapter 4. Panel A of Appendix Table 4.1 describes the experimental design and provides question wording for this experiment. We asked several candidate evaluation questions. First, on the same page as the vignette, respondents were asked, "Based on what you know about this candidate, how likely do you think you would be to vote for him in the upcoming (November 2010) election?" Responses to this item (*Vote Intent*) were recorded on a scale ranging from 0 to 100, where 0 was labeled "not very likely" and 100 was labeled "very likely." Respondents were then presented with a grid on the next page with the header text, "And to what extent do you agree with each of the following statements?"[2] The statements (i.e., rows of the grid, the order of which was randomized) were designed to obtain more specific evaluations of the candidate. The response options for these six questions ranged from "disagree strongly" to "agree strongly" on a seven-point scale. Responses to these six questions were scored so that positive evaluations of the candidate were given positive values and negative evaluations were given negative values, with "neither agree nor disagree" scored as 0, the midpoint of each –3 to +3 scale.

A principal components factor analysis of these six items retained two factors, with all items except for "would focus on serving special interests" loading highest on a single factor. Therefore, we created a standardized index (mean = 0; standard deviation = 1) of the other five items, which we refer to as the *Candidate Evaluation Index* (alpha = 0.93). We analyze the question about serving special interests (reverse-coded: *Candidate would NOT serve special interests*) separately. We create and analyze the same measures for the MTurk experiments, described below.

MTurk Experiments

MTurk 1 and MTurk 2 used convenience samples of U.S. residents recruited using Amazon.com's Mechanical Turk interface. Amazon.com's MTurk population is a convenience sample that appears more representative than student samples, but is not completely representative of the U.S. population. An MTurk sample is typically younger, less likely to own a home, more likely to self-identify as liberal and with the Democratic Party, and more likely to report no religious affiliation (Berinsky et al. 2012; also see Buhrmester et al. 2011 for a discussion of using MTurk to recruit participants for experiments). In their article, Berinsky et al. (2012) illustrate MTurk's usefulness for conducting experiments in several ways, chief among them by replicating important published experimental work that used both student and national samples (e.g., the General Social Surveys).

An overview of the MTurk experiments is provided in the text of Chapter 4. Panels B and C of Appendix Table 4.1 describes the experimental design and provides question wording for MTurk 1 and MTurk 2, respectively. MTurk 1 was fielded from January 23 to April 19, 2012, and was completed by roughly 1,600 participants who were each paid $0.35 to participate. MTurk 2 was fielded from August 12 to 14, 2013, and was completed by roughly 1,700 participants who were each paid $0.50 to participate. The outcome measures used in MTurk1 and MTurk2 are the same as those in the CCES with one exception: *Vote Intent* was asked on a –3 to +3 scale, as opposed to the 0 to 100 scale.

Appendix Table 4.1 Experimental Designs and Question Wording for Studies Reported in Chapter 4

Panel A. 2010 Cooperative Congressional Election Study (CCES)

Vignette: Below is a short biography of a candidate for elective office whose name will remain anonymous. [NAME DELETED] is a [*Party treatment:* Democratic / Republican / NONE] candidate for an open seat (that is, there is no incumbent running for reelection) to the [*Office treatment:* U.S. House of Representatives / U.S. Senate]. [NAME DELETED] is positioning himself as a political outsider who can change the way things are run in Washington. [NAME DELETED] is financing his campaign primarily with [*Funding Source treatment:* money he made in the private sector / money he inherited / contributions from individual citizens and interest groups / contributions from individual citizens]. [NAME DELETED] is married and has two children.

Outcomes: Based on what you know about this candidate, how likely do you think you would be to vote for him in the upcoming (November 2010) election? (Response options: Not very likely—Very likely.)

And to what extent do you agree with each of the following statements? (Response options: Disagree strongly, Disagree moderately, Disagree a little, Neither agree nor disagree, Agree a little, Agree moderately, Agree strongly.)

Statements: This candidate has the experience and skills necessary to represent me in Congress.

> This candidate stands a good chance of winning.
>
> This candidate understands issues that affect people like me.
>
> This candidate would represent me effectively.
>
> This candidate would focus on serving special interests.
>
> This candidate would do a good job as a representative.

Panel B. 2012 Mechanical Turk Study (MTurk 1)

Vignette: Below is a short biography of a candidate for Congress. We would like you to evaluate this candidate based on the short biography. Please read carefully, and then answer the questions about the candidate that appear on this page and the next page.

[NAME DELETED] is a [*Party treatment:* Democratic / Republican] candidate for an open seat (that is, there is no incumbent running for reelection) to the U.S. Congress. [NAME DELETED] is positioning himself as a political outsider who can change the way things are run in Washington. [NAME DELETED] has raised about $1.3 million for his campaign. [*Funding Source treatment:* NONE / $700,000 of [NAME DELETED]'s campaign funding comes from his own money. / $700,000 of [NAME DELETED]'s

(Continued)

Appendix Table 4.1 (Continued)

Panel B. 2012 Mechanical Turk Study (MTurk 1)

campaign funding comes from contributions from individual citizens. / {NAME DELETED}'s campaign funding comes from contributions from interest groups. / $700,000 of {NAME DELETED}'s campaign funding comes from contributions from interest groups, contributions from individual citizens. / {NAME DELETED}'s campaign is funded with a mixture of individual contributions, contributions from interest groups, and his own money.] [*Extra Information treatment*: NONE / {NAME DELETED} is a college graduate and small business owner. He has focused his campaign on economic issues such as growing the economy and reducing unemployment. He is married and has two children.]

Outcomes: Based on what you know about this candidate, how likely do you think you would be to vote for him? (Response options: Very unlikely, Unlikely, Somewhat unlikely, Somewhat likely, Likely, Very likely.)

And to what extent do you agree with each of the following statements? (Response options: Disagree strongly, Disagree moderately, Disagree a little, Neither agree nor disagree, Agree a little, Agree moderately, Agree strongly.)

Statements: <Same as those in Panel A.>

Panel C. 2013 Mechanical Turk Study (MTurk 2)

Vignette: Below is a short biography of a candidate for Congress from the last congressional election in November 2012. We would like you to evaluate this candidate based on the short biography. Please read carefully, and then answer the questions about the candidate that appear on this page and the next page.

{NAME DELETED} was a {PARTY DELETED} candidate for the U.S. House of Representatives. {NAME DELETED} is a college graduate and small business owner. He focused his campaign on economic issues such as growing the economy and reducing unemployment. He is married and has two children. [NO ADDITIONAL INFORMATION / {NAME DELETED} raised $600,000 from individual citizens for his campaign. He also spent $50,000 of his own money. [NO ADDITIONAL INFORMATION / {Super PACs / Interest groups} (1) spent $350,000 in support of his candidacy / 2) spent $1.3 million in support of his candidacy / 3) spent no money in support of his candidacy}, while in support of his candidacy / 2) spent $1.3 million in support of his candidacy / 3) spent no money in support of his candidacy}, while other {Super PACs / interest groups} spent $350,000 in opposition to his candidacy (that is, in support of his opponent).]

Outcomes: Based on what you know about this candidate, how likely do you think you would have been to vote for him in the 2012 election? (Response options: Very unlikely, Unlikely, Somewhat unlikely, Somewhat likely, Likely, Very likely.)

To what extent do you agree with each of the following statements? (Response options: Disagree strongly, Disagree moderately, Disagree a little, Neither agree nor disagree, Agree a little, Agree moderately, Agree strongly.)

Statements: <Same as those in Panels A and B.>

Note: Randomly assigned treatments shown in brackets. Order of statements was randomized. Coding of outcomes is described in the text.

APPENDIX TO CHAPTER 5

To assess how people evaluate presidential ads and, more specifically, whether they differentiate between candidate ads and super PAC ads in consistent ways, we conducted two studies that are reported in Chapter 5. Both of these studies, referred to as Study 1 and Study 2, were administered on Amazon.com's Mechanical Turk (MTurk) interface. The appendix to Chapter 4 provides more detail on the use of MTurk. Each study received human subjects approval from the human subjects committee at the University of Mississippi. Study 1 was fielded on August 19, 2013, and was completed by roughly 725 participants who were each paid $0.75 to participate. Study 2 was fielded from August 21 to 23, 2013, and was completed by roughly 1,200 participants who were each paid $0.25 to participate. An overview of the studies, including details on the ads that were used, is provided in the text and Tables 5.1 (Study 1) and 5.2 (Study 2) of Chapter 5. In this appendix, we provide complete question wording and some additional data and analysis.

Question Wording

Before viewing the eight ads in Study 1, participants read the following text:

> On the following pages, we'd like you to take a moment to watch eight campaign advertisements that aired during the 2012 presidential election between Barack Obama and Mitt Romney and answer a few questions about each advertisement.

Before viewing the (randomly assigned) ad in Study 2, participants read the following text:

> On the following pages, we'd like you to take a moment to watch a campaign advertisement that aired during the 2012 presidential election between Barack Obama and Mitt Romney and then answer a few questions after the advertisement.

After each of the eight ads in Study 1, and after the only ad participants were randomly assigned to watch in Study 2, the following questions were asked:
To what extent do you think the ad was ...

	Not at all	A little	Somewhat	Very
Fair	( )	( )	( )	( )
Informative	( )	( )	( )	( )
Interesting	( )	( )	( )	( )
Misleading	( )	( )	( )	( )
Memorable	( )	( )	( )	( )
Negative	( )	( )	( )	( )
Untruthful	( )	( )	( )	( )

APPENDIX TO CHAPTER 6

To assess public opinion regarding the *Citizens United* decision and public knowledge we conducted several surveys that are reported in Chapter 6. All of these surveys were administered by YouGov/Polimetrix over the Internet.

Appendix Table 5.1   Average Evaluations of the Eight Presidential Ads Used in Study 1

Randomly Selected Ads	"Same Promises" (Priorities USA)		"Disappearing" (Restore Our Future)		"Fair Share" (Obama)		"Dear Daughter" (Romney)	
Fair	1.35	0.03	1.14	0.03	1.68	0.04	0.75	0.03
Informative	1.61	0.04	1.62	0.03	1.79	0.03	1.11	0.04
Interesting	1.93	0.04	1.61	0.04	1.76	0.04	1.14	0.04
Misleading	1.09	0.03	1.44	0.04	0.85	0.03	1.76	0.04
Memorable	1.76	0.04	1.40	0.04	1.55	0.04	1.33	0.04
Negative	2.51	0.03	2.37	0.03	1.86	0.04	2.31	0.03
Untrue	0.85	0.03	1.16	0.03	0.68	0.03	1.49	0.04
Ads Aired Closest to Election Day	**"Connect the Dots" (Priorities USA)**		**"Flatline" (Restore Our Future)**		**"Cynical" (Obama)**		**"Can't Afford" (Romney)**	
Fair	1.20	0.03	1.02	0.03	1.40	0.03	0.98	0.03
Informative	1.52	0.03	1.04	0.04	1.46	0.04	1.26	0.04
Interesting	1.47	0.04	1.23	0.04	1.45	0.04	1.20	0.04
Misleading	1.21	0.03	1.45	0.04	1.04	0.04	1.54	0.04
Memorable	1.14	0.03	1.19	0.04	1.20	0.04	1.12	0.03
Negative	2.26	0.03	2.32	0.03	1.97	0.03	2.23	0.03
Untrue	0.97	0.03	1.28	0.04	0.82	0.03	1.29	0.04

Note: Cell entries are means with standard errors in italics. Number of observations ranges from 705 to 725.

Source: MTurk Study 1

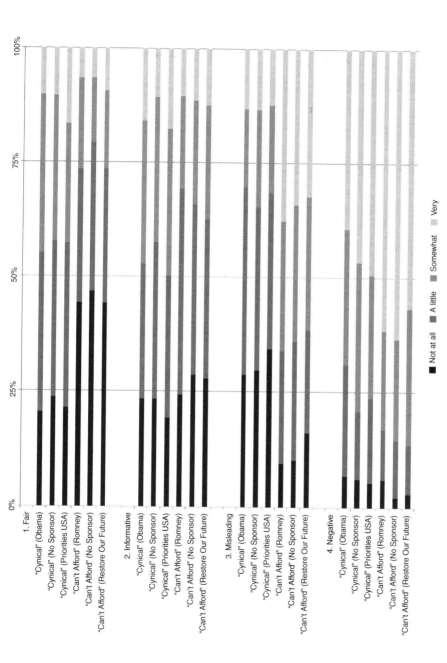

Appendix Figure 5.1 Evaluations of Eight Presidential Ads Used in Study 2, Randomly Assigned Sponsor

Source: MTurk Study 1

Details on YouGov/Polimetrix's sampling methodology are included in the appendix to Chapter 4. Question wording is included in the text of Chapter 6. Here, we present some additional data and analysis that is referenced in Chapter 6.

Appendix Table 6.1   Predicting Beliefs about the Rights of Corporations Compared to Individuals

	Full Sample	Democrats	Republicans	Independents
	(1)	(2)	(3)	(4)
	Are Corporations People? (1 = yes; 0 = DK; –1 = no)			
Elections Prompt (1 = yes)	–0.213	–0.157	–0.512	–0.095
	[0.065]***	[0.101]	[0.150]***	[0.093]
Lobbying Prompt (1 = yes)	–0.071	–0.140	–0.147	0.050
	[0.064]	[0.101]	[0.148]	[0.096]
Age (Years)	0.016	0.014	0.015	0.034
	[0.010]	[0.015]	[0.023]	[0.014]**
Age-squared/100	–0.014	–0.016	–0.005	–0.036
	[0.010]	[0.015]	[0.022]	[0.015]**
Female (1 = yes)	0.049	0.053	0.004	0.115
	[0.055]	[0.084]	[0.126]	[0.081]
Race: Black (1 = yes)	0.085	0.200	–1.166	0.018
	[0.094]	[0.127]	[0.184]***	[0.146]
Race: Hispanic (1 = yes)	–0.137	0.078	–0.255	–0.155
	[0.098]	[0.150]	[0.239]	[0.135]
Race: Other Race (1 = yes)	–0.069	0.026	–0.406	–0.113
	[0.106]	[0.165]	[0.396]	[0.148]
Education (1 = No HS; 6 = Post-grad)	–0.028	–0.047	0.017	–0.026
	[0.020]	[0.029]	[0.049]	[0.032]
Income (1 = <10k; 14 = >150k; 15 = RF)	0.004	–0.013	0.010	0.004
	[0.008]	[0.012]	[0.021]	[0.013]
Income Missing	0.006	0.076	0.042	0.009
	[0.098]	[0.133]	[0.233]	[0.147]
Married/Domestic Partnership (1 = yes)	0.142	0.163	–0.012	0.219
	[0.056]**	[0.080]**	[0.133]	[0.089]**
Republican (1 = yes)	0.252			
	[0.082]***			
Democrat (1 = yes)	–0.020			
	[0.062]			
Ideology (–2 = very cons.; 0 = moderate/not sure; +2 = very lib.)	–0.210	–0.094	–0.179	–0.325
	[0.035]***	[0.058]	[0.093]*	[0.047]***
Registered Voter (1 = yes)	–0.161	–0.251	–0.059	–0.179
	[0.079]**	[0.158]	[0.210]	[0.105]*

	Full Sample	Democrats	Republicans	Independents
	(1)	(2)	(3)	(4)
	Are Corporations People? (1 = yes; 0 = DK; −1 = no)			
Interest in News & Public Affairs (1–4) [DK/ Hardly at all = 1]	−0.040 [0.032]	−0.051 [0.058]	0.058 [0.080]	−0.072 [0.041]*
Region: Northeast (1 = yes)	0.010 [0.076]	0.031 [0.124]	0.210 [0.226]	−0.081 [0.101]
Region: Midwest (1 = yes)	−0.061 [0.069]	−0.042 [0.106]	0.029 [0.159]	−0.147 [0.107]
Region: West (1 = yes)	−0.075 [0.072]	−0.073 [0.110]	−0.015 [0.148]	−0.072 [0.113]
Constant	−0.518 [0.258]**	−0.222 [0.397]	−0.886 [0.664]	−0.843 [0.354]**
Observations	980	342	244	394
R-squared	0.167	0.139	0.155	0.182
Test of Elections Prompt— Lobbying Prompt, Difference	−0.142	−0.017	−0.365	−0.145
Test of Elections Prompt— Lobbying Prompt, p-value	0.024	0.856	0.016	0.120

Note: OLS regression coefficients with robust standard errors in brackets. The omitted treatment condition is the one in which no prompt (i.e., no additional text) was given. *$p < .10$; **$p < .05$; ***$p < .01$.

Source: February 7–10, 2012 YouGov/Polimetrix survey

Appendix Table 6.2 Selected Demographic and Political Characteristics of the 2012 CCES and CCAP Samples

Variable	Weighted
Age (Years)	46.614 [16.2883]
Female (1 = yes)	0.512 [.5000]
Race: White (1 = yes)	0.707 [.4553]

(Continued)

Appendix Table 6.2   (Continued)

Variable	Weighted
Race: Black (1 = yes)	0.130
	[.3362]
Race: Hispanic (1 = yes)	0.086
	[.2808]
Race: Other Race (1 = yes)	0.077
	[.2667]
Education (1 = No HS; 6 = Post-grad)	3.179
	[1.4438]
Income (1 = <10k; 12 = >150 or RF/Skipped)	6.146
	[3.5613]
Ideology (−2 = very cons.; 0 = moderate/not sure; +2 = very lib.)	−0.118
	[1.0149]
Party ID (−3 = Str. Rep.; +3 = Str. Dem.)	0.277
	[2.0757]
Voted in 2008 (1 = yes)	0.685
	[.4645]
Obama Vote % 2008	0.486
	[.5000]
McCain Vote % 2008	0.428
	[.4950]
Interest in News & Public Affairs (1 = hardly at all/DK; 4 = most of the time)	3.055
	[.9927]

Note: Cell entries are means with standard deviations in brackets. $N = 2,000$.
Source: 2012 CCES and 2012 CCAP surveys. Combined responses. Weighted analysis.

Appendix Table 6.3   Additional Question about Legality of Super PACs

	Illegal	Don't Know	Legal
Overall (N = 1,995)	16.8	40.2	43.0
High Interest (N = 1,176)	15.5	28.9	55.6
Low Interest (N = 819)	17.8	48.3	34.0

Note: Cell entries are percentage of respondents selecting each response category. Question wording: "To the best of your knowledge, is it legal today for some groups to accept unlimited donations from citizens if the money is only spent on political advertising or similar communications?
Source: 2012 CCES and 2012 CCAP surveys. Combined responses. Weighted analysis.

NOTES

1. The survey sample is constructed by first drawing a target population sample. This sample is based on the 2005–2006 American Community Study, November 2008 Current Population Survey, and the 2007 Pew Religious Life Survey. Thus, this target sample is representative of the general population on a broad range of characteristics including a variety of geographic (state, region, and metropolitan statistical area), demographic (age, race, income, education, and gender), and other measures (born-again status, employment, interest in news, party identification, ideology, and turnout). YouGov/Polimetrix invited a sample of their opt-in panel of over 1 million survey respondents to participate in the study. Invitations were stratified based on age, race, gender, and education, as well as by simple random sampling within strata. Those who completed the survey (approximately 1.5 times the target sample) were then matched to the target sample based on gender, age, race, region, metropolitan statistical area, education, news interest, marital status, party identification, ideology, religious affiliation, frequency of religious services attendance, income, and voter registration status. Finally, weights were calculated to adjust the final sample to reflect the national public on these demographic and other characteristics. We do not use these weights in the analysis we present in Chapter 4 because our randomization occurs within the selected sample.
2. The full vignette also appeared at the top of this page.

Index

Page numbers for figures and tables are in italics.

Abrams, Floyd 25–8
ABTT (Americans for a Better Tomorrow, Tomorrow) (super PAC) 36, 155
accountability 4–5, 67
administrative expenditures 65, 66
advertising 65; advocacy 40; broadcast 23–4; campaign 14, 20; by candidates 56, 106–31; corporate-funded 21; election day 122–3; expenses for 66, 70–4, 71, 73; impact on elections 78; independent expenditures for 73; misleading 105, 115; negative 74–5, 105–31, 162–3; outside groups and 105–31; political party 107; positive 163; sponsor 48; super PACs and 4–5, 105–31, 111; text of 110–11, 127; voter assessments of 106–31; see also specific advertisement
affluence cues 87
AFL-CIO 38
Alito, Samuel 9, 21–3, 28–9
Amend 2012 campaign 33
American Crossroads (super PAC) 108
Americans for a Better Tomorrow, Tomorrow (ABTT) (super PAC) 36, 155
Austin v. Michigan Chamber of Commerce (494 U.S. 652 (1990)) 17–18, 24–7, 30–3

back-office expenses 66, 72
Bain Capital 35, 113

Bipartisan Campaign Reform Act (BCRA) (2002) 3, 12–25, 31–2, 52–4, 163; candidate advertising and 56; contribution limits and 51; express advocacy and 47; independent expenditures and 68–9; National Defense PAC (NDPAC) and 46; registered corporate PACs and 38–9; soft money and 40; SpeechNow and 42; voter assessments of 133
Bloomfield, Bill 64
Brennan Center (advocacy organization) 33
Breyer, Stephen 20, 27
broadcast advertising 23–4
Buckley v. Valeo 424 U.S. 1 (1976) 16–17, 25–7, 32, 37, 162; contribution limits and 51; voter assessments of 132–4
bundling of contributions 37–9
Bush, George W. 13–14, 41, 105, 108
buying candidates and votes 3, 5, 13, 77–8, 86–7, 158–9

campaign consultants 40
campaign contributions 32; bundling of 37–9; by corporations 4, 6, 17–18, 20–8, 37–8, 50, 54, 77; by individuals 8, 25, 40, 50, 54, 60–1, 64; limits 16–17, 43–4, 50, 51; PACs (political action committees) and 44; Speechnow. org v. FEC (599 F.3d 686 (D.C. Cir. 2010)) 43; voter assessments of 90, 91–3, 96

campaign expenditures 27–9, 60–1; coding system for 64–6; for 2012 elections 64–74, *65*

campaign finance, hydraulic theory of 159

Campaign Finance Institute (CFI) 61

campaign finance regulations 3–4, 8; political speech and 9–10; pre–*Citizens United* 10–19, 37–41; prospects for reform of 155–65; public knowledge of 145–50, *147, 149*; total cost of elections and 58, *58–9*; voter assessments of 5–6, 132–54; *see also* specific regulation

campaign fund raising 60–4

campaign materials *65, 65, 71*

campaign spending: advertising and 72–4; growth of 36–7; by incumbents *83*

Candidate Evaluation Index 90, 91, 94–5, 96–9, 97

candidate funding sources: effect on voters of 84–100, *90, 94–5, 97*; voter assessments of *90*

candidates: advertising by 106–31; Bipartisan Campaign Reform Act (BCRA) (2002) and 56; contributions to 40; effect of funding by 84–100; evaluations of *90, 96–9*; expenditures by *79, 80*; funding profiles of 61–4, *62*; silver spoon *99*; status of *69*

"Can't Afford Another Term" ad *111*, 112–16, *115*, 124–9; text of *127*; voter assessments of *128*

Carey v. FEC, No. 11-259-RMC D.D.C. 2011 44–9, 51, 57, 133–4

CCAP (Cooperative Campaign Analysis Project) 145–50, *147, 149*

CCES (Cooperative Congressional Election Study): 2010 survey 88–93, *90, 96*, 99–100; 2011 survey 137–40; 2012 survey 145–50, *147, 149*

Center for Responsive Politics (CRP) *58, 58–65, 62, 67, 69, 79, 80*

CFI (Campaign Finance Institute) 61

challengers: experience of *62*, 68–9, *69, 80*; impact of spending on 78–102; independent expenditures and 79–81, *80*;

inflow of money to 61–4; party strength of 79–80; quality of 62–3, *80*; share of two-party vote *83*; spending by *80*

charitable donations *65, 65*

CIO (Congress of Industrial Organizations) 37–8

Citizens for Better Medicare 156

Citizens for Strength and Security 156

Citizens United (advocacy organization) 10–34; *Fahrenheit 9/11* and 13–15; First Amendment protections and 19–23; objectives and tactics of 10–11

Citizens United Political Victory Fund (CUPVF) 10–11

Citizens United v. Federal Election Commission (558 U.S. 310 (2010)) 4–8, 25–34, 43, 49–51, 133, 156–7; aftermath of 16, 24, 35–41, 54–7; campaign finance environment prior to 10–19, 37–41; cost of elections since *58, 58–9*; independent expenditures and 67–74; origins of 10–19; reactions to 7–10, 33–4, 77; super PACs and 36–7; voter assessments of 5–6, 134–54, *138, 140*, 163–4

Clean Elections laws 158

Clinton, Bill 11

Clinton, Hillary 11–13, 15, 20, 22, 31; *see also Hillary: The Movie*

Colbert Report, The 35–6

Colbert, Stephen 35–6, 51, 155; Americans for a Better Tomorrow, Tomorrow (super PAC) and 36, 155

Common Cause (advocacy organization) 33

congressional elections *58*, 61–4

Congress of Industrial Organizations (CIO) 37–8

"Connect the Dots" ad *110*, 113, 114–16, *115*, 122–3

constitutional amendments 160–3

Cooperative Campaign Analysis Project (CCAP) 145–50, *147, 149*

Cooperative Congressional Election Study (CCES): 2010 survey 88–93, *90, 96*, 99–100; 2011 survey 137–40; 2012 survey 145–50, *147, 149*

corporate campaign contributions 4, 6,
    17–18, 20–8, 37–8, 54, 77; *FEC
    v. Massachusetts Citizens for
    Life, Inc.* (1986) and 17–18, 23;
    2012 elections and *50*
corporate-funded advertising 21
corporate PACs 39
corporate personhood 35, *55*, 136–45,
    160–2; voter assessments of
    141–5, *142*, *144*, 164
corporate speech rights 5–6, 23, 29, 32
corruption 16–18, 32, 85–7, 134–5
Crossroads GPS (501(c)(4) group) 108
CRP (Center for Responsive Politics)
    58, 58–65, *62*, *67*, 69, 79, *80*
CUPVF (Citizens United Political
    Victory Fund) 10–11
"Cynical" ad 109–31, *111*, *115*; text of
    127; voter assessments of *128*

D'Annunzio, Tim 64
dark money 44–9
"Dear Daughter" ad *111*, 112, 114–16,
    115
dedicated independent expenditures 45
Democracy 21 (advocacy organization)
    33
"Democracy Facts" 157
Democracy Is Strengthened by Casting
    Light On Spending in Elections
    (DISCLOSE) Act 55–6, 133,
    152, 156–7, 160
Democratic National Committee *107*,
    132
Democratic primaries (2008) 11
Democrats: attack advertisements
    assessed by *118–19*, 120–5,
    122–3; *Citizens United v.
    Federal Election Commission*
    (558 U.S. 310 (2010)) assessed
    by *140*; corporate personhood
    assessed by 143, *144*, 145;
    funding sources assessed by *90*;
    independent expenditures and
    67, 68–9
difference-in-differences 117
direct mail expenses 71, *71*
"Disappearing" ad *110*, 113–16, *115*,
    124
DISCLOSE (Democracy Is Strengthened
    by Casting Light On Spending in
    Elections) Act 55–6, 133, 152,
    156–7, 160

disclosure of donors 3, 43, 47–8, 156–7
disclosure statements 37
documentary films 14–15
Doe v Reed (561 U.S. __ (2010)) 156
donations 65, *65*
donors, identity of 3, 43, 47–8, 156–7

Ebay 38
Edwards, John 14
electioneering 14–15, 31; 501(c)(4)
    groups and 48–9; *Federal
    Election Commission v.
    Wisconsin Right to Life, Inc.*
    (551 U.S. 449) and 18; *Hillary:
    The Movie* and 15, 20–1, 25
election outcomes: candidate
    expenditures and 79; impact of
    money on 77–104; independent
    expenditures and 79, 85–9;
    PACs and 86–8; self-funded
    candidates and 85–9, 93
election-related expenditures 48
EMILY's List (political action
    committee) 38–9
event expenses 65, *65*, 71
experienced challengers 68–9, *69*
express advocacy 3, 24, 37, 40–1, 44,
    52, 105; Bipartisan Campaign
    Reform Act (BCRA) (2002)
    and 47; *Buckley v. Valeo* 424
    U.S. 1 (1976) and 16–17; *FEC
    v. Massachusetts Citizens for
    Life, Inc.* (1986) and 17–18, 23;
    *Federal Election Commission v.
    Wisconsin Right to Life, Inc.* (551
    U.S. 449) and 18; SpeechNow
    and 42; 2012 elections and *50*

Fahrenheit 9/11 13–15
Fair Elections Now Act (FENA)
    158–60
"Fair Share" ad 109–31, *111*, *115*, 124
FEC *see* Federal Election Commission
    (FEC)
FECA *see* Federal Election Campaign
    Act (FECA)
*FEC v. Massachusetts Citizens for Life,
    Inc.* (1986) 17–18, 23
Federal Election Campaign Act (FECA)
    12, 16–18, 32, 37, 40, 163;
    contribution limits and 51; PACs
    and 38; SpeechNow and 42;
    voter assessments of 132–3

Federal Election Commission (FEC) 12–15, 17–18, 20–5, 30–1, 73; campaign expenditures and 64–6, *65*; committee expenditures and *60*, 61; independent expenditures and 70–4, *71*; National Defense PAC (NDPAC) and 45–6; *Speechnow. org v. FEC* (599 F.3d 686 (D.C. Cir. 2010)) and 41–5; twelve-part campaign expenditure coding system of 64–6

Federal Election Commission v. Wisconsin Right to Life, Inc. (551 U.S. 449) 18, 20, 24

Feingold, Russell 12, 18

FENA (Fair Elections Now Act) 158–60

First Amendment protections 4–6, 10, 29–33, 51, 137; 527 organizations and 41–5; Citizens United and 19–23; corporations and 24–34, 141–5, *142*; *Hillary: The Movie* and 15, 19–23; voter assessments of 164

501(c)(4) groups 47–51, *50*, 56–7, 156; Crossroads GPS 108

527 organizations 3, 47–8, 52–5; SpeechNow 41–5; Swift Vets and POWs for Truth, SVPT 40–1, 105–6

"Flatline" ad *110*, 113–16, *115*, 124

Forbes Magazine 77

foreign nationals, contributions from 56

funding sources: effect of on voters 84–100, *90*, *94–5*, *97*; voter assessments of *90*

fundraising *65*, 66

Gallup 135

General Motors 20

get-out-the-vote campaigns 40

Gillepsie, Ed 108

Gingrich, Newt 1

Ginsburg, Ruth Bader 20, 25–7

Glass, Russell 77

government contractors, contributions from 56

Greene, Jeff 86

ground campaigns 65

gubernatorial elections 85

hard money limitations 3, 45

Hart Research Associates 136

health PACs 39, *39*

high quality challengers 62–3, 80

Hillary: The Movie 11–13, 24, 31, 36–7; electioneering and 15, 20–1, 25; Federal Election Commission (FEC) and 15, 20–5; First Amendment protections and 15, 19–23

horse-race media coverage 86–7

house elections: effects of funding on 85; expenditures for 64–74, *65*, *67*, *69*, *73*; inflows of money to 60–4; receipts for 62, *62*; self-funded 62; 2012 elections and 60, *60*

hybrid PACs 44–9, 51; growth in numbers of 57; individual contributions to 64; 2012 elections and *50*, 60, *60*

hydraulic theory of campaign finance 159

Hype: The Obama Effect 11

incumbents 62, 63, 68–70, *69*; impact of spending on 78–102; independent expenditures and 80, 81–2, *83*; inflow of money to 61–4; spending by 80, *83*

independent expenditure-only committees 44

independent expenditures 17–18, 41, 59–61, 67, 67–74, *69*, 162–3; 501(c)(4) groups and 48, 56; for advertising *73*; *Carey v. FEC*, No. 11-259-RMC D.D.C. 2011 and 45–9; challengers and 79–81, 80; dedicated 45; election outcomes and 79, 85–9; Federal Election Commission (FEC) and 70–4; increase of 70; incumbents and 80, 81–2, *83*; negative 68–9; purpose of *71*; 2012 elections and *50*, 60

Independents: attack advertisements assessed by *118–19*, 120–5, *122–3*; *Citizens United v. Federal Election Commission* (558 U.S. 310 (2010)) assessed by *140*; corporate personhood assessed by 143, *144*, 145

individual campaign contributions 8, 25, 40, *50*, 54, 60–1, 64; voter assessments of *90*, 91–3, *96*

inexperienced challengers 68–9, *69*

infomercials 22

infrastructure expenditures 66
inherited income, voter assessments of
90, 91–3, 96
Institute for Justice (advocacy
organization) 33, 42
interest-backed candidates, voter
assessments of 5–6, 90, 91–3,
93, 94–5, 96
interest groups 78, 96–9, 97
Internal Revenue Code (26 U.S.C.
§527) 40
Internal Revenue Service 49
Iowa Caucuses (2012) 1–2
Iowa State Fair (2011) 35
issue advertisements 20, 24, 40–1
issue advocacy 3, 13, 16–17, 20–1, 41;
Swift Vets and POWs for Truth,
SVPT and 105–6

judicial activism 33

Kagan, Elena 28–30
Kaminer, Wendy 36
Kennedy, Anthony 20–3, 29–33,
56, 156
Kerry, John 14–15, 40–1, 105–6
Kucinich, Dennis 77

labor PACs 39
labor unions 37–9, 50, 54
Lauer, Matt 2
leadership PACs 38
libel law 26–7
loan repayments 65
lump-sum expenditures 70

March of the Penguins 14
Marshall, Thurgood 17–18
Massachusetts Citizens for Life, Inc.
(MCFL) 17–18, 23
Maurer, Bill 33
McCain-Feingold *see* Bipartisan
Campaign Reform Act (BCRA)
(2002)
McCain, John 12, 59, 61
McConnell, Mitch 25
*McConnell v. Federal Election
Commission* (540 U.S. 93) 18,
24–7, 31, 33
McDonnell, Bob 7
MCFL (Massachusetts Citizens for Life,
Inc.) 17–18, 23
MCFL test 17–18, 30
McGovern, Jim 160–1
meal expenses 71

mean independent expenditures 69
Mechanical Turk (MTurk) 89, 92–3,
96–100, 97, 113, 118–19, 128
media costs 40
media coverage of campaigns 86–7
media exception 14–15
member PACs 39, 39
Messina, Jim 3
Michigan Chamber of Commerce
17–18, 30
Microsoft 38
misleading advertising 105, 115
Moore, Michael 13–14
Morris, Dick 11
Move America Forward (advocacy
organization) 13
MoveOn.org (advocacy organization)
13
MTurk (Mechanical Turk) 89, 92–3,
96–100, 97, 113, 118–19, 128

National Association of Realtors
(political action committee) 39
National Defense PAC (NDPAC) 45–6
National Education Association (NEA)
162
Nation, The 54
negative advertising 68–9, 74–5,
105–31, 162–3
negative expenditures 68–9
newspaper/print advertisements 71
New York City, public election funding
in 158
New York Times v. Sullivan (376 U.S.
254 (1964)) 26–7
Nixon, Richard 132
nonaffiliated PACs 38, 39, 45–8
noncandidate committees 60–1
nonincumbents 63–4
nonparty committees 70–4

Obama, Barack 59, 61; campaign
advertisements for 109–31,
111, 115; on *Citizens United v.
Federal Election Commission*
(558 U.S. 310 (2010)) 7–10;
super PACs and 2–5; 2012
elections and 1–3, 107; voter
assessments of advertisements
attacking 118–19, 120–5,
123, 128
Olson, Theodore 19–22, 25–7
on-demand media 12, 21–6, 31–3
online activity expenses 71, 71
open seat elections 61–2, 62, 68–9, 69

outside groups 4–6, 40–1, 52, 67; advertising and 105–31; campaign fund raising and 60–4; expenditures by 70–4, *73*; impacts on elections of 74–5, 78; voter assessments of 96–9
overhead expenditures 65

PACs (political action committees) 3, 32; advertising expenses and 72–4; bundling and 37–9; *Carey v. FEC*, No. 11-259-RMC D.D.C. 2011 and 44–9; contribution limits and 44; election outcomes and 86–8; EMILY's List 38; Federal Election Campaign Act (FECA) and 38; history of 37–40; hybrid 44–9, 51, 57; incumbency and 63–4; individual contributions to 64; leadership 38; National Association of Realtors 39; National Defense PAC (NDPAC) 45–6; nonaffiliated 38, *39*, 45–8; number of registered, by type *39*; registered corporate 38; trade, member, or health 39; 2012 elections and *50*, 60; *see also* super PACs
"paid for by" disclosure statements 37, 121
party advertising 107
party affiliation, voter assessments and 94–5
party building 12–13, 40
party strength *80*
PCL (Political Communication Lab) 107, *107*
People's Rights Amendment 160–1
phone expenses *71*
Polis, Jared 64
political action committees. *see* PACs (political action committees)
Political Communication Lab (PCL) 107, *107*
political equality 9–10
political party advertising 107
political speech 4–6, 15, 27–8, 37, 41, 54; campaign finance regulations and 9–10
Polk, Shauna 155
polling costs 65, *65*, *71*
positive advertising 163

Prince Albert: The Life and Lies of Al Gore 11
print advertisements 71, *71*
Priorities USA Action (super PAC) 3, *107*, 109–31, *110*, *122*, *127*; advertising by 112–14, *115*; voter assessments of advertisements attacking Romney by *118–19*
prior restraint 31
private campaign contributions 4, 44, 54, 61
private citizen speech rights 5–6, 32
private-sector earned money *90*, *91*
public election funding 158–60

quid pro quo exchanges 25, 32

radio advertisements 71, *71*
refund contributions 65, *65*
registered corporate PACs 38
Republican National Committee *107*
Republican National Convention 14
Republican primaries (2008) 1
Republican primaries (2012) 1–3, 35–6
Republicans: attack advertisements assessed by *118–19*, *120–5*, *122–3*; *Citizens United v. Federal Election Commission* (558 U.S. 310 (2010)) assessed by *140*; corporate personhood assessed by 143, *144*, *145*; funding sources assessed by *90*; independent expenditures and 67, *68–9*
Restore Our Future (super PAC) 1–2, *107*, 108–31, *110*, *119*, *123*; advertising by *110*, 113–16, *115*, *124*; voter assessments of advertisements attacking Obama by *118–19*
retro-coding 64
Roberts, John 18, 21–3, 29–30
Romney, Mitt 35–6, 59; 47 percent comment 109, 112; 2012 elections and *107*, 109–31; campaign advertisements for *111*, 112–16, *115*, 124–9, *127–8*; primaries and 1–2; super PAC campaign contributions to 1–3; voter assessments of advertisements attacking *118–19*, *120–5*, *122*, *128*

Roosevelt, Franklin 8
Rove, Karl 108

salary expenditures *65*, 66
"Same Promises" ad *110*, 114, *115*
Sanders, Bernie 55
Santa Clara County v. Southern Pacific Railroad 118 U.S. 394 (1886) 164
Saturday Night Live 35
Scalia, Antonin 21, 29–30
Schumer, Charles 54–6
Scott, Rick 113
self-funded candidates *62*, 63–4, 85–9; voter assessments of 93, *94–5*, 96–9
self-governance 77
senate campaigns *60*
separate segregated funds (SSFs) 38
silver spoon candidates 99
small donors 61
smoke-filled rooms 87
social networking expenses 71
social welfare groups 47–9, 156
soft money 12–13, 38–40, 52, 55, 133, 162; Bipartisan Campaign Reform Act (BCRA) (2002) and 40; cost of elections and 58, *58*
Sotomayer, Sonia 27–8
Souter, David 20–1, 27
special interests 2, 91, 93, *94–5*, 97
SpeechNow (527 organization) 41–5
Speechnow.org v. FEC (599 F.3d 686 (D.C. Cir. 2010)) 10, 41–5, 49–51, 133–5; aftermath of 54–7; contribution limits and 43; independent expenditures and 68–9; private campaign contributions and 44
spending thresholds 37, 45–9
sponsor advertising 48
SSFs (separate segregated funds) 38
stand by your ad provisions 56
Stevens, John Paul 27
Stewart, John 155
Stewart, Malcolm 21–3, 24
Sunlight Foundation (watchdog group) 49
super PACs 44, 49–54, 57; accountability and 4–5; advertising and 4–5, 105–31, *111*; American Crossroads 108; Americans for a Better

Tomorrow, Tomorrow (ABTT) 36, 155; candidate evaluations and 96–9; *Citizens United v. Federal Election Commission* (558 U.S. 310 (2010)) and 36–7; DISCLOSE (Democracy Is Strengthened by Casting Light On Spending in Elections) Act and 56; election outcomes and 4; funding of 97; growth in numbers of 57; individual contributions to 64; largest donors to 162; Obama and 2–5; Priorities USA Action 3, *107*, 108, 109–31, *110*, 112–13, 114–16, *115*, 117, *118*, 120–5, *122*, 122–3, 125–9; Restore Our Future 1–2, *107*, 108–31, *110*, *115*, *119*, *123*; rise of 35–53; Romney and 1–3; spending and 59; tone of campaigns and 4; 2012 elections and 1–3, *50*, 60, *60*, 105–31; voter assessments of 4, 5–6, 97; voter assessments of attack advertisements by *118–19*, 125–9, 163
swift boat advertisements 54–5
swift-boating 41
Swift Boat Veterans for Truth 105; *see also* Swift Vets and POWs for Truth, SVPT
Swift Vets and POWs for Truth, SVPT (527 organization) 40–1, 105–6

Taft-Hartley Act 37–8
TARP bailout program 56
team contributions *65*, 66
Tea Party organizations 49
television advertisements 71, *71*
Tester, Jon 55, 161
text of advertisements *110–11*, *127*
Today Show 2
Toobin, Jeffrey 33
trade, member, or health PACs 39, *39*
transfer expenditures *65*, 66
travel expenses *65*, *65*, *71*
twelve-part campaign expenditure coding system 64–6
2008 elections 1, 11, 59, *69*
2004 elections 59, 105–6
2010 elections *69*
2012 elections 1–3, 59; campaign expenditures for 64–74, *65*;

committee financial activity during 60; independent expenditures for 69; regulatory landscape during 49–51, *50*; super PACs and 1–3, *50*, 60, *60*, 105–31

Udall, Tom 55, 161
unions 37–9, *50*, 54
United Auto Workers (UAW) 162
United States v. Carolene Products, 304 U.S. 144 (1938) 10

Van Hollen, Chris 55–6
Victory Enterprises 136
Vote Intent 90, 91, *94–5*, 96–8, 97
voter assessments: of advertising 106–31, *118–19*, *122–3*, *128*; affluence cues and 87; of Bipartisan Campaign Reform Act (BCRA) (2002) 133; of *Buckley v. Valeo* 424 U.S. 1 (1976) 132–4; of campaign finance law 5–6, 132–54; of candidate funding sources 84–100, *90*, *94–5*, *97*; of *Citizens United v. Federal Election Commission* (558 U.S. 310 (2010)) 5–6, 134–54, *138*, *140*, 163–4; of corporate

personhood 141–5, *142*, *144*, 164; of financial disclosures 156–7; of First Amendment protections 164; party affiliation and 94–5; prospects for reform and 163–5; of special interests 91, 93, *94–5*, 97; of super PAC advertisements 125–9; of super PACs 4, 5–6
voter mobilization efforts 3
vote shares as function of spending *80*, 81

wages *71*
Washington Chapter of the Institute for Justice (advocacy organization) 33
Washington Post-ABC News telephone survey 136
watchdog groups 49
Watergate scandal 132, 135
Wertheimer, Fred 33
Wesleyan Media Project 108, 125, 162–3
Whitman, Meg 86
Will, George 33
Wisconsin Right to Life, Inc. (WRTL) 18, 20, 22

YouGov/Polimetrix 88, 141–50